Germany: Economic and Labour Conditions Under Fascism

Germany: Economic and Labour Conditions under Fascism

BY JURGEN KUCZYNSKI

GREENWOOD PRESS, PUBLISHERS
NEW YORK   1968

The Library of Congress cataloged this book as follows:

Kuczynski, Jürgen.
Germany: economic and labour conditions under fascism.
New York, Greenwood Press, 1968 [c1945]

234 p.   21 cm.

Bibliographical footnotes.

1. Germany—Economic conditions—1918–1945. 2. Labor and labor-
ing classes—Germany.   I. Title.

HC286.3.K8   1968   330.943   68–30824

Library of Congress   [3]

Reprinted with the permission of International Publishers Co., Inc.

Reprinted by Greenwood Press, Inc.

First Greenwood Reprinting 1968
Second Greenwood Reprinting 1976

Library of Congress Catalog Card Number 68-30824

ISBN 0-8371-0519-6

Printed in the United States of America

CONTENTS

PART II
THE LABOUR POLICY OF GERMAN FASCISM

PREFACE TO THE AMERICAN EDITION

AT the time Jurgen Kuczynski completed his book on November 7, 1943, the German armies were still deep inside the Soviet Union and had occupied a major part of the rest of the continent of Europe. From the Franco-Spanish border to the Arctic Sea and deep into the Ukraine, the peoples were being trampled beneath the Nazi boot. Bulgaria, Romania, Finland, and Hungary were playing the bloody role of Hitler's vassals. Enormous quantities of grain, fats, ores, coal, textiles and machines, plundered from occupied and "Allied" countries, were dragged off to Germany.

The picture has changed radically since that time. Thanks to the opening of the second front, France, Belgium, Holland, and Luxemburg have been liberated. The Red Army has freed all the Soviet Republics occupied by the enemy and by its victories has transformed Finland, Romania, and Bulgaria into allies of the United Nations. Today Allied armies are on German soil in the West and in the East.

This development of the war, so catastrophic for Nazi imperialism, has resulted in a decisive change in the economic position of the German workers. The loss of the reservoir of foreign slave labor, and the enormous losses of the German armies in the West, East, and Southeast of Europe have led to a series of total and super-total mobilization measures in Germany. Even the limits to the exploitation of labor power established by the Nazis are being abolished. Thus, the gauleiter of Hanover decreed: "Old laws and regulations must now be suspended. No one shall say that youngsters are barred from any job by law." In fact, during the course of 1944, twelve-year old children were forced to go to work in the factories.

When Propaganda Minister Goebbels was named "Reichs Director for Total War Mobilization," following the attempt on Hitler's life on July 20, 1944, one of his first acts was the abolition of the "Strength Through Joy" and the "Beauty of

Work" movements. Hitler fascism had organized both of these institutions in order to make the workers forget that they had been robbed of their trade unions and their social gains. The "Strength Through Joy" movement organized vacation trips for a small percentage of the workers, while the "Beauty of Work" organization was responsible for the improvement in hygienic installations, establishment of lunchrooms in the shops, etc. Following the mobilization of the functionaries of these two organizations for the front or for work in war plants, "Strength Through Joy" and "Beauty of Work," which the Nazis advertised as "the greatest social achievements of the twentieth century," ceased to exist.

On October 15, 1944, a decree was issued by manpower dictator Sauckel, which penalizes workers guilty of unauthorized absences by imposing overtime work on Sundays and holidays, cancellation of overtime payments, reduction of vacation time, and denial of food allowances. The employers are entrusted with the execution of these measures. In addition, the men and women workers guilty of absence from work are turned over to the courts. The Nazi newspapers, in the second half of 1944, carried daily reports on sentences imposed for absenteeism. The usual sentence is imprisonment for three to five months, and nine months or longer for a second offense.

The manhunt, which formerly kept the Moloch of German war industry supplied with labor power from the occupied countries, has now been transferred to Germany itself. Neither old men nor mothers of large families are being spared. Of approximately 4,000 German writers, 3,980 have been ordered to work ten hours a day in factories. Actors have suffered the same fate since the theaters closed in the autumn of 1944. The publication of books has been prohibited, and the compositors and printers have fallen victim to Goebbels' total mobilization.

The sixty and seventy-two-hour week has become the rule under conditions which make such long working periods unbearable. Despite reduction of the means of subsistence to a minimum by rationing, and despite the loss of sleep due to air bombardments, the workers are forced to walk for hours to and from work, since transportation in the big cities has been disrupted by air attacks. Drastic fines prevent the workers from absenting themselves from work even after the heaviest bombardments. On May 25, 1944, the publication of the Reichs Labor Ministry reported the result of an investigation in one large plant. Whereas in 1938, with a forty-eight-hour week, production fell off 4 per cent as a result of sickness, in 1942, with a sixty-hour week, this figure rose to 11 per cent, that is, almost trebled!

That was 1942. Since then the concentrated storming of Hitler's "Fortress Europa" has begun, and now the walls of "Fortress Germany" are already being battered in and its roof is being shattered in a thousand places by Allied air fleets. More than 1,600,000 people have been bombed out in Berlin, 800,000 in Hamburg and vicinity, 750,000 in Cologne, 500,000 in Stuttgart. By the end of 1944 more than 18,000,000 were rendered homeless throughout Germany as a result of bombardments. Additional millions are living in homes with shattered windows which cannot be replaced because of the glass shortage.

As a result of heavy damage and military overburdening of the transport system, only a fraction of the required coal has been able to reach the big cities. During the winter of 1944-45 there will be only one heating stove for every one hundred people in Berlin. Grippe epidemics follow one after the other with countless deaths, and the situation is made worse by the fact that most of the doctors have been mobilized for the army. So few doctors have remained that, at present, each doctor must serve an average of 7,000 people and, often these have to work without adequate medicines and antiseptics.

The production of consumer goods has ceased almost entirely. The repair of houses and homes is either prohibited or has stopped because of lack of material. The workers necessary for this have been mobilized for the front or for war plants.

Since October 16, 1944, bread rations have been cut by 8 per cent and further ration cuts in vital necessities have been announced. Almost nothing can be bought for money except inadequate rations. Inflationary tendencies are becoming more and more pronounced. The circulation of banknotes which amounted to 24,400,000,000 marks at the end of 1942 rose to 33,700,000,000 at the end of 1943 and to 40,170,000,000 by September 15, 1944. In the subsequent six weeks up to October 31, 1944, an additional increase of 10 per cent occurred, raising it to 44,700,000,000. This rapid increase in the circulation of paper money, while at the same time there is almost a complete cessation of production of consumer goods, leads to the accumulation of money without a corresponding supply of goods. Confidence in money is vanishing. In order to satisfy the most urgent needs, everyone in Germany today has to resort to the black market where the barter system prevails in almost 90 per cent of the cases.

General decline, overwork, undernourishment, apathy, epidemics, a steady drop in the standard of living among the broad masses of the population—that is the situation of Hitler Germany at the end of 1944. It has sowed the wind, and it is reaping the whirlwind.

The Nazi regime arose in Germany in 1933 as a result of murderous terror. A tenfold terror against millions of Germans who clamor for peace marks its agony today. Hitler and the Nazis rose to power over the corpses of thousands of trade unionists, Communists, Socialists, Catholics, and other opponents of the swastika. The idea of the "master race" was imposed upon their own people with a revolver and the executioner's ax before they enjoyed their frightful triumph over the peoples of Europe. And now, driven back across their own borders, the Nazi leaders and their terror apparatus of the Storm Troopers and Gestapo are destroying everything in Germany that resists the prolongation of their lost war.

According to the *Bulletin of the International Transport*

Federation of September 13, 1944, thirty to forty people, among them many workers, are executed every week in Heiligengeistfeld Prison in Hamburg for criticism of the Nazi dictatorship and acts hostile to it. On a single day, 26 members of an underground organization were beheaded.

The *Arbeiterzeitung* of Schaffhausen, Switzerland, of October 31, 1944, published the report of a former inmate of Urbanstrasse Prison in Stuttgart who saw 256 executions during the course of eleven weeks in 1944. In one day alone he witnessed the guillotining of 35 prisoners, among them one woman and eleven soldiers.

The *New York Times* of October 25, 1944, published the statement of a Swedish sailor by the name of Hagban who spent six months in the Ploetzensee Prison in Berlin for trying to smuggle a letter out of Germany: "Tuesday and Friday mornings are the execution days at Ploetzensee jail in Berlin when between 30 and 40 Gestapo victims are dispatched by hanging or guillotine at each session. Regularly at 10 A.M. on these days I saw the death of the generals condemned for the July plot and of hundreds upon hundreds of other political prisoners."

These are the reports about only three prisons with execution courts, and there are many such in Germany.

The German people did not prevent Hitler's coming to power; millions originally greeted it, and they allowed themselves to be led into a second World War. Today the Nazi regime is trying to destroy all those Germans who represent a new democratic Germany and who would restore it to the family of peace-loving nations by helping, through extensive reparations and the punishment of all war criminals, to heal the wounds inflicted by German imperialism upon the European countries.

The assassination attempt of July 20, 1944, with its subsequent chain of murders, not only of generals but of numerous opposition leaders of all party shadings, from the president of the Communist Party of Germany, Ernest Thaelmann, and representatives of the Social-Democratic Party, to conservative political leaders, emphasizes the fact that anti-fascist groups are making themselves felt in Germany. The Hitlers and Himmlers would not resort to mass terror if they did not see a real danger to the existence of their rule from within Germany. The Nazi leaders are now applying the Lidice method to the Third Reich itself. They are exterminating villages in East Prussia because of resistance to their orders. They are hanging hundreds of men and women on gallows in West German localities and are beating and clubbing many others because they would rather live under Allied occupation than evacuate and perish with the Nazis.

In this way, Hitler and Himmler have succeeded in continuing their policy of suicide for Germany. The power of the opposition, whose centralization has been prevented so far by a raging campaign of terror, mobilization, and mass evacuation, has not yet shown itself strong enough to overthrow the war dictatorship. This is the situation at the end of 1944.

The present book is one of the volumes in a series by Jurgen Kuczynski, the noted statistician and student of the labor movement, dealing with the history of economic and labor conditions in the important industrial countries.

ALBERT NORDEN

December, 1944

INTRODUCTION

THE third volume of this Short History of Labour Conditions under Industrial Capitalism has been subdivided into two parts. The first deals with the period from 1800 to 1933; the second with the years 1933 to 1943, when Fascism reigned in Germany.

To those who abhor "a combination of research with propaganda," such a division may seem inexcusable. Why devote an entire volume to a period of little more than ten years while the preceding 133 years are dealt with in the same amount of space?

Yet I feel sure that the number of those who realize that there is no "pure science"—that is, science divorced utterly from the needs and existence of the people—is great enough to render superfluous a defence of this allocation of space. For reasons of topicality, I wrote the second part of the volume first, and it is published separately, some months before the first part.

There are some who may be uncertain as to whether a real need exists for this study of German Fascism, now that our victory in this war appears to be merely a "question of time," and may, in fact, perhaps already have been achieved when—in these days of slow-motion publishing—this book appears. They overlook the fact that Fascism is not a "native German problem," that, given certain circumstances, Fascism may develop anywhere, and that the study of Fascism in Germany should sharpen our vigilance in noting its primary manifestations in other places.

Therefore, whether or not we have won this war by the time this book appears, its publication, I suggest, is justified if, by providing detailed knowledge of the significance and methods of Fascism, it intensifies the detestation of that tyranny which the great majority of all peoples, and particularly the working class of all countries, share, and strengthens their determination finally to exterminate this monstrous system wherever it may exist or threatens to develop.

And this is not all. A people cannot go through the experience of Fascism without carrying the marks of it for a generation at least. Such bitter experience—bitter for those who opposed it from the day of its inception and even before, in the days of its early growth; bitter for those who followed it in the beginning blindly and enthusiastically and only in time and through cruel experience came to know its character; and for those who merely endured patiently and hopelessly as they had endured lesser evils for generations—such bitter experiences must necessarily affect the life of the German people in the years to ccme.

For those who wish to follow the future development of the German people, whatever course it may take, and from whatever point of view they may desire to study it, a detailed knowledge of the working of Fascism in Germany is necessary. And, as without doubt the German working class will play a decisive rôle in shaping the future of the German people, a close study of the conditions under which it existed during the Nazi régime is especially necessary.

The book deals with the German Fascist system in general and with the development of labour conditions more specifically. No history of the Opposition, of the political movement against Fascism during the years under review, is given—though, of course, the state of the opposition at the time when Fascism usurped power is touched upon, in order to explain how Fascism was able to achieve this. Many will quite justifiably regard it as a serious shortcoming that a parallel history of the opposition movement, or at least of the fight of the Anti-Fascist workers, is missing. Having myself taken a small part in the German underground movement, I feel that this lack not only detracts from the scientific and propagandist value of this book, but also fails to give the rightful place to the endeavours of those with whom I learned first how practically and usefully to study German Fascism: how to look upon every new item of knowledge as something to be turned at once to some use in the fight.

The chief reason why I did not include a history of the opposition movement and combine the history of Fascist reaction with the story of progressive action, is that our knowledge of the full history of the opposition movement is too scanty. Even during the pre-war years, from 1933 to 1939, it was extremely difficult to get a clear and comprehensive picture of the opposition movement—and even more difficult for those inside Germany than for those outside, who received reports through various channels from different parts of the country.

The fact that it was easier for those outside Germany to form a picture of the general character and strength of the opposition movement indicates the degree of terrorism and repression prevailing inside that country, and the consequent difficulty of freely moving around and gathering information. During the war years, it has been even more difficult to form a detailed picture

Thus, while we can obtain a fairly clear view of labour conditions—much having been published on this subject even by official sources—it is not possible to complement this by a similar account of the underground struggle. The seriousness of this omission, however, is, unfortunately, somewhat lessened by the fact that the opposition was very seldom effective enough to influence markedly the development of labour conditions. The ruthlessness of the Fascist régime was not tempered by caution because of actual large-scale resistance. There were no measures of importance which had to be rescinded, no important plans, to our knowledge, which had to be abandoned because of opposition.

Thus, while the history of the opposition movement would have been a tribute to the heroism of a resolute core of German Anti-Fascists, it would not have materially helped our understanding of specific measures introduced by the National Socialists, determining the conditions of labour. Once we realize that, on the whole, the National Socialists had to proceed rather more slowly than they desired because of the existence of two large working-class parties with a loyal following before Fascism seized power, this will be sufficient for our present purpose; for, unfortunately, it was this general knowledge, and not any important large-scale mass action on the part of the labour movement, which was the chief factor reducing the speed of the application of the labour policy of the Fascist régime.

Furthermore, there exist a number of pamphlets which tell the story of the German opposition during the last ten years,* as well as during specific phases in the last three years. While these suffer from the disadvantage of the lack of detailed information, even if the writers themselves have taken part in the underground

---

* Two useful publications of this kind are: *Ten Years of Hitler Fascism*, written by German Anti-Fascists, edited by Siegbert Kahn, and Paul Merker's *Germany To-day . . . and Germany To-morrow?* Both are I.N.G. publications.

fight, they tell the story better than would a necessarily shortened repetition of their accounts in this study. A final reason for not giving a history of the opposition movement in this volume is connected with our general knowledge of the history of the labour movement in Germany. On the one hand, our knowledge is smaller than that of the history of British or American or French labour. On the other hand, on the basis of the experience of the last ten years, a new evaluation of the past is now taking place among many members of the German labour movement: a comprehension of those weaknesses and faulty theories which were already recognized as such but were not sufficiently studied because they seemed "old history"—for instance, the rôle of Lassallianism—and which seem to-day of very much greater importance. Furthermore, inspiring phases of the German labour movement—for instance, the history of the underground fight against Bismarck during the years of the ban on the Social-Democratic Party—also seem to require a much more detailed study and stronger emphasis than they have received up to now. The past, then, has not yet sufficiently become part of our knowledge to yield a considered view of the present; and until this is the case, a really adequate history of the German opposition movement cannot be given, even if we were in possession of much more detailed knowledge.

However, I am confident that, in the near future, first-hand evidence will be provided of the day-to-day struggle of the German opposition, emerging more and more above ground to act in unison with the Allies against German Fascism, following the great example given by the people in the occupied territories of the Soviet Union and in the occupied countries of Europe, until German Fascism is smashed through military defeat and by the hands of the German people who will eventually have found the courage and resolution to liberate their country from the scum which they allowed to dominate Germany, devastate Europe and menace the whole world.

JÜRGEN KUCZYNSKI

LONDON,
November 7, 1943

PART I

THE STRUCTURE AND ECONOMIC POLICY OF GERMAN FASCISM

CHAPTER I

THE GENERAL STRUCTURE OF GERMAN FASCISM

1. ORGANIC GROWTH OR PRODUCT OF SPECIFIC HISTORIC CIRCUMSTANCES?

DURING the twentieth century capitalism entered a new phase of its development, a period which we call the period of imperialism, monopoly capitalism, or finance capitalism. The process of the concentration of capital, of the squeezing out of small and medium concerns, had reached a stage which caused a change in the character of capitalism itself. In some industries a few gigantic concerns began to dominate the field, and by joint action they formed monopolies, price cartels, committees to regulate production, and so on, by means of which society was transformed into one of "monopoly capitalism."

These cartels, monopolies, etc., were, and are, of course, extremely reactionary and oppressive. By keeping prices high, they plunder the people more successfully than was possible before.* They impede technical progress because technical

* Prices of monopoly and other goods in Germany during periods of rapid economic changes (considerable rise and decline of production) developed, for instance, as follows:

RAW MATERIAL—WHOLESALE PRICE INDICES IN GERMANY
(1928 = 100)

Year	Monopoly Prices	Other Prices	Year	Monopoly Prices	Other Prices
1925	101	113	1929	104	93
1926	98	97	1930	101	75
1927	99	97	1931	90	57
1928	100	100	1932	80	47

(Konjunktur-Statistisches Handbuch, 1936.)

progress entails scrapping of old-fashioned machinery.* Because of their overwhelming influence in capitalist society they are the spearhead of anti-labour activity.† Their growth accelerates the process of pauperization among the middle sections of society, including the lower middle classes and petty bourgeoisie.‡

It is from these monopolist sections of society, from the most reactionary, imperialistic and chauvinistic among them, that Fascism receives its support. When Fascism comes to power, the most reactionary groups among the finance-capitalists and monopolists establish a dictatorship and rule by means of terrorist methods. Fascism is, in fact, the dictatorship of these most reactionary elements among the monopolists.

Now, while it is generally agreed that capitalism, as we know it in the nineteenth century, developed organically into finance capitalism, there is much confusion as to the "laws of emergence" of Fascism. As capitalism was not overthrown—as so many labour leaders hoped it would be—in the nineteenth century, it developed on into finance capitalism. Increasing concentration and the formation of monopolies are organic developments of capitalist society. Such a development would only be arrested by the elimination of capitalism itself.

Observing that monopolist society is more reactionary than nineteenth century capitalist society, and that Fascism is the dictatorship of the most reactionary elements of monopoly capitalism, and also realizing that during the period from the beginning of monopoly capitalism around 1900 and the advent of Fascism in 1933, the reactionary character of society in Germany was enhanced in many respects, some people have concluded that Fascism is an organic development from finance capitalist

* In his presidential address to the Engineering Section of the British Association, at Nottingham (1937), Sir Alexander Gibb said: "Many valuable inventions have been bought up by vested interests and suppressed in order to save the greater loss that their exploitation would involve to already operating plant."

† In the United States, for instance, some of the big monopolist concerns employ a private military or police force for use against their workers and use terrorist methods against strikers or workers, trying to build up trade unions.

‡ This process has been accelerated so much that in some countries the number of independent craftsmen and small shopkeepers, for instance, is declining absolutely. One characteristic feature of the decline of the middle classes is the fact that scientific workers are often paid less than skilled workers.

society. They argue that, just as monopoly capitalism grew organically out of nineteenth century capitalism, so does Fascism grow organically out of monopoly capitalism. In fact, as we shall see later, many of these theoreticians believe that Fascism represents a new form of society, a new type of economy and the State. The latest of these theoreticians of the "inevitability of Fascism" is James Burnham in his book on the Managerial Revolution. *

Opposed to this is the conception of Fascism as a product which does indeed develop from a basis of monopoly capitalism, but is by no means inevitable. This conception regards Fascism as a product of certain specific historical circumstances which may or may not occur, during the period of monopoly capitalism. This conception is correct; the other is not only wrong, but it plays into the hands of Fascism and is, therefore, very dangerous and defeatist.

The correct conception points out that it is wrong to base a theory solely on the (undisputed) fact that, under monopoly capitalism, the reactionary elements of society grow in strength and extend their domination. For there is another set of facts of equal importance. These indicate that, during this same period of monopoly capitalism, the elements of progress also grow in strength, and have scored great successes—greater ones, on the whole, than have the reactionary ones. The first proof of this is the existence of the Soviet Union, and her emergence as the greatest power in the world. The second is the development of the united front of freedom-loving peoples against German Fascism.

Since Fascism can come to power only when there exists a tendency for the reactionary elements in society to strengthen and the progressive elements to weaken simultaneously, the theory of the inevitability of Fascism is based on the assumption of a general decline of the progressive forces in society.

Now, there is no doubt that in certain cases there has been a decline. The weaknesses of the non-Fascist and anti-Fascist

* I have mentioned Burnham's book here because it is the most dangerous of all published on this subject. Burnham has had a most varied "spiritual career." The latest transformation he has undergone is from Trotskyite to "Burnhamite." His book has been a social success in the United States, and many liberals and otherwise progressive people have been impressed by it.

sections of society, of which Fascism takes advantage in its advent to power, may have various causes. The working class may be deceived and duped, demoralized, or split. The petty bourgeoisie and the peasants may become affected by Fascist demagogy, may be demoralized by hunger and suffering, or may lack solidarity with the working class. The influence of that section of the big bourgeoisie which does not belong to the ultra-reactionary group may be weakened through economic causes; this section may become desperate and see no way out of its difficulties except by submitting to the Fascist section, or it may even not realize what is happening and thus fall into a trap.

Those who believe in the "inevitability of Fascism" must answer the question: is there a general tendency for the working class to be affected in any of the ways mentioned above? Of course there is always a certain amount of danger that such tendencies will develop. But the question is: has this danger increased during the last twenty years? Has there been a general tendency for the working class to grow weaker and less effective? Has, for instance, the danger of "Social-Democratism," that is, of a labour policy of compromise with capitalism at the expense of the working classes, grown faster in the thirties as compared with the twenties; or was it greater in the years following the last war than before 1914? I do not think that many even of the believers in the "organic theory of Fascism" would maintain this. On the contrary, there have been examples all over the world—Spain, France, and above all the growing influence of the Soviet Union in world affairs—and the united efforts to-day in the fight against Fascism—which show, in some phases, at least, a very considerable growth in the moral, organizational, and political strength of the working class during the last twenty years. *The belief in the "organic theory of Fascism" is inevitably coupled with a lack of confidence in the working class, and a defeatist disbelief in the dynamic strength of the working people.* This attitude is not merely incorrect; it is also very dangerous because its extension would sap the morale of those who are fighting Fascism.

As to the petty bourgeoisie, it has always been unstable, sometimes attaining heights of revolutionary fervour and wisdom —as in one phase of the French Revolution at the end of the eighteenth century—and, at other times, evidencing appalling political immaturity—as, for instance, in France in the fifties of the last century, and in Germany in the twenties and early thirties of the present century. One can neither conclude that there has been a general tendency for the petty bourgeoisie to become particularly pliable to the desires of the ruling class nor especially antagonistic to the working class in a period which includes both, the sorry example of Germany and the Civil War in Spain and concluding with the common fight to-day against German Fascism.

The theory of the organic development of Fascism in the later stages of monopoly capitalism clearly contradicts the facts; it is based on one side only of a dual and dialectical development. Fascism is due, not to any organic development, but to specific historical circumstances. This, of course, does not mean that monopoly capitalism does not provide a basis for the development of Fascism. Of course, it does. Fascism is not possible on any basis other than monopoly capitalism. Nor does this exclude the fact that in all monopolist capitalist countries we find Fascist elements. It does mean, however, that, within the general conditions of monopoly capitalism, certain specific circumstances must first be developed, before Fascism can become strong enough to achieve power. These circumstances may occur in one country and not in another; they may develop in a country with a relatively young and still weak structure of monopoly capitalism (Italy), or in a country where monopoly capitalism has been long established (Germany).

Let us now briefly examine the historical circumstances under which Fascism came to power in Germany. That is, the specific and peculiar historical (not "organic") developments which facilitated the ultra-reactionary elements in Germany in seizing power.

In Germany, Fascism came to power under circumstances which greatly favoured the ultra-reactionary section of monopoly capitalism. The working class, bitterest and strongest enemy of Fascism, was not demoralized, nor was it deceived by the specious promises of Fascism. But it was divided. Two large sections, each embracing millions of workers, were led by the Social-Democratic Party and the Communist Party. Both were anti-Fascist. The

Communists were in favour of mass-action by the German people to prevent Fascism establishing itself. The leadership of the Social-Democratic Party, though animated by anti-Fascist sentiments, was averse to mass action. The Social Democrats underestimated the ruthlessness of Fascism; they had become "constitutionally minded," devotees of gradualism, habituated to compromise; they hoped to defeat Fascism by means of elections, court decisions and parliamentary action. The trade union movement, from the central leadership down to a very large number of small functionaries, gave to the Social-Democratic Party full support. The leadership of the Social-Democratic Party, however, was not only averse to action because of its general "philosophy of social development"; it also deprecated action because it feared that the Communists might, through such action, gain rapidly in influence and strength. For these reasons, the Social-Democratic Party, for instance, declined in January 1933, to issue with the Communists, a joint call for strike action against the Fascists.

These unfortunate, historical circumstances—disunity, and aversion to action among the Social-Democratic leadership—formed one of the conditions which made possible the seizure of power by Fascism. But other factors also played a considerable part.

The second set of circumstances favouring the rise of Fascism was the demoralization of the petty and middle bourgeoisie, and the desperate economic position of the peasants. Taking advantage of this and exploiting the despair and political immaturity of these sections, led by ruthless and cunning gangsters, the National Socialist Party grew into a mass party. The petty and middle bourgeoisie (including the liberal professions, school teachers, etc.) had suffered grievous economic losses during the last war and the subsequent inflation. From 1924 to 1929 there was a lull; one may even say that their position had slowly but steadily improved. By 1929 a part, though not yet the major part, of the damage they had suffered had been made good. Then followed the crisis of 1929–1932 and they lost almost the whole of their small but definite gains. The Social-Democratic Party could not offer them any remedy, and even seemed to them to be partly responsible for their plight as it supported the

Government. The Communist Party had not sufficiently extended its influence among them. Furthermore, some of the petty bourgeoisie—unemployed former officers, and so on—had developed a taste for violence, minor crime, and anti-social tendencies generally. The National Socialists, therefore, succeeded in gaining a considerable following among them. The position of the peasants was unfavourable all through the twenties, and it grew worse during the crisis. These three sections of German society, embracing many millions, natural enemies of monopoly capitalism, of big business and the Junkers, became so demoralized that they lost the capacity for coherent political thinking and became the victims of a crude but cleverly timed demagogy.

It is these sections, which formed the mass basis of the National Socialist Party, to whom the National Socialists appealed with an anti-capitalist and nationalist (Anti-Versailles) programme which they published in a large volume of propagandist literature and innumerable public meetings, towards the expenses of which the big industrialists contributed heavily. In 1931, the coal-owners' association pledged each member to pay into the treasury of the National Socialist Party 50 pfennig (about 6d. at par) for every ton of coal sold. This money was spent in denouncing capitalists both inside (anti-capitalist) and outside (nationalist) Germany. This apparently suicidal investment by the heavy industrialists was safe because the National Socialists could be trusted to lead the indignation of the masses of the people into "harmless channels"—as long as German labour was divided and, therefore, unable to lead the people against Fascism and gain the support of the petty bourgeoisie and peasants.*

The final section of society with which the Fascists had to deal, and which had to be won over, was the element in the big bourgeoisie which preferred to rule in the old established way, without the dictatorship proposed by the Fascist forces. This section of the big bourgeoisie was composed largely of mono-

---

* One of the reasons why Hitler was somewhat hastily installed in the Reichs Chancellorship in January, 1933, was the growing movement of unity among the working class which was still insufficient to lead to concerted action but which certainly had already become dangerous by guiding hundreds of thousands of duped "petty bourgeois" away from Fascism: the National Socialists lost two million votes between July and November, 1932.

polists and large medium employers in the consumption goods industries, shipping, the majority of the banks and assurance companies, and the import and export houses.* These small but powerful groups, in 1932 and in the beginning of 1933, were victims of a pincer movement: on the one hand, they realized the increasing anti-capitalist feeling of the masses, who had suffered so much during the crisis; on the other, they themselves had suffered economic losses as do all capitalists during a crisis, to a certain extent. While they were not specifically and whole-heartedly in favour of the ultra-reactionary policies planned by the Fascist section of industry, nor inclined to so aggressive a foreign policy, they themselves had no plan for extricating themselves from the general mess in which they found themselves, and they naturally shared the interest of the pro-Fascist sections in continuing and, if possible, increasing the exploitation of the people. The breakdown of the biggest German wool concern, the lightly concealed bankruptcy of one of the big five banks—these had beeen warnings, difficult to ignore. Thus, somewhat reluctantly and hoping for the best they allowed themselves to be swayed by the ultra-reactionary section of German finance capitalism.†

We see, then, that the three important historical circumstances which made Fascism in Germany possible were: disunity of the working class, demoralization of the petty and middle bourgeoisie and peasants, feebleness of the less reactionary section of the big bourgeoisie.

One more aspect, however, must be examined, which has been mentioned in the foregoing pages: the weakness of the ruling class as a whole. While Fascism needs as a pre-requisite to power great strength of the ultra-reactionary sections of monopoly capitalism, at the same time, it also is the expression of a considerable weakness of the big bourgeoisie as a whole: a weak-

---

* The chemical and electro industries had representatives in both sections of finance capitalism since, on the one hand, because of their favourable export position, they were not as desperate for a radical change as the iron and steel industry, while, on the other hand, they were sure to profit, as war industries, from an aggressive Fascist policy.

† Yielding to the most reactionary section of the ruling class is an old custom of the German bourgeoisie (1815 f., 1849 f., etc.). The less reactionary centre group of the German ruling class has for a hundred years played the rôle of the not too unwilling weakling.

ness in relation to the masses of the people, to all other sections of society.

Nobody, including the Fascists, the ultra-reactionary monopolists, has any illusions about the dangers entailed in a régime of terror and dictatorship. A democratic régime is, on the whole, better suited to the rule of the bourgeoisie: it gives the impression of solidity, stability, freedom and strength (it is, in fact, a reflection of a certain strength of the ruling class which can afford to concede elementary democratic liberties to the people). Only a ruling class, weakened economically or politically, or both, as was the case in Germany, is prepared to risk all the dangers entailed in such a form of class rule and class struggle as the Fascist system represents.

While the Fascist régime, therefore, rules with ruthless terrorism it is actually the rule of a failing class that goes berserker, or of the invalid who can keep alive only through the use of drugs. If not arrested and destroyed in early infancy, the Fascist régime may temporarily become strong in relation to the forces opposed to it. But it will always have the inherent weakness of being able to reign only with the help of force and oppression.

2. War and Terror as Permanent Features of Fascism

Fascism is not distinguished from other forms of imperialism by the fact that it wants to exploit the whole world. Every imperialist régime must have this fundamental motive. But there are varied ways by which the imperialist powers try to achieve this purpose. Sometimes it has been through "peaceful economic penetration." Sometimes by political pressure added to such penetration—a hint that "there might be complications if . . ." Sometimes military conquest has been used as the most simple and effective means to this end. Great empires have been built by the use of these three methods—but never did the method of military conquest dominate in the building of an empire.

The first really large scale use of the method of military conquest to achieve an empire is the present war of Fascism on mankind. It is a war to conquer the riches of this world and to oppress the peoples, to create an empire and to make the peoples of the world the creators of wealth for the ruling Fascists.

Fascism chose this method—or, rather, this, the Fascist method, was chosen by the most reactionary sections of the German bourgeoisie—not just to try out a third method after the other two had been tried so often and so successfully, but because this seemed the quickest and surest way of achieving their aim. Germany, late-comer on the world market and a late-comer, too, in the distribution of colonies, had been deprived by the Treaty of Versailles of advantages gained before 1914. It had become an imperialism without an empire and a large scale army or navy—but, at the same time, with certain other highly developed attributes of imperialism, such as a heavy industry easily convertible into an armament industry. Under these circumstances, to the most reactionary sections of German capitalism the third method seemed to be the best suited to conditions in Germany.

The Fascist system came to power in Germany to the accompaniment of terrorism, but terrorism was not the means. Fascism was installed in power as a result of political pressure and intrigues within the ruling class, and under the historical class circumstances described above. Austria and Czechoslovakia were conquered through terrorism, bribery and a show of arms, but not in open warfare.

The rest of Europe had to be conquered by arms. The Fascist régime had no illusions that it could go on indefinitely with the methods used in the case of Austria and Czechoslovakia. The Fascists had prepared for war from the very first day. And they prepared for a war to last until the whole world was conquered. The statement of German Fascists that they are satisfied with the conquest of the European Continent, is to be taken no more seriously than their statements, some years ago, that they had no territorial claims after this or that conquest.

However—even were they to conquer the world—there would always be resistance against the Fascists in each conquered country; and even in "conquered Germany" itself Fascism needs hundreds of thousands of S.S. and special police to keep the people down. Thus, under Fascism, there must always be wars and a régime of terror. By its very nature, Fascism must be prepared to wage war continuously and never to refrain from terrorism.

But they are not going to conquer the world. So what is the practical value of ascertaining whether war and terror are permanently features of Fascism? It consists in these two reasons: One, to impress upon everybody's mind the profound danger which Fascism implies to mankind, everywhere, even in the "farthest corners of the world." And two, to make it quite clear that the fundamental measures of Fascism are usually envisaged as long-term measures. Fascists lie whenever they declare that certain measures have been taken under the compulsion of war —either its preparation or prosecution—but that, after victory, they will be rescinded. *There simply is no post-war period for Fascism.* Or, as the *Schwarze Korps*, the paper of the S.S. formations, once expressed it: "the German soldier must give up the conception of 'back home'" (*"Es gibt kein Zuhause"*).

The repressive measures of Fascism, the crimes against the liberty of the people, are measures in permanence. "For the duration," under Fascism means, as in Britain or in the Soviet Union for the duration of the war. But since war is a permanent feature of Fascism, "for the duration of the war" means for the duration of Fascism. The measures giving preference to armament production, distributing food, raw materials and labour power so that war industries have preference, are permanent measures under Fascism. The rationing system already begun in Germany in 1936, the forced labour legislation already introduced on a partial scale in 1934, and the extension and intensification of these measures in Germany and in the conquered territories in the course of the last few years are permanent measures because war and terrorism are the permanent sustaining features of Fascism.

In fighting Fascism, therefore, we are fighting for peace. *As long as Fascism exists, peace cannot exist. Only the root-and-branch destruction of Fascism can ensure no further danger from that source.*

3. Is the Fascist System a Capitalist System?

The German Fascists call themselves National-Socialists. By this they wish to indicate that they are both Nationalists and Socialists.

They are Nationalists in the perverted sense of the word. That is, they distort love for one's own people into hatred and contempt for all other peoples. They distort service to one's own people into the subjugation of all other peoples.

I think there are few, even among those favouring some sort of Fascism, who would maintain that German Fascism is in favour of the free and independent development of every nation in the world.

A. Is it a Socialist System?

As to whether the German Fascists are Socialists, if only in some respects, I devoted some space in some former studies to show that this is untrue.* But I think that, in those countries which this book will reach, there are but few who still believe in the Socialism of the German Fascists. It is no longer worthwhile setting forth a lengthy refutation of the claim of the Fascists to be Socialists. It is sufficient to point to the treatment of the working class by the German Fascists, described in subsequent pages, to show that they are not, have never been, and never intended to be, Socialists. But it is perhaps interesting to discuss in some detail one of the measures the Fascists have cited to prove to the credulous or infatuated that they really are Socialists, a measure which has even puzzled some of the more experienced observers of conditions under Fascism. I refer to the limitation of dividend payments, ordered by the law of March 29, 1934. This law did not really limit dividends, but it forbade any increae of the disbursement of dividend payments from 1933-34 on, if by such increase the dividend was raised above 6 per cent. If a company decided to increase the dividend and this dividend passed the 6 per cent limit, the company was forced to invest the surplus above 6 per cent in public loans.

This law has frequently been used by German Fascists to prove the genuineness of their Socialism, and it has also been quoted widely by non-German dupes of Fascism in almost every country to prove, that the Fascists, even if not pure Socialists, are at least "anti-capitalist."

There are two answers to this. One has been formulated very well by Mrs. Sweezy:†

"Since only 109 of the 585 stocks traded on the Berlin stock

* Cf. for instance, *Germany's Economic Position*, London, 1939, pp. 35 ff.
† Maxine Y. Sweezy, *The Structure of the Nazi Economy*, p. 130.

exchange on March 31, 1934, yielded a dividend exceeding the maximum, and since the law did not concern corporations which had reduced capital stock during the previous three years, its effect . . . was negligible."

And one may add that, as the average level of dividends was very low, it was possible for them to rise considerably on average, as the following table shows:*

But it is not for the sake of this practical refutation that I want to study in more detail this special kind of "case for Socialism." Let us forget for a moment the German Fascists and their dividend restricting decree, and study the role of dividends in highly developed monopolist capitalist society. By far the best material we find for this purpose is in the United States of America, and the most instructive tables have been published in the famous Congress Hearings on the Concentration of Economic Power.†

In Part 17–A of these Hearings we find the following table‡ on dividend payments and on salaries paid to high officials, including directors, of one of the largest oil trusts of the world, the Shell Union Oil Corporation and subsidiaries:

SALARIES AND DIVIDEND DISBURSEMENTS OF SHELL UNION OIL

Year	Payments to Officers and Directors		Dividends Paid on Common Stock	
	Amount	Index	Amount	Index
1929	$697,473	100	$18,285,985	100
1930	734,545	105	9,148,867	50
1931	745,535	107	0	0
1932	598,682	86	0	0
1933	641,364	92	0	0
1934	736,930	106	0	0
1935	728,722	105	0	0
1936	901,309	129	3,267,656	18
1937	969,061	139	13,070,625	72
1938	980,512	141	9,149,438	50

* *Statistisches Jahrbuch für das Deutsche Reich*, 1938, and *Frankfurter Zeitung*, January 17, 1943.

AVERAGE DIVIDENDS AS PER CENT OF SHARE CAPITAL OF ALL CORPORATIONS

1932–33 2·9	1934–35 3·6	1936–37 4·7	1938–39 6·4	1940–41 6·6
1933–34 3·1	1935–36 4·2	1937–38 5·8	1939–40 6·5	1941–42 6·4 [1]

[1] On a considerably increased capital.

† Hearings before the Temporary National Economic Committee, 75th and following Congress, Washington D. C. 1939 f.   ‡ Page 9982.

This most instructive table shows that, while during the severe economic crisis of 1929 to 1932 the dividend disbursements declined by 100 per cent and after 1932 did not again reach pre-crisis level, the salaries of the big company men increased, then declined by less than 15 per cent, and then increased again, reaching record heights. This is a development we can observe not only with the Shell Union nor only in the petroleum industry, but throughout industry in the United States.

What is the meaning of this relative development of salaries and dividends? There are various reasons for it. The most important is that the big employers come to rely, for their personal expenditure, more and more on salaries in contrast to former times when they relied mainly on income from dividends. By cutting down on dividends, they are able to increase the accumulation of capital, strengthen the financial reserves of their companies and thus to increase their wealth and their means of production. By paying themselves salaries and frequently increasing them, they guarantee themselves a luxurious standard of living. By cutting down dividends they skin the small shareholders (who are not at the same time directors) and are able to keep the money for themselves, that is for the purpose of increasing their means of production.

The same tendency in the development of dividends and salaries for the big capitalists also can be observed in other countries, of which not the least is Germany.

By looking afresh at this problem, common to monopoly-capitalism as a whole, and by studying its appearance in the United States we have ascertained that the dividend restriction introduced by German Fascism has nothing to do with Socialism; on the contrary, it is in the interest of the big capitalists. We also note that one cannot overestimate the propagandist astuteness of German Fascism. *Here we have a measure, solely in the interest of the big monopolists, a measure which became common practice, without the introduction of any laws in all big capitalist countries—and the German Fascists presented it as a Socialist measure; and actually convinced numerous people, including several not wholly untrained observers of political and economic affairs.*

B. Is Fascism Corporate or Managerial or State-Bureau-
cratic, etc.?

While the number of those who still see some socialist traits in
the Fascist system has diminished rapidly, the number of those
who see in it something which, they assert, can no longer be
called capitalist has by no means diminished, but has even
increased.*.

Almost all of them have one chief argument in common: they
point to the vast influence of the State in almost all spheres,
whether in price regulation, the regulation of exports and imports, education, arts or propaganda. From this they deduce
that German Fascism is different from the system of capitalism.
In exploding this theory—which is a dangerous theory, indeed,
because any wrong estimate of the character of an enemy as
deadly as German Fascism is serious and may lead to mistakes
in our struggle against it—we can use two methods: we can show
that the undoubtedly accentuated rôle of the State under German
Fascism does not necessarily contradict or detract from its
capitalist character, or we can show that the main traits of
monopoly capitalism are still inherent in German Fascism. That
is, we can study the rôle of the State as an instrument of rule, or
we can show that the main characteristics of the Fascist State are
still those of finance capitalism. I propose to examine both
aspects.

With the exception of the Soviet State, the State has always
been an instrument for the government of the majority by the
minority. There have been times when the part played by the
State was a relatively small one, when it almost disappeared
because of the disintegration of the ruled elements (e.g. during

* We find such theories developed by Peter F. Drucker (*The End of Economic
Man*), James Burnham (*The Managerial Revolution*), Hugh Ross Williamson
("Labour and the Fascist Spectre"—*The Fortnightly*, February, 1939), and
numerous others. Within the German anti-Fascist emigration, this conception
of Fascism has found protagonists in all groups, except the Communists.
Cf., for instance, *Das Wahre Deutschland*, February, 1939 ("Die gesellschaftliche
Umwälzung in Deutschland"), a conservative paper; or *Die Freiheit*, 1939,
No. 3, where the German Social-Democratic theoretician, Georg Decker,
writes in this sense; or the more "left wing" Social-Democratic *Sozialistischer
Kampf*, 1939 (Peter Anders, "Ist Nazideutschland kapitalistisch?"). The
examples could be multiplied hundredfold.

the last stages of the Roman Empire or during certain phases in the Middle Ages). Sometimes in one country the State played a considerable rôle while in the other it played a smaller one. Yet nobody would have denied that both countries belonged to the same kind of society (e.g. Germany after 1870, and the United States). There have also been times when the State played a considerable rôle in two countries and yet these countries belonged to different kinds of society (capitalist England and feudal France in the 17th and 18th centuries).

We see, then, that the importance of the part played by the State at a given period is in itself not enough to enable us to deduce the form of society then prevailing, whether one of slavery, feudalism or capitalism, or even whether it is a society in its early or later stages. The degree of the State's intervention in the activities of the people, including the members of the ruling class, does not depend upon the existing type of society. It depends upon certain historical circumstances which, in some form or other, appear in every kind of society. In every kind of society there occur periods in which the State as an instrument of rule is relatively but little noticeable. Also, in every kind of society, there are periods in which State interference is considerable, in which the State as instrument of rule comes very much to the fore.

Now, if we study the history of German finance capitalism—that is, the history of Germany from about the beginning of the present century—we find that the rôle of the State has been considerably greater than in other countries. The State as regulator, as a centre from which directives are given, the State not only as an instrument of oppression (police, prisons, etc.) but as an active instrument in the various spheres of national economy, has played in Germany a considerably greater rôle than in many other countries. Nobody can say that, with very few and rare exceptions perhaps, the great trusts and monopolies in the United States came into being with the active help of the Federal Government—through pressure, for instance, by this or that goverment department upon this or that big employer or group of employers to come to terms with the rest. In Germany, on the other hand, we find very numerous instances of State intervention to aid in the formation of cartels, trusts and monopolies.

Moreover, we find the State taking over certain branches of industry which in other countries are still under individual management and ownership. The best known example of this is the railways.

The example of the railways can be used to explain one important purpose of State ownership under monopoly capitalism. The railways of Prussia were taken over when they were bankrupt, when their sale to the State was profitable to the owners. But railways have been bankrupt in other countries too, and yet they were not taken over by the State and the owners found other ways to re-imburse themselves. In Prussia, the bankruptcy was not the reason for their transfer to State ownership; it merely facilitated the process. The main reason for the transfer was probably a military one, a reason, therefore, in which practically the whole of the ruling class was interested. For strategic purposes it was advisable to build and maintain in working order a number of railway lines, which, from the purely economic point of view, were unprofitable. By transferring their ownership to the State the ruling class ensured the existence of a military railway network necessary for its purposes of defence or aggression. Furthermore, State ownership meant that the burden of the maintenance of unprofitable lines should fall upon the shoulders of the people through taxation. Another advantage was that the continuous and costly efforts of various industries to secure cheaper transport rates for their products would not require the maintenance of numerous lobbying staffs, as with individual railway companies, but these efforts could be concentrated upon the one State administration.

The history of State intervention in the formation and consolidation of the German coal cartel throws light on yet another aspect of State help to the finance capitalists. The Rhenish-Westphalian Coal Syndicate was first formed in 1893 on private initiative. When it seemed in danger of a breakdown, compulsory cartellization for its members was provided by government decree in July, 1915, and this was extended in March, 1919, when by law the coal cartel became a compulsory syndicate; everybody had to join it. Upon whom was this pressure exerted? Firstly, upon those who believed themselves to be in so strong and favourable a position that they would be able successfully to compete with the others and yet make bigger profits because of their superior technical position (especially in case where mines were integrated into the iron and steel industry). Secondly, upon those who felt so weak that they believed that a trust or cartel would lead to their being squeezed out, to extinction. In whose favour did the State intervene? Not in the interests of the people ; not in the interest of any non-finance capitalist sections of society; but in the interest of the biggest (not necessarily technically and commercially best equipped) and most powerful mine owners, who individually were not necessarily bigger and more powerful than their antagonists but who, when combined, controlled a considerable part of the industry.

Thus we see that State interference, the increased rôle of the State, the State as a factor "meddling" in the most varied spheres of economic activity, is by no means something working against finance capitalism. On the contrary, it is a factor used, as an instrument, to support finance capitalism, helping it to overcome internal strife and to prepare for external war. And by whom is it used? By the strongest and the most powerful sections of finance capitalism.

But while this indicates that the rôle of the State was an active one in Germany even before Fascism came to power, it does not explain the State's vastly increased activity under Fascism. Why has State interference been intensified to a degree unknown, not only in finance capitalist Britain, the United States, France or any other country, but previously unknown even in Germany where it was always prominent?

When we study the history of State interference during the present century, we find that it is not true that the degree of State interference under Fascism—say between 1933 and 1939— has been unique. We find an equal, and in some respects even greater, degree of State interference in Great Britain or in Germany during the previous world war. And this also implies the answer to our question. We can point also to various other occasions which show a sudden and rapid increase of State interference in numerous spheres, especially the economic one. They are the various economic crises, especially during the last twenty-two years. The increase of State interference, not only in Germany but also in the United States, in Britain and in other countries during the crisis of 1921-1923, and especially during the last great crisis of 1929-1933 has been very considerable.

Both crises and wars* have in common the sudden sharpening of numerous issues, the urgent need of increased strength on the part of the ruling class at a time when many factors make for the weakening of their position. This increased strength is needed against external enemies (during the war); it is needed against the enemies at home (the masses of the people); and it is needed also against the internecine strife among the big capitalists which proceeds continuously in many spheres.

Now, if we ask why State interference under Fascism has increased so rapidly, we have the answer ready; especially if we remember the heading of the previous section, "War and Terror as Permanent Features of Fascism." The reason for the increased State interference is that Fascism is nothing but monopoly capitalist rule under conditions of constant war and terrorism. War and terrorism, however, require an extraordinary degree of State interference in modern society as is proved by the fact that State interference was enhanced in all countries during the last and in the beginning of the present war.

Various students of, and commentators on, current affairs have carefully noted the degree and forms of State control in Germany, and have then noted that in other countries there was much less State interference. Consequently, they have argued, that something new is brewing in Germany, a corporate State, a bureaucratic society, a "managerial revolution" (with the capitalists deprived of power, the managers, through the State, ruling supreme), a special form of St. e capitalism which decapitates the capitalists, etc. It would have been more fruitful if these theoreticians had first asked themselves: have we any other experience in the history of capitalism, and perhaps also in other forms of society of a decisive increase in State interference?

Even if they had not found the example of the previous war and of the recent economic crises they might have found other examples. They might have found quite a number in early capitalist society or in the last phases of feudalism. In fact, *whenever a class society is not yet strong enough to be secure against internal or external enemies or both, or when a class society has grown*

* This does not apply in the same way to just wars.

decadent and fears it may have ceased to be sufficiently strong against internal or external enemies, then State interference grows.* If we study the social history of mankind, we realize that the State is an instrument of power but is not the power in itself; State interference is characteristic in certain respects of the stage to which a system has developed, but it is not a system in itself.

Thus we arrive at the negative, but illuminating conclusion that the increased activity of the State in the various spheres of social life does not connote a new system, cannot be taken to denote any modification or restriction of monopoly, of finance capitalism under Fascism in Germany.

On the other hand, the above discussion has not proved to us in a positive manner that monopoly capitalism is still ruling Germany under Fascism. For it is theoretically conceivable that the increasingly active State has become the instrument of some-body or something other than the monopoly capitalist ruling class; in the next section, however, I trust we shall find ample proof that this is not the case.

C. THE MONOPOLY CAPITALIST CHARACTER OF FASCIST SOCIETY

In order to investigate whether capitalism really does still reign in Germany, it is necessary briefly to summarize the chief characteristics of capitalist society.

Capitalist society has gone through many stages. For example, how different in character are the first capitalistically managed farms of England in the 16th century and the Standard Oil Trust in the United States to-day. Yet, they have a number of traits in common. The two chief common traits are that both produce commodities for the market, that both are producing for the sake of profits, and that a considerable proportion of these profits are re-invested in new means of production, in new means of exploitation. Capitalist production does not produce for the home, does not produce the goods needed and desired by

---

* This explains also why State interference, although relatively small, was greater in Germany during the years from 1870 to 1914 than in the other big capitalist countries: the German ruling class with Germany as a late-comer in the world of capitalist nations felt at a disadvantage in relation to that of the other countries.

the individual producer; it produces for the market where the goods are sold for money. Capitalist production is not sold in order to accumulate a treasure in the cellars of the capitalist but in order to enable him to enlarge the basis of his production, to buy new machinery, new factory buildings, more land to be worked with better machinery, and so on.

Can we say that these fundamental traits of capitalist production have disappeared in Germany or even that they no longer determine the character of production there? I think such a statement would be incorrrct. The German owners of the means of production, of the factories and mines, are still producing for the market. Krupp has not turned towards spinning and weaving for his family, nor have his workers done so. They are still producing for the market. The prevailing and determining character of the products of Fascist economy is still that of commodities. Krupp, also, still produces in order to accumulate more capital, in order to increase the means of production, the means of exploitation at his disposal. He does not, as did many Indian rulers, regard his economic activities as means chiefly to accumulate a treasure. What he wants is more capital in order to produce more commodities in order again to enlarge his capital basis.

The fundamental traits of capitalist production have been preserved in Germany. But this statement is not sufficient. It may be claimed that Fascism has maintained the fundamental features of capitalism but has changed the monopolist, finance-capitalist, imperialist character which capitalism has assumed during the last forty years.

Is there then any evidence that Fascism, turning back the wheel of history by forty or fifty years, has erased certain characteristics typical of capitalism in its period of decay? What are some of the chief characteristics of imperialism, of finance capitalism, of monopoly capitalism? The first characteristic is that concentration of production and capital is developed to such a degree that the monopolies thus created play a decisive rôle in the economic life of the country. Is this still the case in Germany, or has the process of concentration been reversed and the power of monopolies diminished?

As to the development of the process of concentration it is

interesting to note the changes in the average size of German corporations under Fascism:*

AVERAGE SIZE OF GERMAN CORPORATIONS
(Million marks)

End of Year	Size	End of Year	Size	End of Year	Size
1933	2.256	1937	3.069	1941	4.597
1934	2,296	1938	3.397	1942	5.378
1935	2.494	1939	3.799		
1936	2.669	1940	3.983		

Looking at this table, nobody can deny that the process of concentration of capital has made rapid progress. During the short period from 1933 to 1941 the average capital stock of a German corporation has doubled.

But has there perhaps been a curious process of more concentration but fewer monopolies? If we look at the present structure of German industry, we find, not only that the old monopolies remain but a number of new ones, which for many years were in the difficult process of creation, have finally been established under Fascism. Among these are a cement monopoly and, quite recently, in the second half of 1942, the shipping monopoly created by the amalgamation of the Hamburg-Amerika line and the North-German Lloyd, after the State had given them back the last of the shares bought from them, before Fascism came to power, in order to save them from bankruptcy. While this process of the creation of a selected number of new monopolies† did go on, the number of small and medium undertakings was ruthlessly cut down.‡ The number of small retail shops, for

* *Wirtschaft und Statistik*, June, 1942 and September, 1943.

† The number of monopolies must not grow too quickly, must in fact always be a restricted one because otherwise the advantages of the monopolization process would disappear. If not only the steel industry ▸ut also the steel-using industries were monopolized there would be no extra profits for the monopolies to squeeze out of the rest of industry. It was one of the tasks of Fascist economy to see that the wave of monopolization which started soon after Fascism came to power was not only stopped but reversed when it clashed with the interests of the old-established monopolies.

‡ This cutting down process, this elimination of the small man was accomplished through various means. Sometimes raw materials were withheld so that they could not go on with their work; sometimes one simply ordered the closing down of all small businesses below a certain turnover, thus forcing many a small craftsman or shopkeeper either to give up his job or to declare a greater turnover than he actually had and consequently to pay ᵗaxes on

instance, declined from June 1933 to May 1939 by about 160,000 or almost one-fifth.* Between May 1939 and January 1943 an additional 80,000 shops were eliminated.† And since then further tens of thousands have been sacrificed.

A second important characteristic of this stage of capitalism is the stepping up of the export of capital as distinguished from the export of commodities. Have the German capitalists under Fascism increased their export of capital? Under the peculiar conditions—Germany being a debtor nation with a large capital import from the United States, Great Britain and other countries—this process of capital export naturally had to consist first in driving out foreign capital, beginning with a partial stoppage of interest payments. Nobody can deny that the Fascists neglected such measures. As good monopoly capitalists, they realized that their first and main object was to deprive the foreign capitalists of the advantages resulting from their exportation of capital into Germany. The next object, attacked chiefly immediately before the war, was to acquire capital interests in other countries. While the Fascists mainly chose the method of simply taking over the foreign capital investments of other capitalists (for instance, after the conquest of Austria, Austrian interests in Czechoslovakia; and, after the conquest of Czechoslovakia, Czechoslovakian interests in Rumania and other Balkan countries) this is just a special Fascist way of "exporting capital"; in effect, however, it is no different from other methods in so far as it leads to concentration of finance capitalist control of less developed countries in the hands of the German impe-

---

this fictional higher turn-over; sometimes instead of closing down businesses below a certain turn-over they were simply deprived of all municipal orders— the effect of such an order was usually the same as that of the more brutal shut-down. During the present war this process of "rationalization" has reached the small and medium factories in a considerable number of industries. In the tobacco industry, especially in cigarette making, almost all factories except the large scale establishments have been closed down. The defeat before Stalingrad and the consequent "total mobilization" led to a renewed combing out with the result that between January and July 1943, when the comb-out was officially declared to be finished, over 150,000 small establishments had been newly eliminated.

* Census statistics. As to the number of handicraft establishments, their decline can be estimated, for 1936, at about 28,000, and for 1937 and 1938, at more than 60,000 in each year.

† *Deutsche Allgemeine Zeitung*, February 9, 1943.

rialists and thus leads to production measures being taken in the interests of German monopoly capitalism. This does not mean, however, that German Fascism did not also make "normal" capital investments in other countries—especially in Spain, Manchuria, and the Balkans. *

A third important characteristic of this period of capitalism is the formation of international capitalist monopolies. Has Germany retired from this activity under German Fascism? On the contrary! She has continued all the monopolies in which she was a partner before the advent of Fascism, and has gone further. The recent investigations into the monopolist activities of American trusts have revealed how much closer became relations between American and German monopolies under German Fascism. The sending of the British private industrial delegation in the spring of 1939 to Duesseldorf was nothing but an attempt by British industry to muscle in and to get a larger share in the distribution of the world markets among the big monopolies. Nothing was further from the Fascists' minds than to impede the process of the international monopolization of the production and distribution of many commodities.

There are a number of other traits, more or less characteristic, even fundamental, of capitalist society under German Fascism as well in the period immediately preceding it, which any student can easily discover for himself. Those mentioned above however, are sufficient to enable us to come to the conclusion that German Fascism is nothing but a particular form of government within capitalist society, to be more specific, within imperialist, monopolist, finance capitalist society.

This does not mean, however, that there have not been quite important changes in the finance capitalist structure of Germany under Fascism. And we should study these changes in order better to understand the enemy, and to foresee and counter his plans and actions. It is perhaps easiest to begin by ascertaining who are the real rulers of Germany to-day, whether they are the same as those before Fascism came to power, from what groupings they come, what their economic basis is, and so on.

* See also p. 45 of this book, and p. 67.

4. ON CERTAIN CHANGES IN THE STRUCTURE OF MONOPOLY CAPITALIST SOCIETY UNDER FASCISM

A. THE RULING CLASS

The real rulers of Germany during the first third of the present century were composed of the most powerful representatives of the chief sections of national economy: the Junkers, representing agriculture; the leading capitalists in transport (shipping and automobiles), in commerce and banking, and in the heavy and consumption goods industries.

Sometimes the Junkers would obtain more advantages, sometimes the heavy industrialists; then, again, a consumption goods industry, or the insurance companies, would forge ahead. But, through all these various phases in which the one or the other of the different sections of the ruling class would be favoured by special legislation or similar well engineered luck, one could discern a certain trend: the section which on balance was most favoured, which grew strongest within the ruling class, was heavy industry, that is, the iron, steel, coal, electro and chemical industries.

When we recall the earlier history of capitalism we are not surprised that one section of the ruling class may grow stronger than the others. If we recall the early days of capitalism in England, we remember the preponderant position of the agricultural capitalist. In France, before the revolution of 1789, the strongest section of the bourgeoisie was banking capital which had in fact grown so strong that it had almost become alienated from the rest of the capitalist class, and even considered it, for a time, possible to come to a special agreement with the feudal class. *
In Germany during the first half of the nineteenth century by far the strongest among the industrial capitalist sections of society was that representing the textile industry. Thus it is not at all unusual to find certain sections among the capitalists in a predominant position. On the contrary, one can say that it is an exception if the main sections of the ruling class are about equally strong.

* The Necker ministry under Louis XVI was nothing but an attempt at a compromise between banking capital and the feudal class.

But while the position of heavy industry in Germany grew stronger in the course of the first third of the present century it would be wrong to say that they had achieved a secure, dominant position before Hitler came to power. On the contrary, the installation of Hitler as Chancellor was the immediate result of the momentarily unique position of heavy industry, of the most reactionary and imperialistic section of the bourgeoisie, and also was considered by heavy industry as a means to make secure permanently their position as the dominant sector of the ruling class. We have touched upon the peculiarly difficult position in which the rest of the big bourgeoisie found itself in the beginning of 1933*; it was in part owing to this embarrassment that heavy industry was able to execute the coup of installing Hitler as Chancellor. At the same time, it was the Hitler-Chancellorship which enabled heavy industry in the following years to solidify its position as the decisive section of the ruling class, the dominant section which in fact directs the policy of the State and uses the State as its own instrument.

Why has the German heavy industry, at first slowly and then suddenly, pushed its way into the foreground? Why, in the course of the last seventy years, has it attained first place in German capitalist society? Can we observe a similar development in all other countries? There are other countries in which heavy industry has gained in relative importance. But there are also some countries where it has grown without coming so much to the forefront. In Great Britain, for instance, we cannot find any evidence for any overwhelming influence on the part of heavy industry.† Was then Britain less imperialistic, less reactionary than pre-Hitler Germany? By no means! But the positions of British and of German imperialism were very different. British imperialism ruled over a large empire, an empire in which the consumption goods industries particularly had very solid roots and were thus in a much stronger position than in Germany, for instance. Britain had a large number of allies.

* See pp. 17–18.
† It is perhaps significant that while the biggest German wool concern was being sacrificed during the crisis of 1929–33, in Britain the Bank of England took the lead in helping to avoid any large-scale bankruptcies in the textiles industry.

Germany had a comparatively small empire and few allies, as the weaker power always has. Consequently, German imperialism, if it intended to conquer a large empire, had to prepare for such a conquest by intensive armaments. Armaments are the business of the heavy industries. Intensive armament means intensive accumulation of capital in the heavy industries, giving to heavy industries special economic and legislative favours, strengthening the position of the armament industries in society, and permitting and aiding the heavy industries to become a more and more influential sector within the ruling class. Here is the chief cause, not for the rise of heavy industry, but for the rapidity of that rise, not for a merely important position, but for the finally dominating position of heavy industry in Germany. Preparation for conquest, for war, and for an imperialist redistribution of the riches of this world, that is the reason for the position of heavy industry in German society, and that also is the reason why we call the heavy industrialist monopolists the most imperialist and chauvinist section of the ruling class in Germany.

With the strengthening of their position the heavy industry trust barons assumed more and more the rôle of the vanguard of the ruling class against the working class, which, of course, was opposed to the above-mentioned developments. After the beginning of this century, all measures to improve the conditions of labour were opposed most bitterly by heavy industry. If workers were shot down in a strike, one could be sure that it was in heavy industry. If a social security measure was bitterly opposed in the press, one could be sure that heavy industry paid the highest contribution to finance this campaign. It is because of this that the heavy industrialists are designated the most reactionary section of the ruling class.

Thus, one can say that, since the beginning of this century, heavy industry in Germany represented the most influential and reactionary single section of the ruling class. Thus, when it came to complete power and erected its dictatorship in January, 1933, Germany was ruled by the most dangerous, cruel, reactionary and aggressive section of the big bourgeoisie.

This definitely represents a change as compared with the first third of this century. It is a change synonymous with the rule of

Fascism in Germany.* The dictatorship of heavy industry, of course, makes for changes in the ruling class. The rôle of the other sections is diminished correspondingly. Where, before Hitler, bankers, textile barons, food manufacturing monopolists, Junkers and heavy industrialists met on more or less equal footing, the scene is dominated to-day by a galaxy of heavy industrial monopolists.†

But this does not exhaust the changes in the ruling class of Germany. The ultra-reactionary section of the German ruling class established its dictatorship with the help of a mass party, the National Socialists. The leaders of this party belong to-day very definitely to the ruling class. They belong to this class as big industrialists. They have taken over numerous directorates; they have bought big packages of shares or accepted them as presents. They have themselves, in fact, become big industrialists and trust barons.

One more important change must be added. Up to 1933 the big industrialists rather kept away from official State positions. They reigned through relatives and friends or hirelings; big industrialists were usually neither M.P.s nor high State functionaries. Since 1933, they have taken over positions in the political and State machinery.

Thus we find that leaders of the National Socialist Party have become directors in industry, sitting at the same table as the

* The reader is warned here when he looks for the economic roots of the Fascist elements in other countries not to concentrate on the heavy industries. While the pro-Fascists in Britain have, of course, contact with all sections of society, the centre of the economic backing of the pro-Fascist forces in Britain will be found to-day in the investment trusts and assurance companies. This is only logical, since in Britain there is no single section to-day dominant among the ruling class or even approaching a position of dominance. The best places to exercise background power, therefore, are the investment trusts and assurance companies which can exert pressure on all sections since they have control over a number of shares of all sections.

† When dealing, in his study "Imperialism, the Highest Stage of Capitalism" with an interesting case of bank "terrorism" against the German Central Northwest Cement Syndicate (Little Lenin Library, vol. 15, pp. 41–42), Lenin remarks: "In substance this is the same old complaint about big capital oppressing small capital, but in this case it was a whole syndicate that fell into the category of 'small' capital! The old struggle between big and small capital is being resumed on a new and infinitely higher plane." The situation, under Fascism is a further reproduction on a yet higher plane of this old struggle—the monopolies and cartels and trusts of the non-heavy industries now playing the rôle of "small" capital.

industrial lords of before 1933, having become one with them. And at the same time we find the industrial leaders as State functionaries, sitting at the same table as the National Socialist party bosses, having become one with them. *A process of merging has taken place between the industrialists and the party leadership.*

One can therefore say: *the composition of the ruling class has changed under Fascism. The composition, especially, of the inner circle of the dominant forces has changed: its basis has become smaller, many big industrialists have been dropped because they did not represent the heavy industries, and many party bosses have come in, as industrialists in their own right.* This new blend rules Germany to-day in the interests of ultra-reactionary imperialist monopoly capitalism.

One example may suffice perhaps to show the "new" ruling class in Germany, or rather the additions to, and eliminations from, the "old" ruling class. In May, 1942, when the whole of the German war machinery, army and economy, was geared for the so-called summer offensive an armaments council (*Ruestungsrat*) was established and attached to the Ministry for Armaments and Munitions, headed by the party official, Speer. The members of this armaments council are:

Field-Marshal Milch (close friend of Goering, prominent in German aviation circles before Hitler came to power, owes advancement solely to party influence; member of the board of Junkers Ltd.);

General Thomas (always a liaison man between army and industry; specially favoured by party; close friend of Goering; on board of Rheinmetall concern);

Colonel-General Fromm (friend of General Thomas);

Admiral Witzell;

General von Leeb (brother of the well-known marshal; on board of Goering trust).

These are the so-called representatives of the armed forces of which Milch is a pure party man and Thomas, Fromm and Leeb are so-called Nazi generals, that is, professional soldiers who owe their recent advancement to the party. Three of these generals are directors in heavy industrial concerns.

To these five so-called military representatives are added eight representatives from industry:

Wilhelm Zangen, an old acquaintance from pre-Fascist times, one of the old-guard leaders of Germany's heavy industry, general-director of the Mannesmann-Roehrenwerke, one of the most aggressive German heavy industrial concerns;

Hermann Buecher, for many years the leading figure of one of the two large German electro trusts, also on the board of Krupps and numerous other concerns;

Hermann Roechling, for many years the leading German Saar industrialist, prominent in iron and steel industry;

Albert Voegler, leading member of the largest German iron and steel trust, the United Steel Works;

Dr. Ernst Poensgen, leading member of the largest German iron and steel trust, the United Steel Works;

Philip Kessler, leading member of the Bergmann Electro Works, belonging to the Siemens trust, together with the A.E.G. (General Electro Works), headed by Buecher (see above), a leading electro trust;

Paul Pleiger, a general director of the Hermann Goering Works, formerly a small iron manufacturer who made his career as a party member;

Helmuth Roehnert, a general director of the Hermann Goering Works, formerly with the Quandt combine (before the Fascists came to power chiefly a machine-construction concern which in the meantime has spread over various fields with a rapidity which would be surprising if one did not know that Goebbels enticed and married the wife of the owner).

If we look at the industries represented we find not a single personality coming from the consumption goods industries, banking, shipping, the insurance companies or transport. The industrial representatives, and they form the majority of this council, come exclusively from heavy industry. Six of them are well-known figures from pre-Fascist times, five of them belong to the most prominent industrialists of the whole Weimar period, Zangen, Buecher, Roechling, Poensgen and Voegler. The two representatives of the Goering concern are special party representatives and owe their industrial position to the party.

If one adds that Goering has become the biggest industrialist of the world, Himmler the largest agricultural landlord, and Hitler the largest publisher, the character of the ruling class, this mixture of old-established industrial barons and new party bosses, becomes sufficiently clear. As a historical comparison by contrast, in the sixteenth and seventeenth centuries the British aristocracy refreshed itself through an admixture of enterprising, progressive capitalists. In Germany Fascism brought an admixture determined by the principle of selecting the unfittest. Under Fascism, the "new" ruling class is the result of a marriage between the old bourbons of exploitation and a new generation of gangsters who in their ruthlessness, brutality and their lust for power and riches are unsurpassed in the history of mankind. Moreover, while in Britain the admixture of the capitalists meant not only new faces but also a new and broader basis from which to rule, the new faces in Germany rule on the rotten basis of monopoly capitalism.

B. Banking Capital

Banking has always played an important rôle in the history of capitalism. Bankers have always been influential representatives of capitalism. Sometimes banks were the dominant section of capitalist society, sometimes they shared in unison with another section the most prominent position.

As I have already indicated, one of the characteristic traits of capitalist economy is production for profit—profit which is not to be consumed, or stored in the form of treasure, but which is to be re-invested in order to enlarge the capital basis; therefore one can say that capitalist production is production for the sake of creating more capital, that is more machines, more factory buildings, briefly, more means of production. The larger the amount of means of production in the hands of the individual capitalist the greater his power in capitalist society.

During the last forty or fifty years, the banks have played a great rôle in the process of enlarging the capital basis of the individual employers or companies. From the bankers' angle, the process was as follows: as the system for getting into their keeping all idle money improved, the amount of potential capital in the hands of the banks rapidly increased. In order to convert this potential capital into real capital they invested (or lent) this money in industrial concerns which were then able to increase their capital basis, their means of production, beyond what the profits accruing from their "own" means of production would have allowed.

From the point of view of the employers and companies, the process appeared as follows: if the individual company made an annual profit of 15 per cent or £15,000, and if £10,000 of this amount were used for the extension of the factory and purchase of new machinery, and if a bank, desirous of putting to use the money at its disposal, offered the company a further £10,000 the rate of increase of the means of production was doubled. The company could, thus, increase its capital twice as quickly as another company dependent upon the same rate of profit.

Private industrial capitalists, as well as bankers, gained advantages. The position of the company improved by its surpassing the average growth of other concerns; this meant more power in capitalist society, more influence, more orders, which in turn strengthened the position of the company. The bank at the same time had a good investment for its money (or had loaned it out profitably). This highly simplified account does not take into consideration the fact that all this happens in a capitalist society, with economic crises and depressions, competition between various banks and concerns, wars and bankruptcies. But the fact is that, in spite of all this, such collaboration was on the whole profitable for both parties and continued to an increasing degree, especially during the last half century of capitalist history.

With increasing competition between individual companies, and the increasing control by the banks of all "idle money" the banks' position grew increasingly stronger, The industrial concerns were eager to expand their capital basis with the help of the banks, and the banks used this eagerness of the industrialists to gain a position of importance within industry. If they lent money to a concern they wanted a voice in its affairs. While the industrialists were not strong enough to oppose this, they were strong enough to secure in return a position for themselves in the directorates of the banks. In this way developed what we to-day call finance capitalism, a system of capitalism in which banks and industrial concerns are merged, intertwined, interlocking, through reciprocal representation on each other's governing bodies. Banking and industrial capital are merged into finance capital. When, for instance, we look through the German press of the period of the Weimar Republic we find equal prominence given to the annual company speeches of the leaders in banking and industry. Before the last war, the Deutsche Bank was prominent in penetrating the Near East on behalf of German imperialism, while the Mannesmann-Roehrenwerke made their similar attempt on Morocco. At the head of each of these concerns stood united prominent leaders of industry and banking, merged into one unit.

This has changed somewhat under Fascism. Finance capitalism, of course, continues to reign. The unity of industrial and banking capital has not been disrupted. But the relation between the banks and the industrial concerns has been altered—not everywhere, but specifically between heavy industry and the banks. The banks have become minor instruments in the hands of the masters of heavy industry. They have been restricted, for example, in the amounts they may lend, for increased investments, to this or that non-heavy industrial branch of national economy. For instance, during the first few years of Fascism, new plant construction was limited by decree, in the following industries, among others:

Jute weaving	Cigars and Smoking Tobacco
Paper and Pulp	Wireless
Wool and Cotton	Nitrogen and Superphosphates
Cement	Rubber Tyres
Hollow Glass	Pressed and Rolled Lead Products

In this way the heavy industrialists have gained full control over the banks, over their investment policy, and the whole process of capital accumulation.

The most reactionary section of finance capitalism, controlling the financial institutions of the State, has assigned to the banks a minor rôle in economic society.* As far as they do business—and they still are very active—they act in the interests of heavy industry.

* It is interesting to read, in this connection, the following statement, in *Monopoly in the United States* (Labor Research Association, New York, 1942, p. 35): "Nevertheless, the T.N.E.C. indicated that financial institutions have not been playing the same dynamic rôle in the organization and extension of monopoly that they had played in the period preceding the First World War."

C. THE ROLE OF "PRIMITIVE ACCUMULATION"*

One of the interesting questions regarding the early history of capitalism is, how did the capitalists get rich? Did they slowly wrest economic power from the feudal class through the superiority of the capitalist mode of production, or did they take more energetic measures?

They used all kinds of means. The superiority of capitalist production methods was an efficient means of driving feudal economy more and more into the background. Through the development of a vast overseas trade they made quick strides. The robbing of the overseas countries was one of the most effective means of primitive accumulation of capital by European capitalists. But probably the greatest rôle in this early period of capitalism was played by robbing other European countries and their own country (that is the feudal ruling class as well as especially the most fruitful expropriation of the small producers, the peasants, the artisans and handicraftsmen). Robbery through the economic weapons, money and price manipulations, and by military means, including pillage and piracy, helped materially in the process of building up early capitalism on a rapidly broadening capital basis.

In the course of later centuries methods of accumulation became more refined, at least as far as accumulation from non-colonial countries was concerned. Trade, between capitalist countries at least, was no longer identical with plain robbery of some kind or another, although some elements of robbery remained.

Fascism brought a return to the more primitive forms of accumulation. It began with a change in trading methods. I do

---

* The term primitive accumulation can really be applied only to the early stages of capitalism. But just as we apply the term slavery to certain aspects of conditions in Fascist Germany in order to emphasize the backwardness of those conditions and in order to stress their primitive cruelty—in the same way I want to use the term primitive accumulation. When one thinks of the methods applied by the Fascists for acquiring Europe's industry, one is forcibly reminded of the famous description of primitive accumulation at the end of Chapter XXVI in the first volume of *Capital*: "The spoliation of the Church's property, the fraudulent alienation of the State domains, the robbery of the common lands . . . under circumstances of reckless terrorism, were just so many idyllic methods of primitive accumulation."

not refer to the various Fascist devices to avoid paying old debts. These have been employed before, even in the recent history of capitalism (although their variety and number, under Fascism, is somewhat unusual). But I refer, for instance, to the following practices. By making use of the trading difficulties of many countries, caused by the preceding economic crisis, the Fascists forced them to accept for their own products all kinds of goods produced in surplus by Germany. A famous example, frequently repeated, is the aspirin deal with Yugoslavia. In part return for a considerable portion of the agricultural surplus of Yugoslavia, this unhappy country was forced to accept from Germany such quantities of aspirin (which Germany produced in large volume) that the Yugoslav demand for this drug was probably anticipated for a decade. The large-scale agricultural interests in Yugoslavia were interested in getting rid of their surplus, and did not care what the Germans exported in return, since, according to the trade agreement with Germany the Yugoslav Central Bank paid the Yugoslav agriculturists on the nail for their exports to Germany. The people and, to some extent, non-agricultural interests in Yugoslavia, had to pay somehow for the unsatisfactory goods which Germany sent them. Mrs. Sweezy expresses all this succintly, and at the same time exposes another Fascist method of "dictatorship by trade," when she writes :*

"The small country had to take what Germany could spare, and could sell only those things which Germany wanted. The last stage came when the small country was practically forced to adjust its economic system to German requirements. Moreover, Germany would sell desirable machinery only if she was given a voice in the management of the small country's industrial enterprises."

But all this was only the beginning and though these methods continued they were largely replaced from 1938 on by even more primitive methods of accumulation through conquest and plain plunder. All these methods were first tried in Germany. I do not refer here to the increased exploitation of the people, with which I shall deal later in detail. But the plundering of capitalists was also begun in Germany. By this I do not refer to the relegation to a minor position of the non-heavy industrial

* L.c., p. 22.

sections of the ruling class although, in a sense, this also was a form of plundering of one capitalist group by another. We are not here concerned with plundering in that sense, but with plain robbery. This was committed on the Jews, and on non-Jewish political opponents of Fascism. The big capitalists in Germany gained considerable advantage through the robbery of Jewish capitalists. Such a crude form of robbery is new in the later history of capitalism and has its parallel only in its early times, during the period of primitive accumulation.

But the robbery of the German Jewish capitalists was only the prelude to the most gigantic robbery of competitors committed in the history of capitalism. This began with the conquest of Austria. It continued "peacefully" in Czechoslovakia. With Poland, primitive accumulation through war began and was continued (with Denmark as a "peaceful" interlude) in Norway, Belgium, Holland, Luxemburg and France. Then followed the Balkans, while a number of countries submitted voluntarily to economic penetration of a kind which resembled in many aspects the "peaceful" conquests of 1938 and the spring of 1939.

The whole process of accumulation was changed. There have always been conquests in the history of capitalism. But if in the nineteenth and twentieth centuries capitalist territories were conquered by capitalist countries, such conquests, though a highly desirable factor in the process of accumulation, did not determine the character of that accumulation. It would be wrong to speak of the nineteenth and of the first third of the twentieth century as a period of primitive accumulation. It is German Fascism which has re-introduced into the history of capitalism primitive accumulation on a large scale. The volume of the means of production, which has been added to that which German capitalism possessed before 1933 has been enormous. This primitive accumulation by means of war surpasses all that had been or could have been achieved by profits, however swollen, and their subsequent investment in means of production within Germany over a period of many decades. The increased accumulation in Germany through profits gained during the ten years of Hitler-Fascism is minute as compared with the gigantic accumulation through conquest.

This is not the place to weary the reader with the enumeration of factories and concerns all over Europe acquired or now controlled by German capitalism. Many books and pamphlets have been published on this subject. It would in fact be easier to enumerate the factories and concerns which are not under German domination. But it will help us to realize the extent of this process if we learn that it took German capitalism more than fifty years before 1939 to increase the means of production by the same amount as it has been increased in three years through primitive accumulation.

These successes have rallied the whole of the big bourgeoisie around German Fascism.* Those sections of the ruling class which had been relegated to a minor place in German economy, and among whom there had been, therefore, some discontent with Fascism, became enthusiastic supporters of the regime which had showered them with gifts and had made them supreme in their own spheres on the Continent of Europe. The return to the method of primitive accumulation has not only enormously enriched German capitalism, but it has rallied all sections of German capitalism enthusiastically to the Fascist régime. Bankers and plutocrats of every sphere in national economy represent to-day the Fascist system.

To this must be added the fact that as in the initial period of primitive accumulation, numerous "small men" have been able to derive profits. But there is one very sharp difference between these two periods. During the early period† the small capitalists who profited, with luck and energy, were able to rise to the position of big capitalists. This chance does not exist to-day. The big trusts monopolize primitive accumulation and the number of small capitalists continues to decline because they are being squeezed out of business. But there is a second group of small men who profit from plundering and pillage. These are the petty agents of the big capitalists and the minor officials of the State, who are given supervisory and other posts in the

---

* Though it closed its ranks at the beginning of the war because of the feeling that the fate of every big capitalist in Germany depended upon victory the really enthusiastic rally took place only after May–June, 1940. Since June, 1941, with the strategically unsuccessful campaigns in the Soviet Union, the former motive has again become more and more dominant. *And with increasing military defeats there will take place a growing disintegration, though on different lines, namely, right through all sections, including the heavy industrial one.*

† That is during the early history of capitalism.

conquered territories. They are petty thieves and petty robbers. They do not profit as capitalists. They profit, as the scum has always profited in every kind of society, in slave-holding or feudal or capitalist society, by bribes and by the large number of new jobs provided by the vastly enlarged supervisory staffs needed by private capitalists and the State in periods of rapid expansion. These lackeys have also become firm followers of Fascism which can transform the pimp or petty bully into the boss of a sub-department of a large factory in France or a dictator over a village in Poland.

*   *   *

These are the changes brought about by Fascism, which make Fascism, not less capitalist, but in some respect different from capitalism as it functions in other countries to-day. They represent an amalgam of methods and traits which have previously existed in separate phases of capitalism. We find monopoly as the dominant force in society in all the older capitalist countries to-day. But primitive accumulation as a dominant factor is something new in recent decades though it was well known in the early history of capitalism. The relegation of the banks to a secondary rôle is also new in recent capitalist history, but there have been earlier phases in the chequered history of capitalism in various countries when the banks were forced to take second or even third place. The rapid absorption into the leading circles of the ruling class of newcomers from a political party is no unique experience in the history of capitalism, though it is unusual in the recent history of the old established capitalist countries.

But these changes in the structure of monopoly capitalism are not all the changes which German Fascism has brought about. There is one change which is more fundamental, and which really affects the capitalist system as such. This change has hitherto been studied very little, yet, curiously enough, it is the only change which, if further extended, might provide a reasonable argument that Fascism is no longer identical with capitalism.

I refer to the growing weight of the elements of Barbarism in Fascist society.

5. ELEMENTS OF BARBARISM

All imperialist, finance capitalist societies are capitalism in decay, capitalism moribund. In order to delay this process—to overcome tendencies towards stagnation in production and technique, for instance, or to overcome the growing resistance of the working class—finance capitalism looks for new methods. One of these—tried so far only to a relatively small extent outside the orbit of German Fascism—is to increase profits by combining the modern means of exploitation, the intensification of the working process,* with older means, such as the prolongation of the working day, the decrease of real wages, increased replacement of men by women, etc.

The small beginnings of this combination of methods in Great Britain, the United States, or France (noticeable, especially, since 1919) were easily and rapidly surpassed by the Fascists, who have become past masters in the application of all the methods of exploitation ever employed in the history of capitalism and who integrate them into their system.

But Fascism not only seeks to employ all the worst features in the history of capitalism and to develop them to new degrees of brutality and effectiveness in the interests of the monopoly capitalists. Fascism has gone further and seeks to make use of the worst features of the whole history of human society. It has borrowed, in the course of the last few years, a considerable number of characteristics of feudal and slave-holding society. *This process of the employment of the worst features in the history of human society means that if Fascism is not beaten, if these features are allowed to develop further, mankind will be well on the way to Barbarism.*

These features, which we shall discuss in more detail when we study the development of labour conditions under German Fascism, are reflected, not only in the conditions of the workers, but also in the life of the peasants, the small shopkeepers, and the independent craftsmen. Before I examine some of these features, it is perhaps necessary to remind the reader that Fascism means war and terrorism in perpetuity, that is, that all

---

* Intensification of the working process is, of course, as old a means of exploitation as capitalism itself, but it has only in the more recent history of ~ 'talism become the dominant means. See Vol. I, pp. 33 and 43.

measures which appear to be only preparations for war or war-time provisions in reality will remain in force as long as Fascism remains in being.

If workers are tied to their factories, not being allowed to leave them without official permission, if they belong to the factory, if they are sold with the factory, if the selling price of the factory increases with the increase in the percentage of skilled workers; if the employer, in case he has no work, can lend his workers to another employer at interest, then this is feudalism on the basis of twentieth century economic conditions.

If the German Supreme Labour Court decides* that employers are justified in fining their workers at will, and that such fines are outside the jurisdiction of the ordinary courts and the labour tribunals—that is, if the employer is to some extent also the workers' juridical supervisor, we have a state of affairs which is reminiscent of some conditions under feudalism and some in a slave-holding society.

If peasants, small craftsmen or shopkeepers can be sent from one country to another—for instance, from Holland to the Ukraine—against their will, and if at their destination they are compelled to become the employees of individual employers or the state, this is reminiscent of similar transactions in slave holding society. This applies also to the compulsory transportation of men and women into Germany from conquered territories.

The entire Continent is treated as a grand colony of German capitalism. But the new feature is not merely that German capitalism exploits a capitalist country as it would a colony. It consists also in the fact that all the countries under Fascist domination, including Germany itself, are subjected to treatment which is not merely colonial, because it affects the "home country," the fundamental basis of German capitalist society, just as it affects the conquered territories. Feudal and slave-holding elements are infiltrating into the very structure of German Fascism itself. The German capitalist, as employer of German and foreign labour, becomes in many respects his own chief of police and judge, and hires out German as well as foreign workers. German capitalism itself, right at home, is affected by these elements of feudal and slave-holding society.

* See RAG 167/41, Decision of April 14, 1942.

German finance capitalist society is on its way to Barbarism. As a dying person visualizes in rapid succession the outstanding moments of his life, so German Fascism, in the dying days of finance capitalism, re-enacts the worst moments in the long history of mankind, going back further and further to the darkness of savagery.

And this is an organic development! Once Fascism gains power its nature compels it to go further on the way to Barbarism, it must grow more and more hellish. Once the wheel of history has been turned back by the vile hands of the Fascists, the backward course of Fascist Society becomes quicker, and ever quicker. How far back can Fascism go? We do not know. All that we know is that when Fascism is in power it can and will not stop until it has destroyed everything of human worth in this world.

It is for this reason that it is so urgently necessary to destroy Fascism so that the danger of its return is averted for ever.

CHAPTER II

THE GENERAL ECONOMIC POLICY OF GERMAN FASCISM

IN the previous chapter we have studied briefly the general structure and main features of German Fascist society. In this chapter it is our task to draw a general outline of the economic policy of German Fascism since its advent to power in January, 1933.* That is, we proceed from theoretical mechanics to practical economics, from the discussion of theoretical problems to the observation of economic practice of Fascism.

Since Fascism means war, terror and suppression in perpetuity it is obvious that the economic policy of the Fascist dictatorship can have only one object: To enable the régime to make as high profits as possible by waging war and keeping the people in a state of subjection. This task implies the transformation of the national and, subsequently, of the European and world economy into one of war and suppression.

Such a transformation introduces numerous changes in economic practice. It is our task to study this transformation in various fields, first, of the German national economy and, secondly, of the German imposed continental economy. The Continent is to-day under German Fascist rule, and its economy must, therefore, be adjusted to the needs and aims of German Fascist society. After we have studied in some detail the general economic practice of German Fascism we shall more easily be able to understand the various features of its policy as regards labour, and the changes in the conditions of labour which Fascism has brought about, which form the main subject of this book.

1. A PARADISE FOR HEAVY INDUSTRY

The transformation of German economy into one of war and suppression implies, as we have already seen, the most vigorous

* See also *The Economics of Barbarism*, by J. Kuczynski and M. Witt.

development of German heavy industry, that is chiefly, of German armament industry. For the major part of armaments are produced in the heavy industries, though uniforms, for instance, are produced by a consumption goods industry. Thus, for practical purposes one can use alternatively the terms "heavy" and "armament" industries.

The rise of German heavy industry under Fascism was phenomenal. The following German official production index shows that already in May, 1935, little more than two years after Fascism had come to power, the heavy industry production index had passed the 1928 level, the year preceding the economic crisis of 1929–32:

INDEX OF PRODUCTION OF HEAVY INDUSTRIAL GOODS*

(*1928* = *100*)

1932		46
1933		54
1934		77
1935	January	84
	February	86
	March†	95
	April	99
	May	101

In May, 1935, the index of production of consumption goods was more than 10 per cent below the 1928 level; and the total number of unemployed, according to the official statistics, amounted to over two million. These few but important data, added to those of the index of production in the heavy industry, show the paramount importance attributed to heavy industry under German Fascism, and how from the very first the Fascists concentrated on increasing the production of heavy industrial (armament) products. At a time when the number of unemployed was still over two million, when—if we include the unemployed excluded from the official register—it was still about double

* In the official index (Produktionsgueter-Index) the production of the following industries is represented : Iron and steel, non-ferrous metals, engineering construction, motor vehicles, chemicals, paper, potash, coal, gas, electricity.

† In these as well as in the figures given in the subsequent paragraph the Saar territory is included from March, 1935, on. Although the Saar production was a most welcome addition for German Fascism it plays only a minor rôle in the whole of the Fascist production. Source, *Konjunktur-Statistisches Handbuch*, 1936.

that of 1928, the production of heavy industry had already reached the 1928 level!

By 1936, production in heavy industry had beaten all records in German industrial history. Before the inclusion of Austria production of heavy industrial products was about one-third higher than the pre-Fascist peak.

Everything was subordinated to helping heavy industry along, by the combination of heavy industrialists and party bosses in their self-interest. Without difficulty the United Steel Works, for instance, obtained the 125,000,000 marks worth of shares (£6,250,000 at par) which the State had taken over in 1932 (at three times the market price!) in order to help the trust to tide over a disastrous crisis. About two-thirds of all capital invested in new firms between 1933 and 1938 went to the heavy industry. Many more examples could be given. They all prove one fact: *The history of German economy since 1933 is one of the subjection of every economic interest to the requirements of heavy, of armament industry.*

With March, 1938, a new chapter* in the history of heavy industrial production is being opened. Up to February, 1935, that is up to the reunion of the industry of the Saar with that of Germany, the heavy industry could increase production only by increased activity in German factories and mines. At the time of the absorption of the Saar territory, German heavy industry had almost reached its pre-Fascist peak. The addition of the Saar territory meant an extension of the capital and production basis of German heavy industry. But it did not mean an enlarged capital basis for the individual German heavy industrial concern.

With the occupation of Austria, began the enormous extension of the general, as well as individual, capital and production basis of German heavy industry. On March 12, 1938, German troops marched into Austria and in their wake followed the German industrialists or their representatives—with the exception of those who had arrived during the weeks preceding the attack. Krupp and Poensgen, Voegeler and Henschel, all the big men of heavy industry, came to Austria and grabbed what they wanted. The United Steel Works and some other

* The preface to this chapter was written in Spain in 1936 and 1937!

concerns had already had considerable interests in Austria before Fascism came. Where they had had a minority share it now became a majority one, and, where they had had no share, they often now took the whole. Not a single Austrian heavy industrial undertaking remained outside German-Fascist control. Accumulation by seizure took place on a gigantic scale. Within a few weeks the whole of Austrian heavy industry had, for all practical purposes, become German property. Iron ore production rose by almost one-third through the acquisition of Austria, manganese ore production by one-quarter.

The methods of acquisition were varied. Sometimes the owners—if they were Jews or political opponents—were simply expropriated. Sometimes German firms exchanged shares with Austrian firms, and, since the capital of the German firms was much larger, even a "fair" exchange—as far as the absolute value of shares exchanged was concerned—really meant that the German firm acquired a majority of shares in the Austrian company while the Austrian acquired only a small minority in the German. When no shares at all were taken over by Germans —perhaps if the owner was a prominent Austrian Nazi—German heavy industry nevertheless acquired control by subjecting Austrian production to German quota regulations—determining the amount of production for each factory.

The acquisition of Austrian economy brought two things of special interest into the hands of the German monopolists: Firstly, the patent rights, and, secondly, the foreign shares which Austrian economic institutions (industrial companies, banks, insurance companies, etc.) held, that is, Austrian capital investments in other countries. The acquisition of Austrian patents helped to rationalize and improve the technique of production in all plants and mines dominated by German heavy industry. The acquisition of Austrian capital investments in foreign countries helped German heavy industry to gain partial or complete control over some foreign concerns, chiefly over a number of Czechoslovakian firms. Through internment of the Austrian Rothschild, for instance, until he handed over all the shares he held in the Czech Vitkovice Iron and Steel Works, the Germans were able to acquire an important position in Czech heavy industry, even before the conquest of Czechoslovakia.

The conquest of Austria was followed by that of Czechoslovakia. First, with British and French help, the Sudeten territory was acquired; then the rest of the country was invaded. This conquest enabled German heavy industry to expand immensely. The largest armament works, the most up-to-date armament industry outside Germany, thus fell "without friction" into German hands. One-quarter of the European production of antimony, a metal which Germany did not produce at all, fell into German hands, and so did the only European source of mercury outside Italy and Spain.

But all these gains were as nothing compared with those of the autumn of 1939, of 1940 and of the first half of 1941. During this short space, the whole of the Continental heavy industry outside the Soviet Union was eventually brought under German heavy industrial control. True, some of the factories and mines had been damaged during the few weeks of warfare in the territories concerned. But this was quickly and efficiently repaired. Everywhere, the key positions were taken by German heavy industry. Everywhere, the patents were taken over and soon applied to the whole of European production. Everywhere, production was technically reorganized in the most efficient manner. Soon, the armament factories of Europe, whose owners had often sabotaged the war effort of their own countries when these were independent, were reaching new production records. French armament production under Daladier or Reynaud came nowhere near the level it reached under German Fascist control. Not a single important French heavy industrialist refused collaboration with Germany, and it is not to be wondered at that French armament supplies to the Fascist war effort between June, 1940, and December, 1941, were higher than those of the United States to all of the United Nations combined, during the same period. *

German heavy industry, however, was not satisfied with taking over the whole of the Continental heavy industry, directly or indirectly. It was not satisfied with rationalizing the factories and increasing their production. It was not satisfied with repairing them if they had been damaged. German heavy industry

* See *The Nation*, New York, April 18 1942.

also began to enlarge the factories and to build new ones. All over Europe new armament plants were being constructed.

From all this two facts emerge: firstly, the whole of Europe is now an armed camp, working for German Fascism, feeding the German war machine*; secondly, the distribution of armament factories all over Europe is developing according to a well-devised plan. Wherever armaments can be produced they are being made in the largest possible volume. Also, new armament plants are erected and others transferred, according to the requirements of German Fascism. The economic policy in regard to the armament (heavy) industry is determined by the need to have Europe covered with a net of armament factories, by economic-geographical conditions, and by the current strategy of German Fascism. This means:

Firstly, since it must be permanently prepared for war and against rebellion everywhere, German Fascism is interested in having everywhere not only armies of occupation with ample stores of weapons, but also the economic means for supplying them on the spot, that is, armament factories. The fact that the German armies of occupation in France or in Belgium, for instance, can be supplied with weapons produced in French or Belgian factories, facilitates the suppression of the people considerably.† *Such decentralization of the armament industry throughout Europe goes hand in hand with technical uniformity as the types of weapons to be produced are standardized and determined by a central office.* Tanks produced in France and sent to the Eastern front can get spare parts from the Skoda works in Czechoslovakia, just as German guns sent from Essen in the Ruhr territory could get munitions from Northern Italian factories.

Secondly, in these arrangements, Fascism is partly dependent upon the location of raw materials, such as coal and iron ore, upon power generating facilities, etc. Whenever possible it erects armament centres in those parts of Europe where natural conditions are favourable. If it builds a large aluminium plant in Hungary, this is due to the extensive bauxite deposits in

* *The Times Trade and Engineering*, July, 1943, write, for instance, on France: "The armament works and affiliated industries are working at full blast."

† The Soviet *Monitor* on March 9, 1942, reported that at a military parade in Paris German troops were equipped exclusively with French arms and not a single German-made tank or lorry could be seen.

that country, and if it has a gigantic plan for converting the Northern countries into electricity generating centres for a large part of the Continent, this is due to the natural facilities these countries offer.

Thirdly, while the Eastern front, for instance, is the chief centre of military activities, German Fascism pays special attention to the armament factories in Central and Eastern Europe. The French factories are, of course, also producing armaments, but if there is a shortage of anything, it is the armament factory in Czechoslovakia or Austria which gets preference, before that in France or Belgium.

Never in the history of industrial capitalism has the heavy industry been in so powerful a position as under Fascism during the last ten years in Germany. The profits of the original German firms are larger than they have ever been, but these are minute as compared with the capital gains through the acquisition of non-German firms. Nobody knows the value of these additions, whether they amount to one thousand million pounds sterling or to two or three thousand millions. Technical progress in the production of goods of destruction has been rapid. By driving some panzer divisions through the Continent, the heavy industrialists have acquired all the best inventions produced during the last twenty years. By pooling these inventions, the heavy industrialists have made great technical progress and increased the efficiency of the armament industry of the Continent very considerably. Through the conquest of the industry of a whole Continent it became relatively easy to eliminate inefficient and obsolete factories without seriously influencing the volume of production. By requisitioning labour power and raw materials they were able, whenever and wherever necessary, to erect new factories. Thus, German heavy industry saw all its plans more than fulfilled and found that its dreams had been but a pale foreshadowing of what reality was to bring—until June, 1941.

But, since June, 1941, the situation has changed. The gigantic requirements of the Eastern front have seriously impeded the freedom of movement and disposition of heavy industry, while the newer acquisition in the East of raw material resources and factories has been disappointing, This does not mean that heavy industry has not acquired some important new iron ore, manganese and coal resources, and that it is unable to exploit them partially. Nor does it mean that heavy industry has not conquered vast territories with a number of factories working in them to-day. German heavy industry has succeeded in turning some valuable industrial properties of the Soviet people into private capitalist means of production and exploitation.

But the vast majority of Soviet factories have been destroyed or damaged through the scorched earth policy of the Soviet peoples, or saved for the Soviet people through the leap-frog policy, so that, even more than two years after the territory has been conquered those enterprises can still not be used by German heavy industry—a very severe disappointment after the successes achieved elsewhere on the Continent. This means that the enormous requirements of the front, necessitating an all-out effort in production, make it more and more difficult to keep the machinery in European factories, including those in Germany itself, in good working order and fully efficient. It means that it is much harder—though by no means impossible—to get the necessary raw materials, man-power and new machinery to build, man and install new factories and have them working in the interests of German Fascism. More recently, since the battle of Stalingrad, in fact, German industry is losing heavily.

2. A Purgatory for the Consumption Goods Industries

The consumption goods industries produce mainly commodities which determine the standard of living of the people. If Goering said he preferred guns to butter this meant also that Fascism favoured the heavy industries at the expense of the consumption goods industries. If man-power, capital, and raw materials are available in insufficient quantities—and they are always insufficient under Fascism which cannot have enough of them in order to increase armament production—every other section of industry must go short of them.

No wonder then that the consumption goods industries were soon in a decidedly unfavourable position, after the advent of Fascism to power. The policy which the Fascist Government pursued was expressed by Dr. Schacht* as follows:

* Speech on November 28, 1938, to the Economic Section of the German Academy.

"*The less the people consume, the more work can be done on armament production. The standard of living and the scale of armaments production must move in opposite directions.*"

Within a few months after Fascism had come to power, the consumption goods industries began to feel the pinch. Their freedom of movement on the various markets where they bought their raw materials and machinery for production began to be restricted. Within a short time a number of them were forbidden by law* to expand their production facilities. During 1934, when it was about 10 per cent below the 1928 standard, the production of consumption goods (excluding the production of goods for the army, air force and navy) had about reached its peak; 1935, 1936, 1937, 1938 and the first nine months of 1939 brought no increase in Germany proper.

This does not mean that the consumption goods industries did not make good profits under Fascism, nor that, until the outbreak of the war, they did not increase their rate of exploitation and benefit considerably from the anti-labour policy of the Fascist Government. Nor does it mean that the big monopolists and trust barons in the consumption goods industries did not profit from the general Fascist policy of squeezing out the small employers.

But it does mean that the consumption goods industries did not share in the same degree as heavy industry in the benefits introduced for industry by the Fascist régime. While heavy industry grew rapidly in strength and power and got the best of everything, the consumption goods industries had to take a back seat. The consumption goods industries got less and less raw materials, and the heavy industries more and more. The consumption goods industries were told to work short-time or to discover substitute materials. When, in 1935, foreign exchange was very short and methods of overcoming this shortage had not yet been developed to the extent we find in 1937 and 1938, the textile factories, for instance, were forced to cut down the number of hours per worker to below the crisis level of 1932. The same thing happened in the clothing industry.

Moreover, heavy industry made serious inroads into the

* See p. 43.

domain of the consumption goods industry by forcing it to introduce substitutes, often manufactured by heavy industry itself. The growing proportion used of staple fibre, for instance, gave the chemical industry an increasing share in textile manufacture. True, the textile industry shared in the production of staple fibre, but it could not prevent the monster chemical trust from muscling in. Similar developments can be observed in other branches of the consumption goods industries.

Thus, for the consumption goods industries things were not so rosy during the first years under Fascism, especially if the magnates of these industries compared their position with that in pre-Fascist society, or with that of the heavy industrial magnates under Fascism.

But the situation began to change with the conquest of Austria and of Czechoslovakia. Both countries had a considerable textile industry, pottery, toy and leather industries, all of them working in serious competition with the German industries. When these countries were occupied the German consumption goods industries got a firm hold upon minor, but nevertheless quite serious, competitors on the all too small world market. Just as the heavy industries of these two countries were annexed by the German heavy industrialists so were the consumption goods industries annexed by their German competitors. Moreover the German industries acquired, together with the factories, not inconsiderable quantities of raw materials which they transferred partly to their own plants, and partly consumed in the "native" factories for their own profit.

The situation was, however, not an easy one. Soon the stocks of raw materials were used up and the textile and other industries could not make full use of the sudden acquisition of new capital, of this enlarged production and exploitation basis. What was the use of the Austrian and Sudeten-German factories, of the buildings, of the fine machinery, of the skilled labour force, if sufficient raw materials were not available, if heavy industry clamoured for labour power from these factories in order to increase its own personnel, and some heavy industrialists even went so far as to demand the scrapping of the machinery in these factories in order to turn it into guns! When the present war broke out the situation of the consumption goods industries, in spite of the large capital gains made, had become very difficult, and it was realized that a new policy was needed.

The present war brought enormous gains for the whole of the consumption goods sector of German industry. It delivered into German hands the Polish, Belgian, and French textile industries the huge food manufacturing concerns in Holland and Norway, and large capital additions to other consumption goods industries. Primitive capital accumulation through the acquisition of the Continental consumption goods industry, proceeded at a rapid pace.

It soon became clear, however, that a well-considered policy for the domination of the Continental consumption goods industries was needed, since in contrast to heavy industry, the raw material resources were not acquired together with the manufacturing centres, and also—a more important reason—because the Fascist system, while it cannot have enough armaments, has no need for unlimited production of consumption goods. On the contrary, the fewer consumption goods needed, the better; for, as Dr. Schacht rightly pointed out: under Fascism, the standard of living and the standard of armaments must necessarily move in inverse directions, and as the standard of armaments has to go up that of living must go down. On this basis, German Fascism decided to follow a policy for the consumption goods industries which is just the opposite to that of the heavy industries. *Instead of decentralizing production all over Europe, as in the case of the heavy industry, it was decided to centralize the production of consumption goods as far as possible within Germany. Instead of bringing the consumption goods industry up to the highest standard of efficiency all over Europe, it was decided to close it down and destroy it.* Those factories damaged by warfare were not repaired. If they were undamaged and in good working order, their working time was cut. A number of them were robbed of their machines which were used as scrap. Some of them were completely gutted, their machinery being taken out and scrapped, and the fixtures used in the erection of heavy industrial plants. *

* In France, about ten thousand establishments were closed, many of the factories producing consumption goods. Of 12,200 textile factories 4,200 were closed by the end of 1942. (*The Economist*, March 13, 1943.)

Here we can observe a most important feature of German Fascist economic policy on the Continent, of the New Order being introduced on the Continent. It is a process which, in some respects, is reminiscent of Britain's policy in India about one hundred and fifty years ago. At that time India was producing large quantities of textile and other handicraft commodities, which represented serious competition for British industry. Consequently, Britain destroyed these "industries" with the result that, within a few decades, the Indian population became more and more dependent upon British industrial products. In a somewhat similar way, but on a different plan, German Fascism is destroying those consumption goods industries of Europe which might compete with German industries. But there is a historical difference: German Fascism is not destroying an obsolete economic system, as did British capitalism in India. It is wiping out the most highly developed factories in Europe which, in the hands of the people, could produce goods so sorely needed by the population of the Continent, and which will be so urgently necessary in order to raise the standard of living after the overthrow of Fascism. Furthermore, while British capitalism brought at least some industrial progress to India (a railroad system, for instance, and later on, a capitalist textile industry) the only, or at least the chief, technical progress which German Fascism brings to the conquered territories is in the production of armaments.

While the conquest of the Continent, as far as the heavy industry is concerned, meant the largest process of primitive accumulation witnessed since the early period of capitalism, for the consumption goods industries it means something unheard of, on this scale, in history: a gigantic process of *negative accumulation*.* When Indian industry was destroyed by British capitalism, something was destroyed which could not be taken over by British industry because it was run on the lines of another and less progressive society. There was no negative accumulation, therefore. Or if there was, another form of production, a less progressive form of production was "negatived." German

---

* On a minute scale, as compared with what Fascism does, we find negative accumulation, for instance, in the case of monopolies buying up a competitor and closing down his works.

Fascism, however, is "negativing" the means of production of its own form of society, leaving a void.

In so doing the Fascist viewpoint is: A fundamental feature of the New Order for the peoples of Europe is a decrease in the standard of living; this means decreased consumption of commodities, and, therefore, a decreased need for factories producing consumption goods. What commodities are needed can be produced by the factories situated in Germany proper, in some of the cheaper producing, neighbouring territories to the East, or in the few factories in France, Belgium, etc., which are worth keeping for the sake of the world renown they have achieved (for instance, Sèvres porcelain), or in the few factories worth maintaining because of their favourable location (e.g. fish canning factories on the coast). As a rule, however, the consumption goods industries are to be concentrated in Germany and the great gain of the German consumption goods industry through the war lies in the elimination of their competitors. Never has the position of the German consumption goods industries been as favourable as in 1940–41. Never have they had so large a market, never have they been so powerful.

The campaign against the Soviet Union has affected the consumption goods industries rather differently than heavy industry. While, through the leap-frog and scorched earth policy, heavy industry failed signally in its attempts to gain through primitive accumulation, the consumption goods industry, out for negative accumulation, lost little. It lost something, of course, through the destruction of stocks. But the chief losses for the consumption goods industries were indirect ones, caused by increased difficulties arising out of the enormous strain imposed upon Fascist economy. The growing shortage of labour, for instance, means that the consumption goods industries, even in Germany proper, are again increasingly restricted by having to give up workers to heavy industry. As it is becoming more and more difficult to replace worn out machinery, add to this the shortage of raw materials which had become intensified, once the stocks in the conquered territories were consumed, and it is clear that the situation for the German consumption goods industries has deteriorated during the last year and a half— though the gains are still enormous.

Once we realize that the consumption goods industries are gaining chiefly by negative accumulation, it becomes obvious that, in their case, the profits they get from current production in Germany play a much greater rôle than in the case of the heavy industries, and this will become even more the case if the method of negative accumulation continues to be applied. That this will indeed be the case is shown by the fact that the increasing needs of the armament industry will require the utmost use of all available resources, resulting in the further destruction of the consumption goods industry all over Europe. Being subordinate to the requirements of heavy industry, the consumption goods industries, while enjoying a splendid position as compared with formerly, have to pay by contenting themselves mainly with negative accumulation* (eliminating competitors) and with profits from current production in Germany.

3. THE POLITICS OF FOREIGN TRADE

Germany's foreign trade has always been considerable. In contrast to that of the United States, for instance, it always plays an important rôle in general economic development. Under Fascism, foreign trade became an instrument for war preparation and fell under the complete control of heavy industry. What does this mean exactly? It means that the questions of what goods should be imported and exported and with what countries German economy should trade were considered from the point of view of their usefulness in the preparation for war and of the interests of heavy industry.

That meant that chiefly such commodities had to be imported as favoured the growth of heavy industry while goods useful to heavy industry required a special export license. At the same time, if foreign exchange was short—and it was always short†— raw materials for the consumption goods industries would be imported in quantities as small as possible, unless the Fascist

* Negative accumulation, for the German consumption goods industries, means missing the chance of exploiting workers in other countries, and foregoing profits from the use of non-German means of production.

† Foreign exchange must be short under Fascism, so long as it has not conquered the world, since foreign exchange is needed to import raw materials useful for war purposes and of those Fascism can never have enough.

régime thought it useful to have some reserves, in preparation for a lengthy war with a blockade.

In order to facilitate the closest supervision of all imports and exports, Dr. Schacht announced, in September, 1934, his so-called New Plan which provided for the official scrutiny of every single foreign trade transaction before it could be undertaken. In the course of time the foreign trade supervisory apparatus was developed to such a degree that it consisted at the top of 24 Import Supervisory Departments, 4 National Offices, 29 Currency Departments, 24 Inspection Offices for the Control of Import Prices, and finally the whole apparatus of the Foreign Trade Service. The *Frankfurter Zeitung*, August 15, 1938, explained that the exporter was required to fill in "on an average over three dozen documents, of which the greater part are schedules, departmental questionnaires and so on."

Through this system of supervision German foreign trade was put into a straight jacket—but those who tightened the jacket were the heavy industrialists who themselves were free to do what they wanted to. To illustrate this it is interesting to contrast a complaint by the Chamber of Commerce and Industry of Bremen, in its annual report in 1938, and a heavy industrial export agreement signed in the second half of the year covered by the report. The Bremen Chamber of Commerce represents chiefly the interests of the exporting and importing houses. These firms, being no part of heavy industry, had to take a minor place even in their specific field of activity. They did not complain of a rapid decline of foreign trade, which in fact had not taken place. The grounds of their complaint are different:

> "Executive organs of the State allot to a private undertaking a monopolist position for the importation of goods of a particular country of origin, thus excluding from first-hand foreign trading certain firms engaged in foreign commerce which formerly were in the market as independent German buyers."

German merchants have been excluded from foreign trade activity to a considerable extent. The state regulates and curbs their activities in accordance with the directions of the heavy industry. But the export departments of the heavy industrial trusts have grown rapidly, have, to an increasing degree, established direct contact with foreign markets, and have sometimes even established contact with foreign governments or semi-governmental institutions. On September 24, 1937, for instance, the heavy industrialist, Otto Wolff, signed an agreement on behalf of a number of heavy industrialist concerns with the puppet government of Manchukuo. This agreement provided for a loan to Manchukuo of £2,000,000, stipulating that the money was to be used to buy from the German heavy industrial firms which granted the loan, machinery for the building-up of a heavy industry in Manchukuo.

These two examples show clearly the effects of the domination of German foreign trade by heavy industry, and the rôle which German heavy industry plays in the execution of its plans.

Let us now look at some broader aspects of the general development of German foreign trade under the Fascist régime. The following table gives the net imports of a number of important commodities into Germany:

NET IMPORTS OF SELECTED COMMODITIES INTO GERMANY
(Quantities, 1,000 tons)

Commodity				1929	1938
Iron ore..	..	..	..	15,794	21,926
Manganese ore		..	..	389	425
Copper ore	..	..	..	430	654
Lead ore	..	..	..	114	141
Zinc ore	..	..	..	95	138
Rubber ..	..	..	..	49	108
Raw cotton	..	..	..	358	351
Raw wool	..	..	..	161	165
Wheat ..	..	..	..	1,820	1,268
Lard	..	..	..	125	42
Cheese ..	..	..	..	64	32
Eggs	..	..	..	168	102

This table fully conforms to the general rules of Fascist policy: everything for heavy industry, for armaments—and as little as possible for the people. Foreign trade is made the servant of aggressive policy. The first six commodities in the above list are of major importance in the preparation of war; they are among the most important raw materials needed by German heavy industry. Iron ore imports have increased by more than one-third and rubber imports have more than doubled. In stark contrast to these stand the six other commodities. These are mainly goods needed by the people to maintain their standard of living; some of them are raw materials for the consumption goods industries. Imports of raw cotton and wool have remained about stable—in spite of the rapid increase in the production of uniforms, etc., for the army; that is, the amount of cotton and wool imported for civilian consumption has declined; wheat imports are lower by almost one-third; cheese imports have been halved.

But German foreign trade policy under Fascism did not only rigorously control the import and export quantities of individual commodities in the interests of heavy industry. It also tried to direct foreign trade towards those countries with which it was most advisable to have close commercial relations in the event of war. Therefore, trade with Eastern Europe, chiefly with the Balkans, became of paramount importance: they were to form the Fascist hinterland in war—if they were not already conquered "peacefully" before its outbreak.

The following table shows how Fascist Germany prepared this Balkan base by constantly increasing her share in the foreign trade of the Balkan countries until they became so dependent upon Germany that German economy dominated that of the Balkans. During all those years some of these countries endeavoured to counteract German influence by establishing closer commercial relations with France or Great Britain, but they were rebuffed. Furthermore, while, in the beginning, German Fascism was prepared to offer bait of favourable terms, later, when it had established itself firmly enough, it had garnered a number of native economic leaders ready to torpedo any plans to oust German Fascism from its dominant position.

GERMAN SHARE IN FOREIGN TRADE OF SOME BALKAN COUNTRIES*

| | Imports | | | Exports | | | Total Turnover |
	1929	*1932*	*1938†*	*1929*	*1932*	*1938†*	*1941*
Bulgaria	22	26	52	30	26	59	80‡
Greece	9	10	29	23	15	39	—
Hungary	20	23	30	12	15	28	59
Rumania	24	24	37	28	12	27	65§
Turkey	15	23	47	13	14	43	20
Yugoslavia ..	16	18	33	9	11	36	—

* Sources, for 1929, 1932 and 1938, official trade statistics of respective countries; 1941 cf. *Twelfth Annual Report, Bank for International Settlements*, p. 47.
† Including Austria.   ‡ Exports only.   § January–June.

The rapid growth of the German share, and its overwhelming superiority by 1938, is obvious.

During the war, German foreign trade at first languished. But, with each new country conquered, it increased again, though the flow of trade became more and more one-sided: German imports from the conquered Continent rose rapidly, while exports to the conquered countries lagged. There are practically no foreign exchange difficulties. These countries are forced to send to Germany what the war machine requires, while Germany sends them only what conforms to the interest of the German war effort. The growing gap between what Germany is taking from, and what she is putting into, these countries is termed their "contribution to the European war effort." But, in spite of this rapid increase in foreign trade, the position of the old established export and import houses has not improved; on the contrary, it has further deteriorated. *While the position of the consumption goods industries has definitely improved with the war and its conquests, that of the German merchant houses has grown from bad to worse.*

4. TRANSPORT: AIR AND ROAD VERSUS RAIL AND WATER

Transport, or rather the production of the means of transport, is mainly a job for heavy industry. The most important means of transport are railways and ships. The last few decades have added the aeroplane and the motor vehicle, which are often the peace-time products of armament concerns.

Germany has always had an excellent network of railways, covering the whole country, and designed often from a purely strategical point of view. General Wavell would probably say that any military leader should excel in logistics with such a railway system. To this must be added the fact that German airways, in their efficiency and extent, were equalled by no other country in Europe. All this, of course, existed before Fascism came to power.

German inland waterways, in spite of some improvement after the last war, had been neglected as compared with the two above-mentioned branches of transport. The motor vehicle industry was relatively undeveloped, owing chiefly to the impoverishment of the German lower and medium middle class in consequence of the lost war and inflation. German shipping, after the terrific losses in the last war and through the peace settlement, had again gained considerable volume.

When Fascism came to power it aimed chiefly at a further improvement in air communications and the building up of a large stock of automobiles, motor cycles, lorries, etc., combined with the construction or reconstruction of roads able to carry a considerable amount of motor traffic. Realizing that the next war would require a large air fleet and a large corps of mechanically trained people, Fascism pressed ahead as quickly as possible in these two fields—neglecting other sections of transport. The following table gives a picture of the development of the means of transport and of their use.*

TRANSPORTATION BEFORE THE CONQUEST OF AUSTRIA

Section	1929	1932	1937	1938†
1. Railways				
Locomotives—1,000	26	24	24	—
Coaches—1,000	90	91	87	—
Freight cars—1,000	660	639	587	—
Passengers—million	2,057	1,352	1,874	—
Freight—million tons	531	308	547	—
2. Canals and Rivers				
River boats with motor power	4,872	4,841	5,440	—
River boats without motor power	14,557	12,944	12,441	—
Freight	110,669	73,744	133,080	—
3. Shipping				
Merchant vessels—1,000 G.T.	4,093	4,164	3,937	4,244‡
Merchant vessels launched—1,000 G.T.	249	81	435	481
4. Airplanes				
Passengers carried—1,000 ..	97	99	323	—
Freight and mail carried—tons	2,456	2,503	8,721	—
5. Motor Vehicles				
Motor cycles—1,000	608	866	1,327	1,513
Automobiles—1,000	423	549	1,108	1,272
Motor buses—1,000	11	12	17	18
Trucks and lorries—1,000 ..	144	174	320	366

The first three transport sections show very little progress under Fascism. The railway system had, of course, suffered

* *Statistisches Jahrbuch für das Deutsche Reich*, 1938; *Statistical Year Book*, *1939-40*, of the League of Nations. † Excluding Austria. ‡ 1939, 4,493.

during the crisis because locomotives, coaches and freight cars which had become too old or damaged were not replaced. But when conditions changed and the railways had to carry an increasing number of passengers, and more freight than before the crisis, Fascism did nothing to improve conditions. The number of locomotives, passenger coaches and, especially, freight cars continued to decline. Conditions on the rivers and canals improved slightly as the number of power driven boats was increased—but the total number of boats declined considerably. Overseas and coastal shipping did not receive any special attention—it was not until 1938 that the total tonnage exceeded that of 1929.

How different when we examine the next two sections! *The "motorization of the German people" made rapid progress! This motorization was in preparation for the Blitzkrieg, for the quick covering of long distances, and for warfare in a country with a different rail gauge such as the Soviet Union.* The tax on automobiles was reduced. The motor industry had to be expanded as quickly as possible. When the number of automobiles in Germany had doubled, as between 1932 and 1937, the Fascists were still dissatisfied. Motorization, in spite of the lowering of taxes on automobiles, the building of the famous auto-roads, and numerous direct and indirect subsidies to the automobile industry, was not going quickly enough; the number of persons who could drive a car was not growing rapidly enough for utilization in mechanized blitz warfare. A new automobile factory, bigger than any on the Continent, was being built at Fallersleben, sponsored by the Labour Front, which advanced fifty million marks for this purpose. Hundreds of thousands of Germans were expected to buy the automobiles it was to produce. By moral pressure numerous skilled workers and salaried employees were forced, not only to order these automobiles in advance but to pay instalments on them long before they were on the market, even before the factory was completed which was to build them. In this way, hundreds of thousands of working people were compelled to finance this undertaking, which was to make of the German people a "nation of motorized warriors." The increase in the number of trucks and lorries was as great as that in automobiles. These vehicles are one of the most important factors in modern mobile warfare for the transportation of troops, munitions and food.

But the greatest progress was made in air communications, that branch of transport which under the Weimar Republic already had been developed so quickly. In spite of the severe economic crisis, the number of air passengers carried was higher in 1932 than in 1929; and the same holds true of freight and mail. When Fascism came to power, the development was accelerated immensely and within five years the number of passengers increased more than three times, while commercial freight and mail carried in 1937 was almost three and a half times as large as in 1932, in spite of the fact that by 1937 Fascist Germany also possessed a large fleet of military aeroplanes, which it did not have in 1932.

The war brought a further very rapid expansion in the two favoured branches of transport: the aeroplane and the motor vehicle. And at the same time it brought about a rapid primitive accumulation. The large and highly developed automobile industry of France, and the first-rate aeroplane industry of Holland were taken over, including their inventions and skilled workers. Within a short time after the conquest of France the transport manufacturing industries of that country were working full blast for the German war machine. The following extract from the *Financial News** illuminates the importance of the French transport manufacturing industry to the Fascist war effort:

> "Current reports from Washington throw an interesting light on the political manœuvres now proceeding between the Laval group of politicians and the German authorities in Occupied France.
>
> "According to these sources, the French automobile industry has been making particularly impressive efforts to supply Germany with manufactures. The Hispano-Suiza concern is concentrating upon engines; the Citroën and Delahaye works are said to be turning out trucks and tanks for Germany. According to Washington, Peugot is now turning out double the pre-war production of two- and four-ton trucks.

* Apr 20, 1942.

... It is claimed that in July last alone French factories took orders from Germany for more than two thousand planes, and that a very large proportion of these units have now been delivered."

But at that time German transport was already in serious difficulties and the provisions made by the Fascists proved completely inadequate. The campaign against the Soviet Union had thrown out of gear the Fascist transport apparatus. Until then, the Fascists had proved to be right in concentrating upon motorization and the aeroplane industry, filling gaps in railway rolling stock by robbing from other countries. French coaches, Belgian locomotives, Rumanian tanker-cars, had made up for the neglect of previous years. But the requirements of the campaign in the East were such that German transport, especially the railway system, almost broke down.

The enormous primitive accumulation in the automobile, aeroplane and shipbuilding industries, and the large quantity of means of production and rolling stock accumulated by the Reichs railway and by the private corporations producing railway equipment, brought them huge profits. But the disappointments of the Soviet campaign, the lack of prospects for new capital accumulation, the strain imposed upon the ... capital of German industry (rapid wear and ... with great difficulty in replacement, etc.) ... exultation inspired by the swollen gains of th...

5. AGRICULTURE: SATED JUNKERS AND PLU...

For reasons connected with its general wa... cultural policy of the Fascist régime was bas... to make Germany as far as possible independe... of food imports and, therefore, to increase home production. Much thought, therefore, was devoted to the development of German agriculture. This did not mean that the consumer would benefit by increased production. On the contrary, *Fascist policy of increased agricultural production was ... of lowering the food standard of the people—and Fasc... standard of agriculture was combined with a policy ... ndard of living of the agri-*

cultural worker and the peasant. The sole object was to enable Fascist Germany to stand a long blockade in the event of war, and before war came, to enable foreign exchange to be used for armament raw materials rather than for foodstuffs.

Before we study the results of this policy, it is worth while to examine the thoroughness with which the Fascist system took all practical measures to implement it. Firstly, the whole of agriculture was organized into the so-called Reich Food Estate, which is a corporation comprising all individuals and organizations concerned in the production and distribution of agricultural commodities. Within a very short time, this organization had the whole of agriculture in its grip. The number of centrally appointed officials and employees soon reached twenty thousand and they supervised everything: prices and profit margins for peasants as well as wholesalers and retailers; the amount of fertilizer used; the amount of fodder bought; the kind of crop raised (rye, wheat, potatoes or flax, etc.); the number of persons employed; the amount of butter used in the household of the peasant; the number of eggs sold to a relative in the city; in short, everything in the daily life of the peasant and in his dealings with others.

Under this strict supervision production of the most important agricultural commodities developed as follows:*

PRODUCTION OF SOME IMPORTANT AGRICULTURAL COMMODITIES
(*Million Quintals*)

Commodity	1932	1933	1934	1935	1936	1937	1938†
Meat‡	3,109	3,151	3,515	3,429	3,375	3,586	3,677
Butter‡	420	448	452	452	496	517	507
Milk§	246	251	249	245	258	258	263
Wheat	50	56	45	47	44	45	56
Rye ..	84	87	76	75	74	69	86
Potatoes	470	441	468	410	463	553	509
Beet sugar ..	10	13	15	15	16	20	18
Hempseed‖	—	—	—	20	34	50	79
Rape-seed‖	74	67	421	809	1,002	793	1,283
Flax‖	—	31	54	138	298	339	292

* *Statistisches Jahrbuch für das Deutsche Reich, 1936, 1938; Statistical Year Book, 1939–40,* of the League of Nations.
† Excluding Austria.   ‡ 1,000 tons.   § Million hectoliters.   ‖ Thousand quintals.

At first glance one gets the impression from these figures that agricultural production under Fascism has been raised to a higher level. There have been fluctuations in the foods as must always take place as long as technical progress in agriculture is still relatively slow. Production of more nutritive foodstuffs, such as meat, butter and milk, had a definite upward trend. Some valuable agricultural products, such as hemp, flax and rape, have been newly introduced, or rather re-introduced.

But this medal has its reverse side. This concerns both the life of the people who consume the products of agriculture, and the life of those who produce them. Let us look first at the consumption side. The table on page 76 is based on official figures and does not take into account one factor of great importance, the gradual deterioration in the quality of the goods. To give only two examples: the increased water content of butter and the decreased fat content of milk. Furthermore, when we compare consumption in 1938 with that of 1932 we must remember that 1932 was the year of the deepest economic crisis in the history of German capitalism.

The table shows that, on the whole, consumption was lower in 1938, when production was very high indeed and in many commodities beat all records, than in 1932, when production was not only lower than in 1938 but when the crisis had reached its peak, and the number of unemployed was over six million and wages were correspondingly low. We see that, under Fascism, increased agricultural production not only does not mean correspondingly increased consumption, but actually lower consumption.

And now as to the conditions of the producers of agricultural products. We can divide the German farmers into two groups, into the large scale and small scale producers. The large scale we can again subdivide into the big landowners and in the medium farmers. The big landowners number about four hundred and between them own about as much land as one million small peasants. Being big capitalists they were, of course favoured by the Fascist régime, by the combination of heavy industrialists and party bosses, as far as possible. Before the conquest of the various European countries, one of the chief means of increasing the riches of the Junkers was to raise the price of cattle-food at the expense of the peasants who, as stock raisers, were the chief consumers. In this way the Junkers who produced fodder enriched themselves at the expense of the peasants producing meat, milk, butter and eggs. Restrictions

CONSUMPTION PER HEAD OF THE POPULATION*
(Kilograms)

Commodity	1932	1938
Meat	42·1	47·8
Eggs (pieces)	138	124
Fish..	8·5	11·9
Cheese	5·2	5·6
Milk (litre)..	105	112
Butter	7·5	8·8
Margarine, other synthetic and vegetable fats	11·3	8·7
Lard	8·5	8·4
Total fats	27·3	25·9
Wheat flour	44·6	51·9
Rye flour	53·5	53·0
Rice	2·9	2·4
Potatoes	191	183
Total starch	292·0	290·3
Vegetables (green)	47·3	47·0
Citrous fruits	8	7
Other fruits	30·8	20·3
Total fruits and vegetables ..	86·1	74·3

on the imports of fodder helped the Junkers to keep prices up or increase them while the foreign exchange thus saved was used for imports of armament raw materials. Another means of enriching the Junkers was by the payment to them of financial

* I have taken the figures as arranged above from Maxine Y. Sweezy, *The Structure of the Nazi Economy*—after having checked them, of course, in the original German statistical publications. The arrangement by Mrs. Sweezy does not come up to the highest scientific standard since in order to check the amount of starch consumed, for instance, it is not sufficient to add up the above-mentioned commodities only, and, furthermore, they do not contain per kilogram, the same amount of starch. But for a rough survey the method is sufficient, has the advantage of simplicity, and is instructive. Original source: *Wirtschaft und Statistik*, 2. Juni Heft, 1939.

subsidies. When one country after another was conquered, first without fighting and then through war, the Junkers had the opportunity of increasing their holdings to an enormous extent. In the East, for instance, the Prussian Junkers gained large estates in Poland, while in Czechoslovakia the beginnings of land reform, started by the Czechoslovak Government, were destroyed and the Sudeten-German large estate owners (the princes and barons with whom Mr. Runciman once went hunting) added materially to their property. Here we see the same phenomenon of primitive accumulation which we have observed in industry.

The medium property owners, or big peasants, were also favoured by the Fascist system. One way was by a reduction in the wages of the agricultural workers in a number of places, the exclusion, in 1933, of all agricultural workers from Uemployment Insurance, and also, in 1934, binding the workers to the land by forbidding anybody to leave agricultural work without special permission of the Employment Boards. All these advantages were also enjoyed by the Junkers in whose interests they were primarily introduced. Most of the big peasants were not affected adversely by the fodder policy of the Fascist system since, like the Junkers, they produced on their land at least the greater part of the fodder needed for their cattle.

While the Junkers on the whole were in a more favourable position than that of the capitalists in the consumption goods industries (as long as peace reigned)—but not, of course, in as favourable a position as heavy industry—the big peasants, or kulaks, were special pets of the Fascist system. They represented, and still represent, the strength of the Fascist following in the agricultural districts and the Fascists were eager, for political reasons, not only to keep them satisfied but to increase their number. If we roughly halve the number of owners of agricultural property in 1933, we find that 50·6 per cent owned farms of less than 15 hectares, while 49·4 owned farms of 15 and more hectares. By 1938, the number of owners of 15 or more hectares had increased to 56·9 per cent, at the expense of the smaller farmers. This policy of fostering the richer peasants also becomes obvious if we study the land settlement policy of the Fascist system. While, under the Weimar Republic, numerous small holdings were created—in 1932, 9,046 new holdings with an average size of about 11 hectares—the Fascist system concentrated on the creation of a much smaller number of considerably larger (kulak) holdings—in 1938, 1,456 new holdings with an average size of almost 22 hectares each. By 1941 the number of new holdings created had declined to 381 with an average size of 25 hectares. *

Finally, both big peasants and Junkers, since long before 1939, had been profiting from the importation of cheap labour from other countries, beginning with Italians and Poles, and largely supplemented by partly—and later on by wholly—compulsory labour on the land by young people in Germany. A year after the war had started, the Junkers and wealthier peasants had millions of prisoners of war at their disposal, for little more than their poor feeding.

The position of the mass of the poor peasants was very different. I have mentioned the fodder policy as one of the factors contributing to the deterioration of their position. There were also the regulated agricultural prices which were manipulated as against the interests of the small peasants; then, the fact that the small peasants, who usually work their land without hired help, drew no advantage from the labour policy of the Fascist system; and finally the policy, directed towards an increase in the use of artificial fertilizers in order to increase the yield. Since the peasants' incomes were hardly increasing, the majority of the peasants were forced to spend a rising proportion of their income for fertilizer, economizing, therefore, on food and other necessities. This fertilizer policy had not only the advantage of partially increasing the yield per acre, but also of providing an expanding market for the chemical industry, an important part of heavy industry. When the peasants reached a point when they were unable to economize further, at the expense of their standard of living, they had to raise money by loans from the banks, thus falling in an indirect manner into the hands of the chemical industry. Thus did the chemical industry, together with the big Junkers, enrich themselves and plunder the small peasants under German Fascism. The war has not improved their condition, though the black market, which has grown

* *Wirtschaft und Statistik*, November, 1942.

rapidly, has brought some small pickings to the peasants. But the dangers of the black market, for the small man (not, of course, for the big one), are very great in Germany, and these small pickings are acquired literally at the risk of death.

Before concluding this short survey of agriculture under Fascism three further points should be mentioned. The first is the creation of the so-called hereditary farms. This measure was boosted as safeguarding the property of the peasants since it forbade foreclosure of a mortgage because of debt, and gave the oldest son the full right to inherit the agricultural property of his father thus making partition impossible. But if we examine the application of this measure we find that it really favours the medium and big peasants. The total number of farms "entailed" under this law amounts to only about seven hundred thousand, that is, about one-fifth of all German farms, and this fifth includes only about 1 per cent of the small farms.

The second point in the Fascist agricultural policy which merits examination is the following: relatively, political life in agricultural districts is usually not very intense and not very progressive. The peasants, more often than the workers, are the dupes of the reactionary propaganda of the ruling class; and since their work is very arduous, their working day very long, and their housing poor, political study, political discussion and meetings are comparatively rare. The current of political life in the country is much slower than in the towns, and flows more often in reactionary channels. The Fascists have made use of this fact, especially in the conquered territories. They employ a policy which drives an increasing number of city workers into the agricultural districts and agricultural jobs. Workers in the consumption goods industries, now closed down, in France, Belgium or other conquered countries, are given the choice of being recruited for forced labour in German factories or going into agricultural work. The German Fascists are supported wholeheartedly in this policy by the native Quislings who have an equal interest in the de-proletarization of the large cities, and in the augmenting of the agricultural population. Both the German Fascists and the native Quislings, while desiring an increase in agricultural production, and the re-population of the agricultural districts, also share the hope of decreased political

opposition through this re-agriculturization policy. They hope
that land workers will be too tired after their work to indulge
in political discussion, that their housing conditions will make it
difficult to read and write in the evening, and that, even if
they are active, their supervision by police and kulaks will be
much easier than in the large cities.

Thus, *one important aim of the Fascist agricultural policy is the
political demoralization of the people, a rapid lowering of their educational
level, and of their political activity.*

Fascist agricultural policy we see, then, serves the following
purposes :

Raising the food necessary for successful warfare and for a
sufficiently high feeding standard to enable armament workers
to do effective work;

Favouring the big peasants and the Junkers, the latter as part
of the ruling class, the former as a basis of political support
within the peasant class;

Lowering the political level of the people through the physical
hardships connected with agricultural work.

The last point to be discussed is the structural change in the
status of the peasant. We have mentioned that agricultural
workers were forbidden to leave the land without special permission, very soon after Fascism came to power. This, in the
course of time, was applied also to members of a peasant's
family working on the home farm and, of course, to the peasants
themselves. They are bound "by blood to the soil" and in order
to enforce "the call of the blood" decrees carrying penalties
have been issued. Now, if the peasant is not allowed to sell his
property but is bound to the land; if he is not free to cultivate
his property according to his own choice; if he is neither free
to sell his produce to those whom he chooses, nor to ask the
price he wants; nor even to spend his income as he wishes (being
obliged, for instance, to spend part of it on artificial fertilizer),
he is definitely no longer a free peasant. He has become a serf
of the State, and, since the State is in the hands of heavy industry,
the peasant has been bonded to heavy industry. In this respect
conditions under Fascism are reminiscent of those in the Middle
Ages. As we found in a former chapter, such measures are taken
for the duration of Fascism, and not as temporary measures;

we are, therefore, justified in speaking of a definite change in the status of the peasant.

But these changes do not only recall the Middle Ages. The war has brought yet other changes which take us even further back, to periods from which we emerged more than a thousand years ago. With the conquest of new territories the Fascists desired rapid and intense colonization. They wanted to settle large numbers of peasants in the conquered territories, especially in the East.* Since the number of peasants ready to give up their land in favour of land in the occupied East was quite insufficient for their plans, large numbers of peasants in the Western occupied territories (Holland, etc.), but also from Germany, are being forced to settle in the East. They are simply ordered off their land and packed off in trains to the East. They are treated like cattle, or, to use the exact term of Roman law: like talking tools. Talking tools was the Roman name for slaves.

We see, then, that *the status of the peasant has not only become partly serf-like, but it has also assumed some characteristics of the period of slavery. The elements of Barbarism of which we have spoken, have entered into the status of the peasant.*

Whatever measure makes the peasant more useful to the Fascist system is applied, whether it is borrowed from the methods of oppression and exploitation of the Middle Ages or one which was used under slavery. Of course, these measures are not exact replicas of those of former times. Everything, after all, takes place on the basis of twentieth century economics. It is easy to point out that some feature or other was different five hundred or one thousand or two thousand years ago. But the difference is not decisive. The importance lies in the similarity and in the fact that the Fascists have revived the ancient methods of oppression and exploitation. The importance lies in the infiltration of the traits of Barbarism into the Fascist economic system. We realize now, therefore, the significance of such terms

---

* The fact that the Ukraine, for instance, is sufficiently densely settled to make full use of the opportunities which agriculture offers is offset by the "need" to permeate the enslaved people of the East who are regarded as the lowest class of serf or slave with a sprinkling of "Herren"-slaves (Germans) and slaves, first class (Dutch peasants), in the hope of playing the one against the other.

as the servile or slave-like status of the peasants. They are not merely illustrative or rhetorical, but convey the harsh reality.

6. NATIONAL FINANCE IN THE SERVICE OF THE FASCIST WAR EFFORT

From the first day of Fascist government, German financial institutions, the big and small banks, the savings banks, the Reichsbank, the budget, even the social insurance system, were used as a means of increasing the war effort. Their dual task was to help finance the production of armaments, and to "de-finance" consumption: to take money away from butter and direct it towards the guns.

The less money people have, the less they can buy; the less is needed from the consumption goods industries, and the more becomes available for the Fascist war effort. If people spend money on a "people's automobile," not yet produced, they cannot buy food or clothing; if they spend their money on railway fares, travelling with the "Strength through Joy" organization, they cannot spend it on consumption goods; if people put their money in the savings banks and if one makes it difficult for them to take the money out again, then they cannot spend it on themselves. The best gauge for the Fascist ability to take money out of the pockets of the people, while leaving them with the illusion that it still belongs to them, is a comparison between the development of savings and the national income.

NATIONAL INCOME AND NATIONAL SAVINGS
(*In thousand million marks*)

Year	National Income	National Savings
1932	45·2	11·5
1934	52·7	12·8
1936	65·0	14·6
1938	79·7	18·0
1940	110·0*	28·0†
1941	120·0*	38·0†
1942	130·0‡	50·0§

* Pre-war figures, official German estimates; figures for 1940 and 1941 see *Frankfurter Zeitung*, February 11, 1943.
† Semi-official German estimates.
‡ My estimate.
§ Figure given by Funk at the 1943 annual meeting of the Reichsbank.

During the ten years under review the national income has risen by about 200 per cent, while savings have risen by over 300 per cent.

Another way of decreasing the spending power of the people is by forced deductions from their wages or salaries, besides the usual tax deductions. Such deductions have been increased continuously since 1933. In 1939 they included, apart from taxes and social insurance contributions, "voluntary contributions" to the Party funds, the Labour Front, the N.S. Welfare, the Air Defence League, the Association for Germans Abroad, the people's car, etc., and amounted to about one quarter of the worker's wages.

Part of this money is, of course, in some form or another, returned to the worker. If he falls ill he receives some benefit from the health insurance. But, while the worker usually has to pay about 3 per cent of his income on unemployment insurance, the amount paid in benefit is almost nil—vast sums being used to support the Fascist war effort. The amounts paid by the Unemployment Insurance Fund to support the Fascist war effort was about 1,880 million marks from 1934 to 1937, and about 3,900 million marks from 1938 to 1941.*

Thus the Fascist government mobilized in the years under review an amount of roughly £290,000,000 (at par), or an amount corresponding to Britain's normal pre-war expenditure on defence in two and a half years, from the unemployment fund alone.

To this must be added the important mobilization of the big banks. They collect a high amount of otherwise idle money and their financial resources—like those of the individual taxpayer or of the savings banks—are mobilized in the interest of the war effort. The following table gives for the end of each year a number of significant items in the balance sheet of the German "big five,"† indicating how the banks, even before the outbreak of war, were actively engaged financially in the preparation of

* *Reichsarbeitsblatt*, May 25, 1942.
† Quoted from *Twelfth Annual Report, Bank for International Settlements*, p. 125. The big five are: Deutsche Bank, Dresdner Bank, Commerz Bank, Reichskreditgesellschaft and Berliner Handelsgesellschaft. Figures for 1929 refer to seven banks, two of them having been taken over in the meantime by the big five: the Darmstaedter und Nationalbank and the Barmer Bankverein.

war, how they were instruments of war at a time when the banks
of other countries were engaged in numerous financial transactions with them and thus furthered the objects of the German
banks:

ASSETS OF THE GERMAN BIG FIVE
(Million Marks)

At the end of the Year	Cash	Business Advances	Bills	Reich Securities	Other Securities
1929	2,271	8,116	2,659	463	371
1937	631	3,145	2,541	844	561
1938	751	3,365	2,146	1,832	547
1939	741	3,495	2,039	2,974	520
1940	886	2,748	2,167	6,310	527
1941	1,005	3,081	2,166	8,834	479

This table shows how the power of the banks is used for the
financing of the Fascist war programme. Cash holdings of the
banks are extremely low, much lower than before Fascism came
to power. Business advances are less than two-fifths of what
they were in 1929. The banks are no longer the chief financiers
of industry. Industry finances a large part of its undertakings
from its own profits, and the enormous amount of primitive
accumulation allows for rapid expansion without much financing.
The amount of bills and of other than Reich securities is small
and not very different from that of 1929. But the amount of
Reich securities has increased by almost 2,000 per cent.; it is
more than nineteen times higher in 1941 than in 1929. The
banks had to invest more and more in Reich securities; they
became one of the chief buyers of Reich loans; they helped to
place the Reich loans and were forced themselves to take an
increasing amount of them. If we add to the "big five" four
other banks with special tasks,* we find that these nine banks
held a total of 18,388,000,000 marks in Reich securities at the
end of 1941. Since the total outstanding debt of the Reich
amounted at the end of 1941 to 128,506,000,000 marks, we find
that the nine biggest banks in Germany alone hold about one-
seventh of the national debt. In 1942 and 1943 this development
has continued—but with one important difference: As the short

---

* The four banks with special tasks are the Deutsche Giro-Zentrale,
Preussische Staatsbank, Deutsche Zentral-Genossenschaftskasse, and the Bank
der Deutschen Arbeit (Bank of the Labour Front).

term debts of the Reich increase proportionally, so the short-time security holdings of the banks rise—sometimes accompanied by an absolute decline of their holdings of long-term Reich securities.

But all these figures and examples of savings, of deductions from the income, of the structure of the assets side of the balance sheet of the big banks are merely illustrations and do not show the whole of the war effort in financial terms. For the financial side is not just an additional factor in the preparation for war but represents and reflects the whole of the preparations for war.

Perhaps the best picture of the Fascist war effort in terms of finance can be gained from the following table which shows, on the one hand, the total national income and, on the other, estimates of the total national expenditure on war preparation and the war, with an additional column giving the percentage of the national income expended on armament and war:

NATIONAL INCOME AND ARMAMENT (WAR) EXPENDITURE*

(Thousand Million Marks)

Year	National Income	Armament (War) Expenditure	Armament (War) Expenditure in per cent of National Income
1932	45·2	1·0	2
1933	46·6	3·0	6
1934	52·7	5·5	10
1935	58·6	10·0	17
1936	65·0	12·5	19
1937	71·0	16·0	23
1938	79·7	27·0	34
1939	95·0	40·0	42
1940	110·0	58·0	58
1941	120·0	78·0	68
1942	130·0	91·0	70

The figures, whether official or otherwise, whether claiming to be merely estimates or not, are, of course, only approximations. But they are more than wild guesses. It is of interest, for instance,

* National income: figures for calendar year; figures for 1932 to 1938 official German estimates; 1939 to 1942 see footnote on p. 82; 1941 my estimate. Armament (War) expenditure: figures for financial years (1932 means April, 1932, to March, 1933); figures for 1932 to 1936 estimates of *The Banker*, February, 1937; 1937 my estimate, 1938 to 1940 League of Nations' estimate, 1941 and 1942 my estimate. Cf. *Statistisches Jahrbuch für das Deutsche Reich*, 1938; and League of Nations, *World Economic Survey, 1939–41.*

that the above estimates of armaments expenditure in pre-war years closely approximate Hitler's statement that, in preparation for the contingency of war the Reich had spent about ninety thousand million marks on armaments since 1933.

On the basis of these figures we can estimate that war expenditure in peace time increased more than thirty times under German Fascism. Under Fascism, the percentage of the national income spent on armaments has risen (in peace time) from about 2 per cent to little less than 40 per cent. In the course of the war armament expenditure has increased to over two-thirds of the total national income.

What do these figures mean? They mean that *before the war broke out, about two-fifths of all paid activities of the German people were directed towards the preparation for war. Of five people in Germany doing paid work, two were actively engaged in armaments work. If we add the considerable amount of unpaid work directed towards the war effort, it would not be surprising to find that, even before war broke out, about half of the active hours spent by the people in Germany were directed by Fascism towards the preparation for war.*

During the war the paid activities connected directly with the war increased to over two-thirds, and if we add the unpaid activities it would not be surprising to find that more than three-quarters of the active hours spent by the German people are spent for the Fascist war effort. This figure is certainly less astonishing than that referring to the last year before the war. It shows that *the difference between active warfare and peace is relatively small under Fascism.* It shows that even in peace time Fascism forcibly directs the major part of the efforts of the nation towards preparation for war.

This concentration upon war preparations and war brings record profits to the big employers, and a worsening standard of living for the masses of the people. This can be illustrated by the following table which shows, for the years 1932 and 1938,

DISTRIBUTION OF NATIONAL INCOME BETWEEN WORKERS AND CAPITALISTS

Year	*Percentage of National Income going*	
	To the People	*To the Capitalists*
1932	59·8	19·1
1938	52·2	28·0

the percentage of the national income which goes to the masses in form of wages, salaries, pensions and relief, and the percentage which goes to the capitalists in form of profits and rent.*

We see that the percentage of the national income going to the people in form of wages, etc., has declined considerably under Fascism, while profits and rent for the capitalists have increased considerably.

If we keep in mind these two movements, the rapidly increasing proportion of the national income spent on armaments and war generally, and the parallel declining share of labour in the national income with the increase in profits and rent, we perceive two of the most important economic trends of the Fascist régime.

But we cannot leave this short financial survey without touching upon some of the problems connected with the conquest of foreign countries. If we study financial developments in countries conquered by Fascism, we find not only that Fascism takes over all the big banks, directly or indirectly, determines the State budget and ruthlessly cuts all welfare and educational expenditure while increasing the amount spent for war purposes. We also find a very considerable inflationary trend in all territories conquered by German Fascism, with the exception of those which for all practical purposes have been incorporated into the Reich. The table on page 88 illustrates this very well.

I have divided the countries into three groups: the incorporated or practically incorporated countries for which we have regular statements by their central banks; the countries conquered by war; and finally the allies of German Fascism. Inflationary conditions are worst in the satellite countries. That is not surprising, for in these countries the German Fascists can leave all the economic and political difficulties to the "native" administration, and by creating a certain amount of disorder and increasing the inflationary trend by their economic-military demands, they force the native governments to assume an ever increasing degree of economic-political dictatorship. Such measures need not be taken in countries occupied by German

* Computed from the official statistics; cf. *Statistisches Jahrbuch*, 1938; *Wirtschaft und Statistik*, 1939, Heft 8, 21 and 22.

troops such as France, Belgium and Holland, though a certain inflationary trend is allowed, such being regarded as useful for the occupation troops. But such a trend must be avoided inside "German territory," such as the Protectorate, for instance.

Thus financial manipulations are cleverly used by the Fascists as a further means of exploiting the people in the conquered

INDEX OF NOTE CIRCULATION
(*June, 1939 = 100*)

Country		End of 1940*	End of 1941*	End of 1942†
Protectorate	..	101	146	219
Slovakia‡	..	119	145	197
Belgium ..	..	157	218	306
Denmark ..	..	166	189	220
France	..	178	220	312
Holland ..	..	149	202	304
Bulgaria ..	..	225	466	658
Finland ..	..	252	333	437
Hungary ..	..	157	224	334
Rumania ..	..	166	251	303

Continent, and of intensifying dictatorship in the allied countries. But by the end of 1942 and during 1943 a certain similarity of development could be observed: all countries under German Fascism came, because of the general deterioration of the situation, under severe inflationary pressure.

7. BESTIALITY

In dealing with the general structure of Fascism we concluded with a short study of the elements of Barbarism in the system of Fascism. In concluding our short survey of the general practice of Fascism it is right and necessary to give thought to the subject of Bestiality as a practical means of translating Fascist plans and laws into reality. Such a study is all the more important since *Bestiality is the Fascist counterpart to the most important spiritual factor on our side, the morale which helped us at Sebastopol and Stalingrad and in many an exploit of the R.A.F. and British Navy.*

* League of Nations, *Money and Banking*, 1940–1942.
† League of Nations, *Monthly Bulletin of Statistics*, 1943.
‡ December, 1939 = 100.

Our morale is high because we know that we are fighting for a just cause, to preserve the finest traditions of progressive mankind, that we are fighting against an enemy who stands for all which the best men and women of all countries and all ages have fought against. The bestiality of the Fascists is so great because they know that nothing but their ruthlessness stands between them and their end.

The importance of the factor Bestiality on the side of the Fascists must not be under-estimated. Many methods, which we could not use, are at the service of the Fascists. Certain temporary difficulties can be overcome by the Fascists because of their Bestiality.

Let me illustrate by a few examples. We know that food conditions on the Continent are poor. The harvest is not sufficient to feed the whole of the people at a standard of health and decency. At the same time, we know that Fascism only cares about things conducive to destruction. We are not surprised, therefore, when we hear that—just as the factories which produce armaments are well cared for, while those which produce consumption goods are neglected or systematically destroyed, just as the workers who produce weapons of destruction are less poorly fed than those who produce consumption goods—so whole countries are treated according to their capacity to produce for destruction. Czechoslovakia has, in the second half of 1942, been elevated to the highest standard of rationing, being now in many respects equal to Germany, because of the very high percentage of the population actively engaged in the production of armaments. Greece, on the other hand, with almost no heavy industry, is so badly off for food that the people are simply starved to death. This is planned Bestiality. Fascism does not care if a whole people dies. But the people who are sacrificed are not chosen haphazard, but according to their ability or inability to produce goods for destruction. Now if a régime is ready to sacrifice whole populations its difficulties are less, *temporarily*, than those of a régime which seeks to overcome such difficulties in a humane way.

We all know, and the Fascist leaders have admitted it, that the German transport system almost broke down in the winter of 1941–42. Hitler had said that 1942–43 conditions would be different. And they were. Not because of the higher morale of the people, and especially of the railwaymen, or because of any important technical progress—though some has been made—but because of planned Bestiality. For in the meantime, throughout 1942, the German Fascists systematically looted the countries of Europe of what had been regarded as the minimum of railway stock needed. In France, for instance, a Council of Ministers in Vichy, on July 3, 1942, decided to hand over to Germany 1,000 locomotives, 40,000 trucks, 35,000 lorries and several thousand miles of rails. If one remembers that the French railways were in a sorry state before the outbreak of the war, that they suffered severely during the war, and that after the armistice the Germans took away a not inconsiderable part of the rolling stock, one can understand the effect of this new expropriation on the French railways. Passenger traffic has probably been cut to less than 10 per cent of that of peace time. But this is the less important side. Freight traffic is much more important. Food and health depend to a very large extent upon it. Now, those parts of France in which large heavy industrial works are situated are still able to get sufficient freight to keep the factories and people going, while those parts where there are no armament industries are sometimes in a condition resembling that of Greece. Again we have an example of how certain difficulties are temporarily diminished by the application of Bestiality.

In discussing the meat situation on the Continent with an agricultural expert he explained to me that it will be impossible to keep up the meat rations in Germany because of the lack of cattle. When I mentioned the herds in some occupied countries the expert said that it was impossible to increase the percentage of slaughtered cattle since that would mean the slaughter of cows which provide milk. It would be absolutely inadvisable, he said, to cut down the stock any further. The expert was right in one way. It is true it would be inadvisable, from our point of view, because sufficient fodder is available in those parts of Europe to keep the herds fed, and the milk and butter are urgently needed by the people of those countries. But what this expert had forgotten is that his standard is not the Fascist standard. If through increased meat rations the "morale" of the German people can be kept from cracking, if the productivity of the European armament-workers can be maintained by a little more meat, then the children of the occupied territories will have to suffer, then the cattle will be destroyed and the agricultural capital of a country may be lost.

One final example, which will be of special interest to British workers. In Germany, too, there is a shortage of coal. Coal production tended to decline, partly for reasons which are valid also in Great Britain, such as the gradual exhaustion of the working capacity of the miner, not so much for lack of food but because of the drive for ever increased intensity of work. How did Fascism try to meet this difficulty? It tried to meet it by rapidly increasing the number of miners at work. Not only in Germany, but also in Belgium, Luxemburg, France and Poland, more miners are working to-day than in many peace-time years. These miners are partly those who always worked in the mines, partly miners who were formerly unemployed, and partly miners who had left the industry and had to return to it—but to an increasing extent they are also workers brought in from other countries against their will. In the French mines we find to-day Belgian and Dutch workers who were conscripted and sent there; we find an increasing number of Polish workers transported from the East. And, since 1942, we find all over the West, including the Ruhr territory, a rapidly increasing number of people from the Soviet territory; men and women, boys and girls, arrested, herded into railway cars, sent to some concentration camp, where they are checked up like slaves going on the market for sale, and then sent to various factories, and especially to the mines. While constantly trying to increase the intensity of work in the mines, the Fascists are also putting an ever increasing number of people to work in them, regardless of the death and accident rate, regardless of the number who have to be sent out of the mines because of their inability to stand the work. When new miners are needed they are imported from the East.

These examples are sufficient to show the importance of the factor of Bestiality on the side of the Fascists. It is an important economic weapon, for it creates new economic strength—temporarily.

Bestiality is the only weapon the Fascists have to counter our morale. It will prove to be an inadequate weapon if we live up to the great task before us—but it is an efficient weapon within certain limits. It is being used by the leaders of industry and the party bosses; we can hear it through the speeches of the leaders of the Fascist régime. But it is being also used by the smallest functionary of the system in the village he dominates, in the factory department he helps to manage, or in the block of houses he supervises. It permeates the Fascist system everywhere and is part of the ideology of every Fascist.

PART II

THE LABOUR POLICY OF GERMAN FASCISM

CHAPTER III

LABOUR CONDITIONS IN GERMANY, 1933 TO 1937

A STATISTICAL SURVEY

IN this survey of labour conditions under Fascism we will first study the development during the first five years of Fascism. In these five years the fundamental policies were worked out—before the conquest of Austria, Czechoslovakia or any other country. In these five years a status of labour developed which, even if we leave the political upheaval out of account, involved such a complete change that measures taken in the following years, including the war years, are nothing but a further tightening-up, an added degree of degradation, a further development in a direction which had been determined and begun to be practised during the previous five years. While, for instance, the outbreak of war brought about many radical changes in the conditions of work in Britain, this was not the case in Germany. The transition from peace to war was smooth, in many respects barely noticeable, under German Fascism—in stark contrast to the same process in France or Britain for instance. And even if, in 1938, we find that, in many respects, quantity changes into quality, it is in the first five years that the quantity is created.

In studying the conditions of labour under German Fascism during the period under review we must pay special attention not only to the development of the standard of living and to working conditions in general, but also to the equally important study of the deprivation of the workers of the elementary liberties, such as free speech, free assembly, the right to elect their own representatives in certain organizations, and so on. This includes the study of the infiltration of elements of serfdom and slavery into the worker's status. These problems cannot all be studied concurrently because their development was a very unequal one, and the influence of certain occurrences reacted in various ways upon the various aspects of labour conditions under Fascism. To give only one example, while the outbreak of war had relatively little influence upon the food standard in Germany it had a great influence upon the man-power development in the factories. In the following sections of this chapter we shall now study the various aspects of the conditions of labour under Fascism between 1933 and 1937.

1. ABOLISHING THE ELEMENTARY RIGHTS AND LIBERTIES OF LABOUR

In the course of the last hundred years, labour had won in Germany, as in other capitalist countries, a number of elementary rights and liberties. These were gained in a sharp struggle with the ruling class, in the course of two revolutions (1848 and 1918) and many a political campaign. Under the Weimar Republic the following main elementary liberties of labour existed: the right to organize in trade unions and political parties; the right to a free labour press which found practical expression in the existence of hundreds of labour papers; the right to free speech which was practiced in thousands of public and ten thousands of closed meetings annually; the right to vote for every man and woman, regardless of economic status, in the election of municipal bodies and State and Reich parliaments and the right to stand for election; the right to elect in all industrial and other establishments above a certain size workers' representatives whose position made it possible for them to exert a minor influence on working conditions. The importance of all these rights must not be over-estimated; they are not sufficient in themselves to bring about a real change for the better in the conditions of the workers; but their loss is very grave indeed because it contributes to the further deterioration of the conditions of labour, and, worst of all, their loss makes it infinitely more difficult for the working class and its leadership to fight and destroy the government by monopolists and vested interests in general.

As soon as the Fascists came into power in Germany they closed down most of the newspapers of the Communist Party and made propaganda for the elections in March, 1933, impossible for Communists and very difficult for Social-Democrats. Before the newly-elected Reichstag could meet many deputies of the Communist Party had been arrested, while the Social-Democratic press experienced increasing difficulties. On March 24th, an enabling act was passed by the Reichstag, called significantly an Act to Relieve the Distress of the People and of the Reich, which gave almost unlimited legislative power to the government, and enabled it to act regardless of the constitution. It is important to emphasize here that the government which put through these measures contained three National Socialists only, while the rest of the nine ministers had an "old-fashioned conservative past," having represented for decades the interests of the big industrialists (especially heavy industry) and the Junkers. While the Communist Party had virtually become illegal, even prior to the meeting of the first Reichstag under Fascism, the Social-Democratic Party continued to function legally until May 26th, when its property was confiscated, although many leading functionaries of that party had already been arrested. In addition to the confiscation of its property a decree of June 23rd prohibited any party activity, including any activity of its representatives in the Reichstag, in State parliaments and municipal councils. This action against the Social-Democratic Party had been preceded on May 2nd by a general storming and wrecking of trade union offices, bookshops and other institutions, and the "co-ordination" (Gleichschaltung) of the trade unions. *Thus, all the elementary liberties which labour had fought for and gained in the course of a hundred years were abolished in little more than one hundred days of Fascist government.* Only one minor liberty remained in existence for some time: the right annually to elect delegates to the works councils. The National Socialists hoped to control these elections, and through pressure and terror to prevent the election of Social-Democrats and Communists. But they did not succeed in this, and numerous workers, who were leading members of the opposition movement in the factories, were elected and re-elected. Therefore, the **National Socialists,** after 1935, ceased holding these elections.

They dismissed those who strove to represent the interests of the workers, and filled their places with their own nominees. Thus vanished the last remnant of the elementary liberties of labour and the full darkness of tyranny descended over Germany.

2. INTRODUCING THE FIRST ELEMENTS OF BARBARISM

After having deprived the workers of their political liberties the Fascists began to take away their liberty of movement. I do not refer here to the fact that tens of thousands of workers were thrown into prisons and concentration camps. I refer to the restriction of the freedom of movement of labour by tying the worker down to his place of work.

The first measure of this kind was introduced in May, 1934; it applied to agricultural workers and did not as yet bind them to a particular employer or estate but only to their occupation, which they were forbidden to leave for any other one. At the same time all industrial workers who had entered industry from agriculture during the preceding three years were liable to be returned to their former occupation if employment was available. At that time unemployment was still relatively high.*

UNEMPLOYMENT, 1932 TO MAY 1934

	Date	Number
	1932	5,575,000
January	1933	6,014,000
	1933	4,804,000
May	1934	2,529,000

While unemployment in May, 1934, and in the following months was still high, the distribution of the unemployed among the various occupations had already undergone a considerable change. As the decree of May, 1934, indicates, in agriculture it had already become so small that the Fascists had to take measures to avoid a shortage of labour which would lead to declining agricultural production.

In the course of the year 1934 rearmament got under way to such an extent that soon many of the unemployed workers in occupations connected directly or indirectly with armaments

* *Statistisches Jahrbuch für das Deutsche Reich, 1938.*

manufacture were absorbed, and the beginnings of a labour shortage became apparent. By the end of the year, a decree, similar to that for the agricultural workers though somewhat stricter, was introduced. On December 29, 1934, all skilled metal workers were forbidden to take employment, even as metal workers, outside the jurisdiction of their Employment Office (Labour Exchange) without special permission of that Office. While the agricultural workers had only been tied to their occupation as such, the metal workers were tied to their occupation within a relatively small geographical area. No further measures as sweeping as those were taken during the following years, while unemployment developed as follows:

UNEMPLOYMENT, MAY, 1934, TO DECEMBER, 1936

	Date	Number
May	1934	2,529,000
	1934	2,718,000
	1935	2,151,000
	1936	1,593,000
December	1936	1,479,000

By the end of 1936, the number of unemployed metal workers had declined to little more than is usual when the workers move freely from one job to another. The unemployed in the metal industries were usually without work because they were on the look-out for a better job. In order to stop any loss of working hours owing to the mobility of labour a decree, issued on November 27, 1936, practically forbade the skilled as well as the unskilled metal workers to change their job without special permission of the Employment Office.

Less than a year later, on October 6, 1937, carpenters and masons were subject to the same restraint of movement. By the end of 1937 a general labour shortage began to develop. Not that the number of unemployed was exceedingly low, but the distribution of the unemployed had become so uneven, occupationally and geographically, that the number of factories needing labour was considerable and varied. This, the beginning of a general labour shortage, led to the introduction of measures designed to increase the number of workers available. The first of these measures was the retraction in November, 1937, of the

* *Statistisches Jahrbuch für das Deutsche Reich, 1938.*

order introduced at the beginning of the Fascist régime when unemployment was still very high, that women who had received marriage loans from the State were forbidden to take employment. A second measure of this kind was introduced on December 10, 1937, when the tax on itinerant trades was raised in order to drive as many of these traders as possible into industrial employment.

UNEMPLOYMENT, DECEMBER, 1936, TO DECEMBER, 1937

Date		Number
December	1936	1,479,000
	1937	912,000
December	1937	995,000

In 1937 unemployment was lower than in the year of "prosperity," 1928, when it was 1,391,000; and during September, 1937, unemployment reached the low figure of 469,053, less than half of the 1928 low figure for the best month, which was still above one million.

*   *   *

What is the significance of these measures? Mrs. Sweezy calls the measures relating to the restriction of freedom of the worker Labour Feudalism* and says:

"By gradual steps, government decrees which provided for mobilization of workers in industries and occupations engaged in military work created a modern equivalent to mediæval feudalism. The serf of the Middle Ages was considered part of the estate of his squire or lord. He was attached and fixed to the estate and had no right to move away. The German worker also has become attached and fixed to his job, whether agricultural or industrial."

She is right, and she is also right in connecting these measures with the military preparations of the German government. *Fascism means war and terror. Fascism means transforming peace time economy into a war economy and replacing elementary liberties and a certain freedom for the worker by terroristic measures of forced labour. Political terror measures are followed by economic terror measures, by introducing barbaric elements into the status of the worker, in this case by robbing him of his freedom of movement.*

These measures are taken against the interests of the workers,

* L.c., p. 169.

in the interests of preparations for war, in the interests of heavy (armament) industry, in the interests of the most reactionary and most imperialistic elements in society.

While, in all other capitalist countries, unemployment was high and millions had to go hungry and were without work often for several years at a stretch, the fact that during these years unemployment had begun to disappear in Germany impressed a number of observers. But what were the tasks at which the formerly unemployed were set by Fascism? They were set to produce the weapons to attack the whole world, especially that country which is the inspiration of every progressive movement, the Soviet Union. Furthermore, by producing armaments the workers, at the same time, were forging the chains which were to shackle them ever faster until they became that combination of slaves and serfs which they are to-day. Fascism gave employment to millions of unemployed—but their work was directed against their own interests. Fascism, in putting tools into the hands of the workers, converted the workers themselves into tools in the most nefarious crimes known to history.

This becomes obvious when we study in more detail the development of employment for various categories of working people. The first and more generalised comparison is given in the following table:*

EMPLOYMENT IN 1932 AND IN 1937

Categories	1932	1937
Wage and Salaried Workers	100	148
Wage Workers†	100	160
Salaried Workers	100	127
Wage Workers in Factories, Mines and Construction	100	179
Wage Workers in other occupations ..	100	122

* The increase in the number of wage workers is computed from the difference in the development of average weekly gross wages and the total wage bill as given in the official statistics (see below, p. 103). The increase in the number of all wage and salary earners is computed from the official employment statistics. The increase in the number of wage workers in factories, mining and construction is also computed from officially published data. The increase in the employment of other workers was computed from the above figures for all wage workers and for wage earners in factories, mining and construction, with the help of weights as taken from the 1933 census; in the same way the increase in the number of salaried workers was computed.

† If we compute the number of employed wage earners according to the same method for the intervening years, we get the following rough index of employed wage earners:

1932 100; 1933 111; 1934 130; 1935 139; 1936 151; 1937 160.

This table is very interesting because it shows on a large scale that the increase of employment is the greater the nearer we come to the armament industries. The Fascists are all out for increased production. For this reason the number of manual workers has increased more than that of salaried workers. * Furthermore, if we compare the development of the employment of workers in factories, mines and construction work on the one hand, and in all other sections of economy on the other (for instance, transport, agriculture, etc.), we find a much larger increase in that section in which the armament industries are situated.

If we now subdivide the workers employed in factories only, we get a much clearer picture still. We see that it is those industries which are producing weapons of destruction which employ more workers and employ them longer per day than the industries which produce goods for consumption by the people:

TOTAL NUMBER OF MAN-HOURS IN SELECTED INDUSTRIES
(*1932 = 100*)

Industries	1929	1932	1937	Change 1937 over 1929
Iron, steel and other metal production	230	100	280	+ 22 %
Machine building	228	100	327	+ 43 %
Vehicle building	263	100	402	+ 53 %
Leather industry	170	100	156	− 8 %
Woodworking industry ..	198	100	184	− 7 %
Textile industry	143	100	133	− 7 %

The difference between the development of employment in the first three and the last three industries is striking. In the first three the number of man-hours worked is between 180 and 302 per cent higher in 1937 than in 1932, and between 22 and 53 per cent higher than in 1929. In the other three the number of man-hours worked is between 33 and 84 per cent higher in 1937 than in 1932, that is at best less than half as much higher

* Part of the difference in the increase, though not a very large one, between the employment of wage earners and salaried employees may be due to the fact that during the preceding crisis the number of salaried employees declined less than that of wage earners. For industry alone employment of salaried workers was by 1 per cent higher in 1937 than in 1929, while that of wage workers in the same period rose by over 6 per cent (cf. *Statistisches Jahrbuch für das Deutsche Reich, 1938*).

as in the case of the other three industries; and while the first three industries also showed a not inconsiderable rise in the number of man-hours worked in 1937 as compared with 1929, the second three industries show a decline of 7 to 8 per cent as compared with 1929. The reason for this very uneven development of employment, of man-hours worked, is, of course, that the first three industries are closely related to rearmament and war preparation while the second three are chiefly consumption goods industries, closely related to the general standard of living. Thus, the employment statistics are a true reflection of some of the general economic trends we have already observed of Fascist economy as a war economy.

3. The Development of Wages

A. Wages in General

The standard of living is determined to a considerable extent by the development of wages. In studying the development of wages during the first five years of Fascism, it is necessary to note briefly the standard of wages before Fascism came to power. The last month of pre-Fascist government was January, 1933, when unemployment was very high indeed and wages were very low. At that time average wage rates and average actual wages in industry were as follows:*

WAGE RATES AND WAGES ACTUALLY EARNED PER WEEK IN INDUSTRY, JANUARY, 1933

Weekly Wage Rate..	38·90 Mark
Average payment above wage rate	1·15
Losses through short-time	2·40
Losses through unemployment	18·70
Taxes and insurance payments	2·65
Unemployment insurance benefits†	3·75
Actual Weekly Earnings	20·05 Mark

* Cf. "Die Konjunktur fuer den Arbeiter," by Juergen Kuczynski, *Finanzpolitische Korrespondenz*, Jahrgang XIV. Nr. 7/8.
† Benefits, if received, are actually much higher, but many unemployed had been deprived of the right to benefits.

Actual weekly earnings were only about half of what they were in 1928. The wage rate also had declined not inconsiderably as compared with pre-crisis years; it was about 20 per cent lower. How did wages develop during the first five years of German Fascism from this all-time low represented by January, 1933—in fact, by the level of the whole thirteen months since January, 1932? Let us first examine three tables on the development of money wages, all based, of course, on official Fascist statistics:

AVERAGE WAGE RATES, 1932 TO 1937

		(*Pfenning per hour*)				*Index, 1928*
		Men			*Women*	= *100*
		Semi-		*Skilled and*		*All*
Year	*Skilled*	*skilled*	*Unskilled*	*Semi-skilled*	*Unskilled*	*combined.*
1932	81·6	68·8	64·4	53·1	43·9	86·2
1933, January	79·2	68·3	62·8	52·2	43·5	84·2
1933	78·5	68·2	62·3	51·7	43·4	83·6
1934	78·3	68·2	62·2	51·6	43·3	83·5
1935	78·3	68·3	62·2	51·6	43·4	83·5
1936	78·3	68·3	62·2	51·6	43·4	83·5
1937	78·5	68·4	62·3	51·5	43·4	83·6

AVERAGE WEEKLY GROSS WAGES

(*Mark and Pfenning*)

Year	*Amount*
1932	22·88
1933	21·88
1934	22·83
1935	24·04
1936*	25·25
1937*	26·50

TOTAL WAGE BILL, 1932 TO 1937

(*Million Mark*)

Year	*Amount*
1932	11,320
1933	12,051
1934	14,642
1935	16,483
1936*†	18,837
1937*	20,915

All three tables, as I have stated, are taken from official publications,‡ and the three seem to contradict each other. The first table indicates a decline in wages; the second table shows a moderate increase; the third one shows an enormous increase in wages, almost a doubling within five years. All three, however, are reasonably accurate and confirm each other.

The first table shows the development of wage rates. It shows that (in contrast to the development in all other countries), under

* Including Saar-territory.   † Excluding Saar-territory the sum is 18,576.
‡ Source for the first table: *Statistisches Jahrbuch für das Deutsche Reich, 1938.* Sources for second table: *Wirtschaft und Statistik,* 2. April Heft, 1936; 1. April Heft, 1937; and 2. April Heft, 1938. Sources for the third table: *Wirtschaft und Statistik,* 2. April Heft, 1936; 1. April Heft, 1937; and 2. April Heft, 1938.

German Fascism, wage rates have actually declined since the deepest point of the crisis was reached; a unique development in the history of wage conditions.

The second table shows the development of gross weekly earnings, that is, actual weekly wages without deductions for taxes, contributions and collections, and without taking into account losses through unemployment and short-time. These gross wages have increased while wage rates remained stable chiefly because the number of hours worked per worker has increased. If the number of hours worked per worker increases more than the wage rate declines, then weekly gross wages must increase.

If, in addition to the number of hours the number of workers employed also increases, then the total wage bill must show a greater increase than the average weekly gross wage per worker, as the third table shows.

Summarizing the development shown in the previous three tables we arrive at the following:

WAGE INDICES, 1932 TO 1937

(*1932 = 100*)

Year	Wage Rates	Gross Weekly Wages	Total Wage Bill
1932	100	100	100
1933	97	96	106
1934	97	100	129
1935	97	105	146
1936	97	110	166
1937	97	116	185

In order to measure wage developments in terms which indicate their relation to the workers' standard of living we must compare them with the cost of living. According to the official statistics, the cost of living has developed as follows*:

COST OF LIVING, 1932 TO 1937

(*1932 = 100*)

Year	Index
1932	100
1933	98
1934	100
1935	102
1936	103
1937	104

* Cf. *Statistisches Jahrbuch für das Deutsche Reich, 1938.*

According to these statistics, prices have gone up very slightly during the years under review. If we now apply these cost of living figures to the above index figures for wage rates, gross weekly wages and the total wage bill, we get the following results:

REAL WAGES INDICES, 1932 TO 1937

(1932 = 100)

Year	Real Wage Rates	Real Weekly Gross Earnings	Total Real Wage Bill
1932	100	100	100
1933	99	98	108
1934	97	100	129
1935	95	103	143
1936	94	107	161
1937	93	112	178

From this table we get the impression that real wage rates have declined under Fascism by about 7 per cent, that gross real wages per week have increased by about 12 per cent, and that the total real wage bill has increased by more than three-quarters. But this impression is inaccurate because the official cost of living index does not indicate the real increase in the cost of living. Furthermore, the gross wage index does not (according to definition) take into account the fact that deductions from wages have increased under Fascism.

Let us begin with the second factor and turn the gross wage index into a net wage index for the employed workers. Official estimates of deductions in 1932 for tax payments and social insurance amounted roughly to 12½ per cent. For the following years official estimates assume an increase of these deductions by about 1 per cent. But in 1932 no worker had to pay for "Winter Help," for air raid protection, for "Strength through Joy," and similar purposes which at that time were either non-existent or were paid for by the Reich. If we assume that the average payment for these purposes was only 1½ per cent of the wage received, we arrive at a minimum figure of 15 per cent for such deductions, a figure which quite probably is too low. If, then, we take these deductions into account, we arrive at the following more accurate picture of wage rates, weekly earnings and the total wage bill:

REAL WAGE INDICES, 1932 TO 1937
(1932 = 100)

Year	Net Real Wage Rates	Net Weekly Real Earnings of Employed Workers	Net Total Real Wage Bill
1932	100	100	100
1933	96	95	105
1934	94	97	125
1935	92	100	139
1936	91	104	156
1937	90	109	172

We now come to the rectification of the official cost of living index. The chief faults of this index are the following:

Firstly, it is based on the assumption that the worker spends about 40 Marks per week, while actually he cannot spend anything like that amount. Since, under Fascism, the more expensive kinds of food have increased less in price than the basic necessities, Fascist statisticians, when computing the cost of living, assumed that the worker has a better standard of living than was actually the case, as this made possible the inclusion of more expensive foods (the prices of which were more stable) into their computation of changes in the cost of living. Furthermore, the official cost of living index included certain cheap foodstuffs which were really no longer obtainable and which had to be replaced by more expensive, as for instance, imported lard or, to a certain extent, margarine. Finally, there has been a deterioration in the quality of food. One pound of butter in 1937 contains less fat and more water than one pound of butter in 1932, and the same holds true of milk, cheese, and other foods. As to clothing, the quality has also deteriorated. A winter coat, for instance, is not only less substantial than formerly, affording the owner less warmth, but, because of its poor quality, must be replaced much sooner than a winter coat bought in pre-Fascist times. Unfortunately, it is not possible to take into account all these and other factors which tend to increase the cost of living above the official scale. But I have made some computations of the increase in the cost of food, basing them on official price quotations, and taking into account the need for replacing some foods which are no longer available by other foods, as well as deleting a number of foods which the worker could not afford to buy with his meagre wages.* Taking these facts into account, the food price index rises by 19½ per cent between January, 1933, and January, 1938, instead of the official cost of food index's increase of only about 9 per cent. If we assume—but incorrectly—that the other items in the official cost of living index have increased only as much as the official data show, and assuming that food makes up about half of the cost of living (not too high an assumption if we take into account the low level of wages), we arrive at an increase in the cost of living between 1932 and 1937 of about 7 per cent instead of the officially indicated increase of roughly 4 per cent. If we now apply this corrected cost of living index to the wage indices given above we arrive at the following results:

THE COST OF LIVING AND THE NET REAL WAGE INDICES

Prices and Wages		1932	1937
Official Cost of Living Index		100	104
Corrected Cost of Living Index		100	107
Net Real Wage Rates		100	87
Net Weekly Real Earnings of Employed Workers		100	105
Net Total Real Wage Bill		100	166

Thus, under Fascism, net real wage rates have declined by 13 per cent during a period of rapidly increasing business activity —a unique departure from conditions and trends as observed throughout the whole history of capitalism!

Net real wages per week per employed worker have increased during the first five years of the Fascist régime by roughly 5 per cent. This increase, if an increase has taken place at all, was in fact much smaller for reasons explained above. But even this does not yet explain the wage situation. It is not sufficient to take into account only the development of prices in order to understand the meaning of a wage table. Other factors must be mentioned.

First, there is the development of the intensity of work. We shall show later that this has increased considerably. Now if the intensity of work increases, the worker needs more purchasing power, not in order to live at a higher level but in order to maintain his present standard. For increased intensity of work

---

* Cf. for a detailed description of the methods by which this corrected index was computed: Juergen Kuczynski, *The Condition of the Worker in Great Britain, Germany and the Soviet Union, 1932–1938,* pp. 18–20.

means increased expenditure of energy which in turn requires more food or food of a more nutritious quality and more repose.

Furthermore, we must remember that an average wage increase does not necessarily mean that wages have increased in every industry. What happened in Germany was that there was a transfer of workers from lower paying industries to higher, or rather less poorly, paying ones; for instance, from textile and clothing to the metal industries. Such a transfer may lead to an increase in average wages while wages in the individual industries (in metal or in textiles, for instance) have increased much less or not at all. That is what took place in Germany. We may even check up on the influence which this shifting of workers had upon the development of actual wages. The following table shows the development of hourly wage rates and of average actual hourly earnings : *

WAGE RATES AND EARNINGS PER HOUR, 1932 TO 1937

Year	Rates	Earnings
1932	100	100
1933	97	97
1934	97	99
1935	97	101
1936	97	102
1937	97	105

From this table it is obvious that the shifting of workers from low to less lowly paying industries must have had a considerable influence on the development of average wages in industry.†

Taking all these factors into account, we are fully justified in saying that *the average worker received real wages which moved around the lowest level reached during the crisis of 1929–32 and for these wages had to work more intensively and for longer hours. Also the average real wage paid in individual industries was definitely lower than that paid during the crisis at its deepest point, and the worker had to work more intensively and longer for this low wage.*

*   *   *

But our survey of general wages is still incomplete. We still have to compare average wages and the average cost of living in

* Cf. *Statistisches Jahrbuch, 1938,* and *Wirtschaft und Statistik,* 2. Februar Heft, 1938.

† A slight part of the increase in average earnings may be due to the increase in the percentage of overtime earnings.

absolute terms. The average gross weekly earnings per week amount to about 26·50 Marks. If we deduct from this about 15 per cent for taxes and other payments, we arrive at an average of roughly 22·50 Marks per week. When computing the official cost of living index the *Statistische Reichsamt* assumes that, to keep his family and himself decently and in health, a worker needs something like 40 Marks per week.* This means that *the wages of the worker in 1937 had to be increased, on the average, by about 80 per cent in order to reach even what the Fascist statisticians regard as a minimum standard of health and decency.* If we add that this standard is, in fact, much too low (nobody who knows what Fascists understand by a decent standard of living for the workers can quarrel with this statement) we can realize that wages would have to be increased by over 100 per cent in order to reach a minimum standard of health and decency—a standard which, let us add, is definitely below that, which, for instance, the United States Bureau of Labour Statistics or the United States Bureau of Home Economics regard as a health and decency standard.

B. Wages of Specific Categories of Workers

In studying wages in general, many peculiar features of their development are concealed. It is necessary, therefore, to split up the general averages into specific categories.

The first, and still very general, division is into fully employed workers, short-time workers and unemployed. We know from the above figures that the wages of the not inconsiderable number of workers who in 1932 were still fully employed and who in the first five years under Fascism did not work more hours per day than formerly (for instance, many workers in the consumption goods industries) have declined; and that their real wages have gone down by at least one-eighth. But many workers whose hours of work have been increased are receiving real wages below the crisis level in spite of this fact. For, even if we include overtime pay, the number of hours must be increased by more than 10 per cent in order to make up for the loss of purchasing power through increased deductions and the rise in the cost of living. According

* Cf. my computations in *Finanzpolitische Korrespondenz*, December 17, 1929.

to official statistics,* the proportion of workers employed full time was about one-third in 1932. If we apply this proportion to the total number of workers and deduct about one million, chiefly metal and construction workers, who are working considerably longer hours than in 1932, we arrive at a figure of about four million workers who were fully employed in 1932 and who received in 1937·a real wage lower than that paid in 1932.

The percentage of short-time workers, according to the same statistics, amounted in 1932 to about 23 per cent; related to the total number of workers, this corresponds to a figure of over three million. Most of those who in 1937 worked full time have received an increase in their real income because the increased deductions and the increased cost of living do not amount to as much as the average wage loss through short-time in 1932, which amounted to about one-quarter of the normal wage. But in 1937 there were still a considerable number of short-time workers. No statistics of short-time were published by the authorities. I estimate that about half the textile workers worked short-time (we must also count those who in 1937 worked 40 hours per week as a "normal working week" as short-time workers, compared with 1932) and many workers in other consumption industries worked less than their normal working week; to these we must add a considerable number of temporary short-time workers in other industries, usually forced on short-time by raw material shortages, and so on. All in all, it is no exaggeration, but rather an under-estimate, if we assume that in 1937, about one million workers in Germany worked short-time to such an extent that their real wages were lower than in 1932.

As to the unemployed, there is no doubt that those who were unemployed in 1932 and who were fully employed in 1937 were receiving a definitely higher real income. On the other hand, those dependent upon unemployment benefit in 1937 received a lower real income than the unemployed of 1932. The number of unemployed in 1937 amounted to about 900,000. To the latter category must be added those who were unemployed in 1932 and who were working in 1937, but were not receiving standard wages; these were all those persons employed in the Labour

* *Statistisches Handbuch der Weltwirtschaft, 1936.*

Service, as Agricultural Service workers, and at forced labour on road construction and fortifications, etc. On the whole their income, measured by its purchasing power, was lower than in 1932; the number of workers employed in this way was probably little less than one million.

If we total all those workers receiving a lower real income in 1937 than in 1932 we get the following:

> 4 million workers already fully employed in 1932.
> 1 million short-time workers.
> 1 million workers not normally employed.
> 0·9 million workers who are unemployed.
>
> ---
>
> Roughly 7 million workers.

From this we can conclude that, even if we take the official Fascist statistics as correct, in 1937, the real income of almost half the German workers was lower than at the time of the worst economic crisis in the history of Germany.

Another aspect of wage conditions is opened up to us if we study the development of wages in factories, mines and building construction on the one hand and in all other sectors of national economy, on the other. The following table gives us the annual income per worker in all sectors of national economy and then in the above-mentioned three sectors which, for the sake of brevity, I combine under the head of "industry."*

GROSS ANNUAL WAGES, 1932 TO 1937
(Mark)

Year	Total Economy	Industry
1932	1,197	1,404
1933	1,141	1,435
1934	1,190	1,540
1935	1,253	1,613
1936	1,320	1,687
1937	1,381	1,754

We see, then, that wages in industry have been rather higher than in national economy as a whole; they began to increase as

---

* Wages for industry as a whole compare *Statistisches Jahrbuch*, 1936 and 1937, and *Wirtschaft und Statistik*, 2. Februar Heft, 1938. Wages paid in national economy as a whole are computed from the official data for average weekly wages.

soon as Fascism was established in contrast to wages as a whole; later, they increased more rapidly. From the above figures we can also compute wages in all non-industrial sectors of national economy and it is of interest to contrast them with wages in industry:

ANNUAL WAGES IN THE INDUSTRIAL AND NON-INDUSTRIAL SECTOR
(Mark)

Year	Industrial Sector	Non-Industrial Sector
1932	1,404	783
1933	1,435	553
1934	1,540	490
1935	1,613	533
1936	1,687	586
1937	1,754	636

The picture presented is staggering. We find that the non-industrial workers, the workers in many cases the least related to war preparations, receive less than half the wages of the industrial workers. But, more important, we find that the wages of non-industrial workers, even without taking into account the problem of purchasing power, declined continuously from 1932 to 1934, and the following increase did not bring them up even to the crisis level of 1932; on the contrary, they remained about 20 per cent below this level. Here, the question arises: how can workers live under such conditions? It can be answered partly (but only partly) by the fact that not all these workers are solely dependent on their wages for their living. They include domestics and agricultural workers who are either fully fed and housed at their place of work (many domestics) or who receive products in addition to their wages (many agricultural workers) or who may buy cheap meals at their place of work (forced labour on road construction, etc.). But all this does not invalidate the fact that their money income has declined considerably under Fascism, and that, at a modest estimate, they could buy with their money income in 1937, at least 25 per cent less than in 1932.

We now come to an investigation of the development of wages in individual industries:*

* Cf. *Statistisches Jahrbuch für das Deutsche Reich*, 1936 and 1937, and *Wirtschaft und Statistik*, May and June, 1938.

GROSS WEEKLY WAGES IN INDIVIDUAL INDUSTRIES
(April, 1933 = 100)*

Industries				1934	1935	1936	1937
Production industries ..	..	..	..	105	107	109	110
Consumption goods industries		..	..	101	98	102	102
Iron and other metal production		..	..	111	114	115	115
Metal goods industry ..	..	..	..	109	115	117	122
Iron and steel goods industry..		..	..	111	114	114	115
Machine building	..	..	..	113	118	120	122
Electrical industry ..	..	..	..	121	124	127	129
Building materials industry ..	..	..	..	103	102	109	109
Woodworking industry	..	..	..	101	98	103	104
Textile industry	..	..	..	102	97	100	102
Clothing industry	..	..	..	96	91	96	95
Food industry ..	..	..	..	101	101	101	102
Beverages and Tobacco industry	..	..		107	106	107	108

This table is of the very greatest interest because it shows the terrible wage conditions of all those workers under Fascism who do not produce weapons of destruction. There are two general groups of industries: first, those producing production goods, which generally form the heavy or armament industries. Wages in these industries, taking into account the increased deductions and the increased cost of living, have in a number of cases probably increased slightly. But even here we find so important an exception, apart from many minor industries. as the industry producing building materials which (and this explains everything) to a considerable extent caters for the ordinary consumer in the form of housing accommodation. The other group is formed by the consumption goods industries which have relatively little to do with armaments; they paid the workers less in 1937 than in 1932, as measured by the increase in the cost of living, taking into account also increased deductions from wages. Again we see confirmed, as so often already, that the producers of weapons of destruction are favoured, or at least less badly treated in some respects, than those who produce goods for general consumption.

If we investigate wages by geographical subdivisions† we again find the military factor to be of great importance:

* Unfortunately, no comparable data are available for an earlier period.
† Cf. *Wirtschaft und Statistik*, 2. April Heft, 1936, 1. April Heft, 1937, and 2. April Heft, 1938.

WEEKLY GROSS WAGES BY GEOGRAPHICAL DIVISIONS
(Marks)

District	1932	1933	1934	1935	1936	1937
East Prussia	16·06	15·17	16·09	16·99	17·68	18·38
West Prussia	14·61	14·33	14·99	16·00	16·76	17·84
Berlin..	29·37	28·12	28·55	30·80	32·64	34·40
Brandenburg.. ..	18·87	18·47	19·83	21·06	22·15	23·00
Pomerania	18·21	17·61	18·55	19·34	20·42	21·05
Silesia	18·32	17·63	18·64	19·15	19·79	20·53
Saxony-Anhalt ..	20·82	20·63	22·14	23·87	25·14	26·44
Schleswig-Holstein ..	22·19	21·08	22·35	23·58	25·34	26·08
Hanover*	21·33	20·02	21·23	22·34	—	—
Oldenburg	20·46	19·18	20·00	20·23	23·50	24·30
Westphalia	23·89	23·35	24·60	25·70	27·10	28·67
Hessia-Nassau ..	23·68	22·56	22·61	23·46	24·78	26·65
Rhine Province ..	25·52	24·48	25·32	26·60	27·93	29·25
Upper Bavaria ..	22·01	20·00	21·47	22·48	23·59	24·44
Upper Palatinate and Lower Bavaria	16·93	15·71	16·06	17·10	17·63	18·85
Palatinate	22·63	21·77	22·38	23·46	24·82	26·43
Upper and Central Franconia	19·98	19·61	20·51	21·46	22·52	23·54
Lower Franconia ..	20·95	20·31	20·96	22·27	23·62	24·67
Swabia	19·99	19·12	19·82	20·48	21·71	23·30
Saxony	22·73	21·94	23·07	23·64	24·49	25·31
Wurtemberg	21·58	21·26	22·73	23·66	24·76	25·96
Baden	21·96	20·78	21·69	22·62	23·53	24·42
Hessia	22·27	20·97	22·52	23·59	24·35	25·43
Mecklenburg.. ..	19·46	18·97	20·39	22·04	23·00	23·85
Thuringia	19·82	19·15	20·39	21·50	22·59	23·57
Brunswick	20·82	20·32	21·80	23·17	24·23	25·50
Hanseatic Towns ..	31·74	29·07	27·89	29·70	31·51	33·69

At first sight these figures seem to give too complex a picture to indicate any developments of importance. But there is an easy way to their interpretation if we examine first those districts which in 1932 paid the lowest, and those which paid the highest wages.

DISTRICTS PAYING THE LOWEST WAGES
(Wages in Marks)

	1932	1937
West Prussia	14·61	17·84
East Prussia	16·06	18·38
Lower Bavaria ..	16·93	18·85

DISTRICTS PAYING THE HIGHEST WAGES
(Wages in Marks)

	1932	1937
Hanseatic Towns ..	31·74	33·69
Berlin	29·37	34·40
Rhine Province.. ..	25·52	29·25

* Combined with Oldenburg since 1936.

In 1932, the lowest wages were roughly less than half of the two highest wage payments. In 1937 the lowest wages are more than half as high as the highest wage payments. There seems to have been a certain levelling of wages, although the extent is very small. Let us investigate this further. Let us find the six districts in which wages increase most. They are:

West Prussia	Brandenburg
Saxony-Anhalt	Wurtemberg
Mecklenburg	Brunswick

This surprises us at first sight, for all these districts pay very low wages and they are largely agricultural districts. Did the Fascists decide to raise relatively the earnings of the agricultural workers? We know that this is not the case. But remembering

DISTRICTS IN WHICH WAGES IN 1937 WOULD HAVE HAD TO BE INCREASED IN ORDER TO REACH THE MINIMUM

1. By over 100 per cent

East Prussia
West Prussia
Brandenburg
Pomerania
Silesia
Upper Palatinate and Lower Bavaria
Swabia

2. By 50 to 100 per cent

Saxony-Anhalt	Lower Franconia
Schleswig-Holstein	Saxony
Oldenburg	Wurtemberg
Westphalia	Baden
Hessia-Nassau	Hessia
Rhine Province	Mecklenburg
Upper Bavaria	Thuringia
Palatinate	Brunswick
Upper and Central Franconia	

3. By less than 50 per cent

Berlin
Hanseatic Towns

that all developments which we do not at once understand in Fascist economy usually find their explanation in connection with war preparations, we find the solution. The Fascists erected in, or transferred to the agricultural districts a number of armament factories, and, since wages in armament industries are higher than in agriculture, the average wage level in these districts has been raised more than the national average. *The wage level in the various districts in Germany has thus become more even, because war industries spread over all Germany and especially to the agricultural districts.*

Before concluding this survey of wages by geographical regions, it is of interest to compare the average wages with the official cost of living minimum and to see by how much wages in the various districts must increase in order to reach it. The table on page 114 subdivides the various districts into three groups according to the percentage by which wages would have to be increased to attain the official Fascist cost of living minimum.*

There were, thus, only two districts in 1937 in which wages would have had to be increased by under 50 per cent in order to reach the Fascist cost of living minimum. And there are seven districts in which wages would have had to be increased by over 100 per cent in order to reach this minimum. In the remaining seventeen districts wages would have had to be increased by between 50 and 100 per cent This is probably one of the most impressive indictments against the economic labour policy of Fascism during the first five years of its reign.

C. RELATIVE WAGES

In the preceding pages we have studied the development of money wages and of real wages. We have also tried to give a rough picture of the relations between the absolute amount of wages and the minimum cost of living as computed by official Fascist statisticians. The next step would be the computation of relative wages, of the relation between the wage income of the workers and the income of the ruling class. Unfortunately, not enough material is available to make such comparisons.

But it is possible to give a rough picture of the development of the income of wage earners and salaried workers, on the one hand, and of all other income receivers, on the other. This is a very unsatisfactory way of "computing" relative wages since the non-workers' income includes that of the small independent

---

* I have deducted from the above gross wages 15 per cent for taxes and other deductions.

craftsman, whose income has suffered a decline under Fascism in many cases, and that of the monopolist whose income has risen rapidly. It includes the income of the peasant whose income has developed unfavourably, as well as that of the Junker who has definitely benefited from Fascism. If we add to this the previously mentioned unsatisfactory nature of our figures on wages, we realize that the following figures are no more than rough approximations. Yet the results of the computations are so striking and show such a definite trend that we are really justified in making them, for an error of 5 or 10 or even 20 per cent would not materially change the conclusions.*

RELATIVE WAGES IN GERMANY, 1932–1937

Year	Income of Wage and Salaried Workers	Income of Employers and other Non-Workers	Relative Wages
1932	100	100	100
1933	97	119	82
1934	103	154	67
1935	110	177	62
1936	117	199	59
1937	124	248	50

According to these figures, the relative position of the worker in Germany under Fascism has deteriorated by about 50 per cent. The income position of the rich has improved so much that even if we must count among them (because of poor statistical material) shopkeepers, small craftsmen, and so on, we find that their income has doubled, as compared with that of the workers. Not only has the purchasing power of the individual worker had a tendency to hover around the crisis minimum of 1932—but in addition his income as compared with that of the rich, declined rapidly. The abyss between the two nations, the rich and the poor, which exists always under capitalism and widens from trade cycle to trade cycle, widening yet more rapidly in the period of finance capitalism, has broadened with infinitely greater rapidity under Fascism. *Fascism has not only succeeded in keeping down real wages during a period of increasing trade activity— which has never happened before in the history of capitalism—it has also succeeded in widening the division between the income of the worker and that of the rich to an extent and with a rapidity hitherto unknown.*

* Originally published in my *The Condition of the Workers in Great Britain, Germany and the Soviet Union, 1932–1938*, pp. 58 and 59.

4. PRODUCTIVITY AND INTENSITY OF WORK

While the general purchasing power of the worker has at best remained stable on the crisis level of 1932, while that of a considerable number has, undoubtedly, declined considerably, the intensity of work per wage earner has increased.

This fact, together with a number of others which we shall study on the following pages, is of the greatest importance, for all these factors are of considerable influence upon the general standard of living and working of the wage earner. While wages —money wages, real wages and relative wages—play a great rôle in determining the standard of living, they are by no means of exclusive importance.

The following table gives a preliminary survey of the development of productivity per worker. The figures are based on official data* and the picture which they give is approximately correct. Of course, these figures are not accurate to the last fraction, and the material on which they are based is not ideal (productivity in the vehicle industry, for instance, is based on an index including the production of ships and an employment index referring only to industries producing power-driven land vehicles and locomotives), but the trend of the development emerges so clearly that the table is most useful as an illustration of what actually happened:

PRODUCTION PER EMPLOYED WORKER IN INDUSTRY, 1932 TO 1937

(*1932 = 100*)

Year	All Industry	Production Goods	Consumption Goods	Iron, Steel	Vehicles	Textiles	Foodstuffs
1932	100	100	100	100	100	100	100
1933	101	101	101	115	135	109	99
1934	102	105	99	130	145	104	96
1935	107	118	95	143	163	96	98
1936	110	121	98	149	173	103	96
1937	111	124	97	144	187	101	100

* Based on statistics given by the Institut fuer Konjunkturforschung, *Halbjahresberichte zur Wirtschaftslage*, 3. Jahrgang, Heft 2; *Statistik des In- und Auslandes*, 13. Jahrgang, Heft 3; *Wochenberichte*, 1938, No. 42 and 44 of the same Institute.

The results of this computation are surprising in their variety. In industry as a whole production per worker has increased by somewhat over 10 per cent, a composite figure of an increase by about one-quarter in the production goods industries and a decline in the consumption goods industries. Five years of Fascism have driven up the productivity of the worker in the vehicle industry by roughly 90 per cent and in the iron and steel industry by little less than 50 per cent, while in the textile and food industries it has remained almost stable.

How much of this increase has been due to an increased number of hours worked, and how much to greater productivity per working hour? The following table gives an answer:*

HOURLY PRODUCTIVITY PER INDUSTRIALLY EMPLOYED WORKER

Industry	1932	1937
All Industry	100	100
Production Goods	100	108
Consumption Goods ..	100	91
Iron and Steel	100	119
Vehicles	100	163
Textiles	100	96
Food-stuffs	100	97

The results of this table are not only surprising for their variety—each is surprising in itself. The first surprising fact is that productivity per hour in industry as a whole has remained about stable. That is, the increased production per worker is due to an increase in the number of hours worked. Has there been no technical progress? Has there been during those years so much sabotage and ca'canny, that in spite of technical progress, productivity has remained stable? Has ca'canny been especially widespread in the consumption goods industries? Has technical progress been concentrated upon a few industries only? Has there been no increase in the intensity of work? Or has the intensity of work been increased only in a selected number of industries?

The answer to these questions again shows the nefarious character of the Fascist system. The first point of importance is

* Same sources as for previous table and *Statistisches Jahrbuch für das Deutsche Reich, 1938.*

the difference between the development of hourly productivity in the armament and related industries, and those which produce for the people. Industries such as the iron and steel or the vehicle industry show a considerable increase in productivity, while others, like the textile or food industries, actually show a decline in productivity.

But this decline in productivity is not due to technical regression, nor is it due to general sabotage and ca'canny. During the period under review, from 1932 to 1937, there have been numerous cases of ca'canny and some of sabotage; but they have not been so widespread as seriously to influence the development of hourly productivity. Nor has the food situation been such that the productivity per worker was seriously decreased because of poor nutrition. Or rather, let us express it in this way: the food standard was already poor before Fascism came to power, and in this respect the first five years of Fascism made relatively little difference. What difference it did make was counter-balanced by a drive for increased intensity of work, by slave-driving, speed-up, increased terror against "slackers." One must, however, not over-estimate these factors during the first five years of Fascism; they must be mentioned but, as compared with the second five years of Fascism, they are not of such decisive importance. They already play a considerable rôle in some sections of industry, but they are not yet of any decisive importance for the development of productivity, as compared with the last pre-Fascist decade.

Thus, we are driven back to the argument of technical regression. But has there really been technical regression under Fascism? No doubt, there has been much technical progress under Fascism in all matters concerned with war production. In fact, probably no war industry, with the exception of that of the Soviet Union, made such technical progress during these five years as did the German.

Can we then say that, while much technical progress was made under Fascism in the war industries, the consumption goods industries were neglected? This would not be correct. On the contrary, curious as it may seem at first, much technical progress was also made in the consumption goods industries. The reason for this is that, because of the shortage of many raw materials (caused by the confiscation of foreign exchange by the heavy industries for imports of armament raw materials) the German consumption goods industries were forced to devote much research to the production of substitutes. The substitute industries in Germany during these years made considerable progress, and it is quite possible that, with further development, the final results of this research, under another form of Government, will benefit mankind. But Fascism, of course, was not out to benefit mankind. Fascism was out to replace foreign raw materials by home-made substitutes in order to be able to withstand a blockade in case of war, and in order in peace time to save all the foreign exchange possible for the importation of armament raw materials.

Consequently, the mass production of substitutes was introduced at a time when they were not fully developed, when their quality was still inferior and when their production involved relatively much labour power. *Thus, we have the perverse situation under Fascism of technical progress damaging, instead of benefiting, the people, even when applied to consumption goods; technical progress, thus, increasing instead of diminishing production difficulties.* The changeover in the textile industry, for instance, from cotton and wool to a mixture of these two raw materials with staple fibre, considerably decreased the productivity in this industry.

Additional factors leading to decreased productivity per hour have been the introduction of large numbers of unskilled workers into semi-skilled occupations because of a shortage of labour in certain industries, increased fatigue because of the lengthened working day, and the wear and tear of the machinery. While the first and second factors apply, in this period, chiefly to the metal industry, the third plays a considerable rôle in the non-war industries. Machine-building was concentrated more and more upon the production of such machines which were needed in the armament industries while many textile factories or food manufacturing industries had to use worn-out machinery, with increasingly frequent break-downs.

A further factor of importance is that, particularly in the first few years of Fascism, many workers entering industry after years of unemployment had lost some of their skill. This and the other factors are to a certain extent offset by the elimination of numerous small factories with less up-to-date machinery, in the process of increasing trustification and the concentration of industry in general.

In conclusion, we can say that in spite of increased driving and rationalization, in spite of the elimination of a number of small and technically less advanced factories, the productivity of labour per hour remained, on the average, the same, because of wear and tear of machinery in some industries without the possibility of quick replacement, because of the premature introduction and use of substitutes, because of the influence of poor nutrition and too long a working day, because of the introduction of long unemployed and unskilled labour, and lastly because of sabotage and ca'canny. *Starting with the fact of increased intensity of work, one can conclude that during the first five years of Fascism the individual worker, while driven ever harder, was unable to produce more.*

5. Accidents and Health Conditions

I write in the preceding section that the drive for more output per hour, the increase in the intensity of work, must not be over-estimated during the first five years of Fascism. When I wrote on this problem five years ago I laid considerable emphasis on this increase. I did not then foresee that, in the next five years, there would be such a degree of slave-driving as the German worker had not known in his entire history. Yet those were right who, five years ago, laid stress upon the terrible increase in the intensity of work—terrible because every degree of intensity added to that prevailing before Fascism came to power bore so heavily on the workers. This is obvious from the following statistics which show the development of accidents.* Accidents are one of the few auxiliary means at our disposal in attempting to assess the increase in the intensity of work. Long hours of work, poor food and increased intensity of work per hour are, under Fascism, the chief reasons for increased accidents.† (See page 122).

The number of accidents has risen very rapidly; within five years it has more than doubled. And these statistics give only

* Accidents are much more sensitive to changes in food conditions and to speed-up than the productivity of work.

† For this and for all other tables dealing with accidents see *Reichsarbeitsblatt*, 1938, Heft 15, and *Statistisches Jahrbuch für das Deutsche Reich*, 1934 ff.

those accidents which were so severe that they have to be notified to the insurance authorities. If we bear in mind the fact that, under Fascism, the notification of accidents is even more discouraged than before, we realize the full importance of these figures.

NUMBER OF ACCIDENTS, 1932 TO 1937

(*In Thousands*)

Year	Number
1932	827·0
1933	929·6
1934	1,173·6
1935	1,354·3
1936	1,527·3
1937	1,789·2

But, one may ask, while it is true that accidents have more than doubled in number, was this not to be expected, with increasing employment? Let us see how accidents developed, taking into account the increase in the number of employed.*

ACCIDENTS PER 1,000 INSURED (EMPLOYED) PERSONS,
1932 TO 1937

Year	Accidents
1932	33·9
1933	36·8
1934	44·1
1935	47·2
1936	50·5
1937	56·5

The table shows that only part of the increase in the number of accidents was due to the increase in the number of employed workers. The table shows that not only the number of accidents has increased rapidly, but that in addition the rate of accidents has risen by about 70 per cent. In other words, the risk that the employed worker may be seriously injured has increased by roughly 70 per cent. If we assume that every worker works at least forty years then *this accident rate means that every worker can expect during his working life to be injured at least twice, so seriously that his accident has to be notified to the accident insurance, even under Fascist conditions as they prevailed in 1937.* To-day, they are, of course, still worse.

* *Reichsarbeitsblatt*, 1938, Heft 9.

In this connection it is important to compare the development of accidents and of the number of cases for which compensation was paid:*

NOTIFIED ACCIDENTS AND COMPENSATED CASES, 1932 TO 1937
(Per 1,000 Insured)

Year	Notified Accidents	Cases of Compensation
1932	33·9	3·6
1933	36·8	2·9
1934	44·1	3·1
1935	47·2	3·1
1936	50·5	2·9
1937	56·5	3·0

Although the rate of accidents has risen by about 70 per cent, the rate of compensation has not merely failed to rise correspondingly, but has declined by about 20 per cent. This gives us an inkling of the influence of Fascism upon social insurance. While social insecurity increases (while accidents rise), the palliatives bestowed (compensation) become less and less. The whole extent of the decline in compensation becomes clearer from the following table showing the percentage of notified cases which received compensation:

PERCENTAGE OF COMPENSATED CASES AMONG ALL NOTIFIED CASES OF INJURY, 1932 TO 1937

Year	Percentage
1932	11
1933	8
1934	7
1935	7
1936	6
1937	5

The percentage of cases compensated has been halved under Fascism. While in 1932 about 11 per cent of notified injuries were compensated, the percentage after five years of Fascism had declined to 5. No wonder, under such circumstances, that in spite of the fact that the total number of accidents more than doubled, total payments by the accident insurance increased very little:†

* Statistisches Jahrbuch für das Deutsche Reich, 1938.
† Based on figures given in Statistisches Jahrbuch für das Deutsche Reich, 1934 ff.

ACCIDENTS AND COMPENSATION PAYMENTS, 1932 TO 1937

(1932 = 100)

Year	Accidents	Payments
1932	100	100
1933	112	92
1934	142	96
1935	164	101
1936	185	104
1937	216	111

If we now divide the index of accidents into the index of compensation payments we arrive at the following index of payments per notified accident:

PAYMENTS PER NOTIFIED ACCIDENT, 1932 TO 1937

(1932 = 100)

Year	Payments
1932	100
1933	82
1934	68
1935	62
1936	56
1937	51

Thus, the amount of accident insurance paid per notified injury has declined by half, as compared even with 1932, the year of the greatest crisis and the worst financial conditions of the social insurance system! So much for social insurance under National "Socialism.'"

*   *   *

How did health conditions develop during these years? Because of the German health insurance system we have, in contrast to most other countries, some statistics of value indicating the development of health conditions among wage and salary earners.

The following table vividly illustrates the miserable condition into which Fascism has brought the ailing worker. It gives the number of days the average insured member has been ill and the number of cases of illness per insured member:*

HEALTH CONDITIONS, 1932 TO 1937

Year	Days of Illness per Insured	Cases of Illness per Insured
1932	8·8	2·1
1933	8·9	2·3
1934	8·3	2·6
1935	8·8	2·8
1936	8·8	2·8
1937	9·0	2·8

* See *Wirtschaft und Statistik*, 1938, Heft 9.

Before studying this table let us be clear as to the following. While to-day illness is regarded as sabotage, even in the years under review it was dangerous for a worker to become ill. Often, when workers stayed at home because of illness, they found, when they returned to work, that their places had been taken by others and that they were relegated to worse paid or more disagreeable or arduous work. This caused a general tendency for ailing workers to stay at work as long as possible, and, when their illness had made it impossible for them to continue at work, to return to work as soon as possible.

Having taken this into account we can realize the implications of the preceding table. The first fact of importance is that, under Fascism, the days of illness per insured member remained about stable. The second is that, while the days of illness per insured member remained stable, the number of cases of illness increased. It would be wrong to conclude from this that, under Fascism, the worker is ill more often but his illnesses are less severe. Keeping in mind what we said in the preceding paragraph, we can quite easily interpret these data. They show that, because of increased intensity of work, poorer food, and the general deterioration of working conditions, the number of illnesses per worker has increased so much that, in spite of the intimidation of the sick workers, even the official Fascist statistics indicate *an increase in the number of illnesses per insured worker of about one-third*. They also show that, in spite of this fact, the total number of days the individual worker is absent from work has remained stable, that is, *the ill worker ventured less and less to stay away from work*. The following table, giving the number of days the individual worker was away from work during each illness, shows this even more clearly:

DAYS OF ILLNESS PER ILL WORKER, 1932 TO 1937

Year	Days
1932	4·2
1933	3·6
1934	3·2
1935	3·1
1936	3·1
1937	3·2

The table shows that, as time went on, the worker feared more and more to stay away from work, even if the Fascist health insurance authorities recognized his illness as genuine and serious. The most tragic figure in this table is the one for 1937: it shows an increase in the number of days the worker kept away from work because of illness—slight, but nevertheless an increase. This was not due to any humane attitude of the Fascist health insurance authorities. It was due to the fact that health conditions had deteriorated so much that even Fascist terror did not then succeed in reducing further the number of days the sick worker dared to keep away from work.

Accident and health conditions during the five years under review show a continuous deterioration. This is a further clear indication of the fact that the intensity of work has increased under Fascism. At the same time the statistics which we have added to those giving the number or rate of accidents and sickness, reveal the deterioration of the social insurance system under Fascism, a process which can best be described as a systematic undermining of the gains which labour had made in Germany, in this respect, during the preceding half century.

6. The Social Insurance System

After the impressive figures on the decline of social insurance under Fascism given in the preceding pages, the table* on page 127 which shows the movement in pensions paid by the invalidity insurance can hardly surprise us, but it will enhance the impression we have gained from the foregoing figures.

Here we become acquainted with a new feature in Fascist social insurance policy. *The number of pensioners is being rapidly reduced—while at first one is cautious about reducing the amount paid to the individual pensioner.*

From 1932 to 1937, the number of pensions paid for prolonged illness has been cut down by almost one-third; the number of old age pensioners has been reduced by over 50 per cent; the number of widows' pensions paid has remained about the same, but this is in reality a decline if we keep in mind the growing number of widows which Fascism creates even in peace time (Spanish intervention, the increased fatal accident rate, etc.).

* Cf. for this and the following table *Statistisches Jahrbuch für das Deutsche Reich*, 1934 ff.

The number of pensions paid to sick widows has been cut by more than one quarter, and orphan pensions, a very important item, have declined by almost half—one of the cruellest cuts!

NUMBER AND AMOUNT OF PENSIONS PAID, 1932 TO 1937

	Sickness Pensions		Old Age Pensions		Pensions to Widows	
	Number	Million	Number	Million	Number	Million
Year	Thousand	Marks	1,000	Marks	Million	Marks
1932	18·4	4·2	40·2	13·4	0·65	141·4
1933	14·1	3·6	35·4	10·5	0·56	130·4
1934	16·7	3·4	30·9	9·1	0·58	135·8
1935	14·9	3·3	26·2	7·8	0·59	141·4
1936	13·7	3·1	21·3	6·7	0·61	146·2
1937	12·9	2·9	18·0	5·5	0·63	151·3

	Pensions to Sick Widows		Pensions to Orphans		Total Pensions	
	Number	Million	Number	Million	Number	Million
Year	Thousand	Marks	Million	Marks	Millions	Marks
1932	2·1	0·5	0·55	58·6	1·26	218·0
1933	1·9	0·4	0·35	48·2	0·96	193·1
1934	1·9	0·4	0·35	47·7	0·98	196·1
1935	1·7	0·3	0·33	44·4	0·97	197·3
1936	1·6	0·3	0·31	40·9	0·96	197·3
1937	1·5	0·3	0·29	38·3	0·96	198·3

All in all, the number of pensioners under Fascism has been cut by about one quarter!

Turning from the general pension system to the payment of pensions to the invalids of labour, we find the situation as follows:*

PENSIONS PAID TO DISABLED WORKERS AND OLD AGE PENSIONERS, 1932 TO 1937

Year	Number (Millions)	Payments (Million Marks)
1932	2·29	921·2
1933	2·30	865·6
1934	2·39	893·1
1935	2·42	911·6
1936	2·44	920·0
1937	2·46	925·9

During the five years from 1932 to 1937 the number of recipients of disability and old age pensions has increased only by about 8 per cent, in spite of the rapid increase of serious accidents and the increasing percentage of older people in the population! A sure sign of the rigid determination of the Fascist officials to

* *Statistisches Jahrbuch für das Deutsche Reich*, 1936 and 1938.

keep the number of recipients as low as possible and to interpret the rules more and more strictly against the workers. At the same time, the amount of pensions paid increased by less than 1 per cent, an indication that even if a worker succeeded in getting a pension, the amount paid was reduced.

Before we come to a final survey of the social insurance system as a whole it is well to remember some data given in a previous chapter, which showed the development of the unemployment insurance system, how, in spite of declining unemployment, the contributions which were increased during the period of rapidly rising unemployment in the crisis, remained the same, while benefit payments declined rapidly and the enormously swollen surplus was used to subsidize the war efforts of the Fascist system.

The following table* shows the development of the finances of the whole of the social insurance system, excluding unemployment insurance, during the five years under review:

SOCIAL INSURANCE FINANCES, 1932 TO 1937.
(Million Marks)

Year	Revenues	Expenditures
1932	3,316	3,304
1933	3,305	3,140
1934	3,780	3,356
1935	4,060	3,579
1936	4,457	3,750
1937	4,709	3,816

During the five years, total revenues rose by 1,400,000,000 marks, or over 40 per cent. This is almost exclusively due to the fact that a rapidly increasing number of employed workers had to pay the high contributions introduced in the course of the crisis. (In Britain, for instance, the contributions were also increased during the crisis, but they were reduced again when it was over; at the same time, the benefit paid—which had been reduced during the crisis—was again increased afterwards.)

While revenue increased by over 40 per cent, expenses rose only by about 15 per cent. The rise in expenditure is explained by the increased payments which had to be made under health

* Cf. the annual surveys of the social insurance system published in *Wirtschaft und Statistik*.

and accident insurance—a growing expenditure in absolute terms, but, as we have seen, declining rapidly as compared with the number of accidents or cases of illness! One additional item of expenditure must not be forgotten: the increased administrative costs caused by high salaries and the creation of special posts for minor party careerists!

The growing discrepancy between the income and expenditure of the social insurance system resulted in a rapidly growing surplus which developed as follows:

SOCIAL INSURANCE FUND, 1932 TO 1937
(Million Marks)

Year	Amount
1932	4,628
1933	4,774
1934	5,194
1935	5,721
1936	6,495
1937	7,439

The rise in the fund was very rapid. Within five years it increased by almost 3,000,000,000 marks or by about 60 per cent. By 1937, the fund was more than double the total expenditure during the crisis year of 1932. Why did Fascism allow this rise in the social insurance fund to continue? The reason is a very simple one. Like everything else that Fascism touches, the social insurance system was transformed into an instrument of war and oppression. Fascism did not reduce the contributions because this would have placed more money in the hands of the workers and this, in turn, would necessitate increased production of consumption goods. *The social insurance system, to a certain extent, became an auxiliary tax system, a method of taking money from the workers.* The funds which in this way accumulate are invested in government bonds. That is, like unemployment insurance, the rest of *the social insurance system was used as a means of financing the war preparations of Fascism.* During the five years under review the investments of the social insurance system in Reich loans rose by roughly 2,000,000,000 marks, that is, during these five years, the social insurance system, excluding unemployment insurance, financed armament expenditure to the extent of about 2,000,000,000 marks. While allowances to orphans were cut by half, the insurance money contributed by the workers was used to finance the preparations for war. Such is the social insurance policy of German Fascism, of that party which calls itself the National Socialist Workers Party and which lies when it calls itself national, when it calls itself socialist, and when it calls itself a workers' party.

7. CONCLUSION

We have come to the end of our first survey of the conditions of labour during the first five years of Fascism. We have been restrained in our language, much more restrained than we were five years ago, when we were unable to envisage how much more terrible for labour conditions under Fascism would become. But for those who have never lived under Fascism, for those who have been spared the terrible fate that has fallen upon more than four hundred million people, the story of the first five years must be cruelly impressive.

Fascism succeeded in keeping wages to the low level of the year of deepest crisis, 1932. Fascism increased the intensity of work, and accidents have risen rapidly. Health conditions deteriorated and the social insurance system was transformed into an instrument of war. All the political liberties which labour gained in a hundred years of painful struggle were abolished. The first elements of slavery and serfdom were injected into the status of labour. And all this within five years! Yes, Fascism has proved its efficiency when it is a matter of degrading the worker, of debasing working conditions and the standards of living, of preparing large scale brutal destruction for the sake of enslaving and exploiting hundreds of millions of people. If we study carefully the story of the first five years of Fascism we find there all the elements of the nefarious "new order" which crushes so cruelly to-day the continent of Europe.

CHAPTER IV

LABOUR CONDITIONS IN GERMANY

1933 TO 1937

THE STORY OF THE LIFE OF THE GERMAN WORKER BASED ON THE ANNUAL REPORTS OF THE GERMAN FACTORY AND MINE INSPECTORS

IN the preceding chapter, we have surveyed labour conditions as a whole on the basis of the statistical material published by the Fascist German Government. This survey gave us a broad, general picture of the year-to-year development of many important aspects of living and working conditions of German wage-earners under Fascism.

In this chapter, we present another survey of the same period, which complements the first and which consists of important detailed material on the life of the German wage-earner as presented through the medium of the annual reports of German factory and mine inspectors for 1935 and 1936, published by the Reich Ministry of Labour in 1937.

THE FACTORY AND MINE INSPECTORATE UNDER FASCISM

Naturally, the working of the factory and mine inspectorate suffered considerably under the conditions of Fascist dictatorship. Some officials quitted the service because they "simply couldn't and wouldn't work any longer." Others were dismissed as "unreliable," while, at the same time, those remaining in the service were burdened with numerous new tasks. In general then we find that in the period under study, the number of inspections carried out in factories and mines has diminished. Here is what the reports state on this matter:

> "As a result of the lack of personnel, a number of executive and expert positions were unoccupied for periods

varying in length (Frankfort-on-the-Oder, Coblenz, Magdeburg, Merseburg, Liegnitz, Upper Silesia, Stettin). Furthermore, there was a very large decrease in personnel through sickness. Also, calling-up for army service had a pronounced effect in the reduced personnel. Owing to an increase in their duties—of which, for reasons of convenience as many as possible would be carried out in the course of one visit—the inspectors remained longer than formerly in each particular factory, so that, in the same given period, the total number of inspections decreased." I. 4.*

"Since the beginning of 1933, altogether 12 technical-expert and 21 non-expert inspectors—about 38 per cent of the total of the Saxon inspectors—have left the Saxony inspectorate and have been replaced by newly enlisted forces. On account of the continually increasing pressure of duties in all departments, the large number of officials still to be trained, and thus not yet capable of assuming their positions, was making itself painfully felt." III. 5.

"Inspection visits covered about 25 per cent of large undertakings, 14 per cent of medium sized ones, and 17 per cent of small concerns. This state of things shows that the percentage of factory inspection visits cannot be regarded any longer as satisfactory; an improvement in this direction is only possible through an increase in the number of inspectors." IX. 3.

Among the new tasks with which the inspectors are charged are the following:

"The heads of the factory inspectorate departments were drawn into the recruiting weeks and the particular events arranged by the German Labour Front . . . among these being the opening of the Winter Help Work." I. 9.

* The annual reports are in 17 parts, as follows: I. Prussia; II. Bavaria; III. Saxony; IV. Wurtemberg; V. Baden; VI. Thuringia; VII. Hessia; VIII. Hamburg; IX. Mecklenburg; X. Oldenburg; XI. Brunswick; XII. Anhalt; XIII. Bremen; XIV. Lippe; XV. Lubeck; XVI. Schaumburg-Lippe; XVII. The Saar District. If, therefore, at the conclusion of a quotation there stands the figures I. 4, it means that the Part is on Prussia and the page is 4; and so on throughout this section.

"The factory inspectors frequently took part in A.R.P. and blackout practice in the industrial concerns, so that they could draw attention to the secondary dangers connected with an air attack, and could also initiate the necessary measures for the protection of the employees against, for instance, accidents in darkened factories." I. 12.

"The decrease in visiting activity by 3·9 per cent, as evidenced in relation to the annual report for 1934, the last one previously published, is chiefly owing to the considerable requisition of the inspection personnel by the increase in enquiries relating to armaments and other production problems." II. 8.

We see that with a diminished staff whose training has also considerably deteriorated in quality, the inspectorate has far more work to perform. But of what does this added work consist? It is no longer the inspection of factories and mines in order to investigate the conditions of the workers and the maintenance of existing regulations. It is an increased activity caused by the opening of Winter Help weeks, by air raid precautions practice (in 1935 and 1936!), through measures imposed by the attempt to establish self-sufficiency in raw materials and through the growth in armaments production; in other words, through things which have absolutely no connection with the inspection of working conditions, but are primarily related to preparations for war. The aim of Fascist factory-inspection policy is to make the inspectors into supplementary supervisors of the preparations for war.

But let us do the Fascists justice. Not only have they increased the duties of the factory inspectors. On the other hand, they have also seen to it that these overworked officials have, in certain fields, rather less to do. For example:

"There is no longer any connection with the Reich Labour Service and its camps, as, with the introduction of Labour Service Duty, through the Reich Labour Service Law of June 26, 1935, the responsibility of the factory inspection officials for the supervision of accident prevention in the Labour Service has been abrogated." IV. 7.

Working conditions in the Labour Service were so bad that before the issuing of the above-mentioned decree, the factory inspectors found themselves compelled to make frequent complaints, which by no means suited the book of the Labour Service chiefs. Therefore, they saw to it that from then on neither the Labour Service workers nor their conditions came under investigation by the Factory Inspection department.

The fact that, in spite of all these difficulties, factory and mine inspectors did render reports on workers' conditions, as quoted below, is proof that there were then still a number of decent, honest officials in this department. While these people were unable to counteract the pernicious measures enacted by the Fascist government, they did at least discover one way by which they could let the world know something about what was happening under Fascism, by means of submitting and editing reports which reveal such facts as those disclosed in the following pages.

*   *   *

1. CHILDHOOD

A. Before Birth and Infancy

The exploitation of the worker starts before he is born. Hardly has the child's primary existence begun, than it must suffer the effects of capitalism. Women of the wealthier class are able carefully to nurture themselves and their unborn children: repose, good food, and the services of first-class, expensive doctors. All this costs money, but the money is forthcoming.

With the workers, it is different. There is a lack of money, of nourishing food; and housing conditions are poor. Also, pregnant women are often compelled to continue working so that their families shall not go hungry. Sometimes the working mother is the sole bread-winner in the family, so that everything depends upon her to keep the family from starvation—and the family must not starve.

When a mother works during pregnancy, it has evil consequences both for mother and child. Frequently they both carry through life the marks of this social evil in the form of permanent weakness, chronic sickness or some sort of disability. During the last weeks of pregnancy it is particularly important that the mother should not go to work. The law, therefore, provides that pregnant mothers shall not work six weeks before, and six weeks after, childbirth, and that they shall receive a certain proportion of their wages, even if they cease work. This was a good law, passed after many decades of hard struggle on the part of the working class. But of what use is the very best of laws under Fascism when conditions are such as to compel the working-woman to ignore the law?

"It is generally admitted that pregnant women usually cease work only a very short time before delivery. . . . But otherwise the pregnant women usually leave work, even when of the most unsuitable nature, only in the last phase of pregnancy. Thus a number of pregnant women were discovered in the winding-rooms of textile-mills; in one concern, a woman in the last month of her pregnancy. Whenever a thread breaks, the winding machines are stopped by pressure by the upper part of the thigh or the belly, perhaps some 3,500 times in a shift. This causes danger of a premature birth or a miscarriage." I. 459.

"In general the working women avail themselves but very little of the rest period to which they are entitled before confinement, because of the losses in earnings which it entails. According to the reports, the introduction of a rest-interval in working hours for breast-feeding is only observed in one single large factory." II. 41.

"The prospective mother thinks less of the injury to her own health through the long protraction of industrial work, than of the money sacrifices involved in the child's birth." III. 40.

"The women supervisors repeatedly found that women workers continued their industrial labour until shortly before confinement. According to the Reich Insurance Law, the women workers, even if capable of work, receive sick benefit four weeks before confinement. Because of this, and in order to lose as little wages as possible before confinement, the women work on until the very last day." VI. 21.

These, then, are the conditions prevailing under "German Socialism." Pregnancy is kept a secret, right up until the moment of confinement, in case the woman may be given lighter and worse paid work to do. To the injury of the infant, no advantage is taken of the breast-feeding rest-intervals for mothers, for to do so would mean either loss of wages or perhaps dismissal. In spite of their physical disability, pregnant women stay at their industrial work for as long as possible, so as to lose as little wages as possible.

B. CHILD LABOUR

A Ten-and-a-Half Hour Day—Service in the Hitler Youth lowers the Age of Child Labour—Five Pfennigs (Halfpenny) an Hour's Pay

There are no reliable estimates of the extent of child labour in Germany.

> "The statistics on child labour compiled by the factory inspection officials are based upon children's reports to their teachers, and must be treated with caution. . . . In 1936, 31,183 children of school age (in Saxony—J.K.) were in employment. Of every 100 children, 5·5 per cent were working. . . . In the higher classes of the schools, the proportion of children engaged in industry and otherwise will be greater, probably three times as great," III. 43.

This means that, during the later school years, from one-seventh to one-sixth of all school-children are working. And then, when we have deducted from this total the children of the bourgeoisie, we see that not much less than one-third of all working-class children have to go to work in Hitler's Germany before they reach school-leaving age.

By how much child labour increased under Fascism during the years under study we are not able to ascertain, owing to the lack of statistical material. It is definite, however, that child labour begins at a considerably earlier age.

> "In all parts of Saxony the despatching of goods and newspapers by children is still greatly favoured. Unfortu-

nately, younger children than formerly, those under 12 years of age, are often brought into this work, as so little time for such work is left to the older children, what with their long school hours, confirmation lessons and service in the Hitler youth. . . ."

"The powerful revival of the accordeon industry in the Vogtland has unfortunately led to the fact that the home-workers, who have always put fairly large numbers of children to work, have now drawn in many children aged under 12, as the somewhat older children are now entirely occupied with the more difficult work of riveting and adjusting the tongues." III. 43.

"Most child labour is illegal. It is established that, in Hessia, about 50 per cent of all child labour is illegal." VII. 21.

The law is applied just as infrequently in the case of child labour as in that of pregnancy. Although the law prohibits child labour under certain circumstances, while the earning capacity of the parents is such that both they and the children are near to starvation it is obvious that the children themselves will have to try to get work, even if illegally. One cannot prohibit certain forms of child labour and at the same time pay starvation wages, as occurs now under Fascism.

While still in the mother's womb, the child must suffer from this contradiction between the law and the actual facts. Then, a few years after his birth, the child is once again the victim of this contradiction. Again it must suffer. It has to go to work early on winter days, delivering through snow and frost the morning rolls or newspapers. And, on stifling summer days, children sit in dust-filled factory workshops, rising from their beds at 5 a.m. sometimes not going to bed until 11 p.m.

"In the market-places of the Arnsberg district both home and country children, aged from 9 to 10 years, were already working in the early morning between six and seven o'clock, putting up the market stalls. . . . In a snack-bar in Cologne-Altstadt, a 10-year-old schoolgirl had to work at dish-washing, run errands and do other work as a help until 10 p.m." I. 112.

"In one newspaper print-shop, a schoolboy, not yet 14 years old, who had been engaged chiefly as messenger, was also occasionally used for small jobs in the printing proper. One day, when he was helping a printing assistant, on the latter's orders, to start a mechanical press, he slipped and caught one hand between the cylinders, thus losing four fingers. . . ." I. 113.

"How much child labour still needs careful supervision is shown by the case in which a 6-year-old girl was engaged in making leather buttons from four to six hours a day, together with her 13-year-old brother who had been released from elementary school." II. 43.

"At a basket-maker's, five boys had to work during holidays from morning till night, and during school time five hours per day, at peeling osiers, for 14 pfennigs (about 1¾d.) per hour." III. 48–49.

"One knitting firm . . . increased the working-day for a child to nine-and-three-quarter hours. A paper-box manufacturer employed women and juvenile labour for 11 hours a day, and children for nine." IV. 31.

"Proceedings were brought against the manager of a canning factory who, during the season, kept a 13-year-old girl working for 10½ hours instead of six, per day." IV. 35.

"Still worse was the case of a small mineral water factory which employed numerous children for an hourly wage of five pfennigs (about half a penny)." V. 25.

In truth, it would appear that the exploitation of working-class children cannot begin too early. Fascism has brought back the most cruel excesses of early industrial capitalism.

C. Apprentices and Juvenile Labour

"Apprentices rush for War Work"—Universal Compulsory Labour Service increases Working Hours for Juveniles—Twenty Hours' Work per Day—The W.C. as Bedroom—Amnesties for Exploiters.

About one-third of German working-class children in their last years of school age must go to work either before or after school hours or during the holidays. Once these children are out of school, however, the factory or workshop, mine or farm, swallows them up. A working-class child, on leaving school, either becomes an apprentice or begins work as an unskilled juvenile worker. The factory and mine inspectors' annual reports contain rich material with which to provide us with a picture of the working and living conditions of apprentices and juvenile workers.

Into what industry does the greater number of apprentices go during these years? Naturally, into the industries connected with preparations for war. Under Fascism, German youth is systematically diverted into war industries. The most important skilled labour learned by German young workers are the various forms of work in the war industries.

> "The young people still have a particular inclination towards the metal and engineering trades. They prefer apprenticeship in the large and medium-sized concerns. . . . Besides the trades so favoured in recent years, * such as those of automobile engineer, engine-fitter, mechanic and electrician, the trade of turner has now entered the list of favourite callings. Motor engineering is still the most favoured trade, for which there are many more applications than openings. . . . Some of the youngsters hope later to find good advancement in the army." I. 100.

And a report from Hamburg states:

> "It is true that just now the apprentices are leaving the artisan workshops for the industrial concerns, often also for the army (as precision-tool mechanics, electricians, motor mechanics), where they sign up for long terms of service." VIII. 9.

While apprentices are driven or lured in masses into the armaments industry, and are received with open arms as cheap labour power, some of the artisan workshops are complaining that they cannot get enough apprentices; on the other hand, there are cases where artisan enterprises, because of their difficult eco-

* In 1933 and 1934.

nomic position, cannot take on all those who apply for apprenticeship.

> "On the other hand, many artisan employers refuse to engage the number of apprentices to which they are entitled." XI. 9.
>
> "Part of the boys and girls who have not found employment as apprentices are at first sent by the employment exchanges to work in the Land Service." VII. 20.

Contradictions of this nature, the apprenticeship, on a vast scale, of young people to the war industries, while others, who desire to learn a skilled trade, are sent on to the land to do the unskilled jobs, are typical of a Fascist economy.

However, cases in which youngsters leaving school can find no opportunity of getting themselves apprenticed are fairly uncommon. More frequently, we find instances in which an altogether undue proportion of the entire staff of a factory consists of apprentices.

> "In one Berlin engineering works, 22 apprentices were employed to six workmen. . . . In engineering works in Sleswig, there were 95 apprentices and 120 skilled and unskilled workers." I. 102.
>
> "In one locksmith's workshop, there were 11 apprentices to the two proprietors and one journeyman." XIII. 14.

Next to children, apprentices are the cheapest labour power which the employers can obtain, and the more work is available, the more apprentices are engaged, as has been quite candidly stated by the factory inspectors:

> "From all appearances, the appeal to engage apprentices is answered primarily by those concerns which are already considerably overcrowded with them. In contrast to this, the respective proportions in some of the artisan trades, such as baking, butchering, tailoring and printing, have not improved in 1935-36, which can be explained by the unemployment in these trades which has led already to retraining of apprentices." XIII. 14.

"The appeal, 'Engage apprentices' was answered by a doll factory and a marble-cutting shop in a unique manner. They prepared indentures to cover several years' apprenticeship, which were signed, but the actual work was purely mechanical and could be learnt in a few weeks. Naturally they paid the so-called apprentices well below the standard wage." III. 42.

And the following report reveals yet another method of cheating apprentices:

"As has often been established, dressmakers evade the apprenticeship regulations by accepting young girls, on payment of a fee, for a course of instruction at which the girls are supposed to learn sewing and dressmaking necessary to the household by working on materials they bring with them. In this case, a so-called instruction notice to the guild is prescribed. An instruction notice instead of apprenticeship conditions with indentures is only permissible for a period of six months. But there are master dressmakers who continually extend the period of the course, thus employing these young girls for the purposes of their trade and saving themselves the expenses of wages to assistants and also obligations and payments to apprentices." VII. 20.

In such cases, then, we see that these young people have to pay something, even if they do not learn the trade properly, for they are not even real apprentices.

In many ways, the apprentice is worst off who has to reside in his master's house. Sleeping accommodation, as described by the factory inspectors, is sometimes so appalling that it appears improbable even to those who may have imagined they knew something of apprenticeship conditions. However, Fascism has so often wrought the incredible, that even this can now be believed.

"In bake-shops, with butchers, in mills, dairies and brickyards, complaints had not infrequently to be made against the sleeping arrangements, and police proceedings had to be taken. . . . In the Osnabrueck and Aurich district, in 21 cases two apprentices, or one apprentice and one journeyman, occupied the same bed. In many cases, bedrooms or

dormitories were without windows or other ventilation. . . .
In some instances, water-closets and bathrooms were used
'for sleeping purposes.' " I. 343.

While apprentices stand in a different relationship to the
employers from that of the ordinary workers, cases of outrageous
mistreatment of apprentices are more frequent than among
young workers in general.

"A master baker struck the boy with an oven-peel and
broke his jaw. . . . A butcher's apprentice, in an accident
when riding the faulty bicycle supplied by his employer,
incurred an injury to his knee which rapidly became worse.
Although there was a doctor on the spot, the butcher caused
the apprentice to be treated by a quack with the result that
the apprentice died from the results of his accident. What
contributed materially to this result was the fact that the
apprentice was not able to obtain proper care but, in spite
of his grave condition, was forced to go on with his work
and was even beaten because he was so slow." I. 108.

The exploitation of apprentices through long hours and too
heavy work is best described in relation to youth labour in
general, as follows:

"One glass bottle factory in Upper Silesia and three
glass-works in the Dusseldorf district were permitted to
employ apprentices under 16 years of age on alternate nights
in eight-hour shifts with one half-hour break." I. 93.

Night-work by youngsters under 16, officially permitted!
Such is the care which Fascism takes of the youth!

"In some cases, apprentices of from 14 to 15 years of age
were kept working for as much as 16 hours consecutively,
partly by night." I. 107–108.

A sixteen-hour working day for boys under 15! And here are
other cases:

"In many cases, employers working on public contracts
showed but little regard for the legal protective regulations.
Not infrequently, they used the labour power of young

workers and women in a manner which bordered on exploitation. Also, the factory inspectors repeatedly complain that the penalties inflicted by the courts only too frequently bear no relation to the gravity of the injury to the people's health. For instance, one factory-owner of a machine-building firm was fined 200 marks, or 40 days' imprisonment, for employing young people on the night shift. On appeal, this was reduced to a fine of 20 marks. As reason for the appeal court's decision it was stated that the employer had demonstrated his social attitude by providing daily one-quarter litre milk (worth six pfennigs!) for the young workers." I. 94.

The above is literally reproduced, including the exclamation mark after the "6 pfennigs." One can imagine with what indignation these lines must have been written. And also what reserve had to be exercised, when the writer stated that this form of working young people "bordered on exploitation." It approaches about as near to exploitation as Solomon did to polygamy, when he took to himself 1,000 wives.

"In a factory producing electric lamps, etc., women and young people were worked up to 14 hours. . . . In a machine-shop young people were made to work after 8 p.m., and worked 12 hours daily together with the adults. . . . In another machine-shop young and adult workers were working 11 and 13 hours daily. . . . In a silk mill young workers and women worked 11 to 12 hours daily . . ." I. 94.

"The continual increase in economic activity also demanded the working of overtime by women workers over 16 years of age, especially in export and arms trades." II. 37.

This means overtime for girls between 16 and 18 in the armaments industry, in the years 1935 and 1936. Thus does Fascism protect young womanhood! Here is a somewhat different example:

"Endeavours have been made to extenuate infractions of the regulations enforcing rest-intervals for young workers by the argument that minors are now occupying the places in industry of persons who have been called up for the army.

In the inspectorate district of Lower Franconia, continuation-school pupils, under 16 years of age, have been illegally put to work on threshing machines." II. 39.

"In the Chemnitz textile industry, illegal working hours, work before 6 a.m. and after 10 p.m., and the ignoring of rest-intervals (for young people) developed like a plague which the control, warnings and prosecutions instigated by the factory inspectors were unable to stamp out and which demanded the active co-operation of the police." III. 39.

We conclude this review of conditions of young workers with the following:

"The lessee of a box factory employing about 100 workers could not abide by the existing working time regulations. In the most irresponsible manner, and in spite of warnings received, he made his employees work on some days as long as 20 hours, sometimes on several consecutive days, and even forced young workers of 14 or 15 years of age to work these immoderate hours, so that the work people had only a pause of three to four hours between work-days." V. 18.

There we have the life of apprentices and young workers under the German Fascist régime. A work-day extending even to 20 hours, and for several consecutive days, leaving only four hours for travelling to and from their homes and for sleeping and meals

Furthermore, we have other instances of the mistreatment of young people, enough to drive them to their deaths. Particularly unfavourable working conditions are here described for young people in factories which are favoured with numerous public contracts—in other words, factories which enjoy the favour of the Fascists and work for armaments orders. There is also proof that the law now permits night work for young people under 16 years.

All this is revealed by cases which have been uncovered by the investigations of the factory inspectors themselves. And we must remember that these inspectors, because of the added multiplicity of their work, were able to cover only a constantly diminishing field in the course of their duties. How many cases, then, were never discovered by them! Obviously, however, the cases cited above are by no means unusual. In one of the reports we are told that instances of illegal working hours "developed like a plague." Then, again, the penalties inflicted when action is taken because of contraventions of the law! And frequently enough even these modest penalties are revoked by the amnesties which the Fascist institute from time to time. Here we have one of the real bases for the amnesties which Hitler, with a flourish of trumpets, announced about once a year—among the beneficiaries are employers who have been sentenced to pay small fines for infractions of the labour protective regulations.

Apart from the fact that inspection and control have become far less widespread and stringent, a factor of particular importance in the increase of the exploitation of apprentices and young people was the vast expansion of armaments.

We see, therefore, that the exploitation of young people has increased, not only because Fascism means a freer hand for the employers, but also because Fascism, by its very nature, makes for war and therefore uses larger and larger numbers of young workers for purposes of the armaments industry.

*   *   *

2. THE ADULT WORKER

We have followed the life-course of the worker from birth, or, rather, from the time of his earliest existence, through the years of apprenticeship or of his status as a young worker. Now he attains his industrial coming-of-age, and becomes an adult worker.

A. The Work Place

Armaments Production leads to Overcrowding of Working Space—The Courtyard as Workshop—Overheated or Unheated Workrooms— Primitive Sanitary Arrangements—One Washbasin for Fifteen Persons—A Factory with no Drinking Water.

As it is not within the purview of their duties, factory inspectors mention nothing of the housing conditions of German workers.

But we do not need such reports in order to realize under what poor conditions the greater part of the workers live in Germany. For example, in an article summing up one year's achievements —or lack of achievements—in the *Frankfurter Zeitung*, on December 31, 1937, we read that there is a "deficit" of one million dwellings.

The worker leaves his dwelling, often an entirely unsatisfactory one, in the morning to go to his place of work. What are the conditions he often encounters there? Here we have plentiful evidence, from the factory inspectors' reports, as, for instance, the following:

"There are occasionally drawbacks arising out of lack of proportion between the space available and the number employed. In some instances, the space formerly used is now much too great for the present use, so that heating and ventilation are extremely expensive and are therefore neglected. Sometimes, the space is too little and, because of urgent orders, it is crowded. For instance, Dr. Groetschel reports that in a man's tailoring shop, the 120 workers were confined in a space of about 1,000 cubic metres, a good deal of which was occupied by sewing machines and ironing-boards. There was no mechanical ventilation, and the natural lighting was so poor that artificial light had to be used all day. . . . In small workshops, which rent space in industrial buildings, there is often no possibility of improvement, from the point of view of space. But, in frequent cases, even where that possibility exists, there is lack of good will, so that the workshops fall into pronouncedly deteriorated conditions." I. 449.

"In a cement works, the roof threatened to fall in; and in a brickyard, it was one of the walls. . . . In a rag-sorting establishment, there were no special safety stairs, nor fire-resisting ceilings. This case was aggravated by the fact that, below the rooms, was a store-house for condensed and liquefied gases. . . . The frequently rapid increase in the number of personnel, particularly in the metal, clothing and leather industries, often led to an overcrowding of work-rooms and to the requisitioning of any space which could possibly. be used, such as attics and basements, sheds and even open courtyards." I. 322–323.

"In a big cigar factory and its branches, overcrowding was discovered, amounting in some rooms up to 50 per cent." IV. 65.

"An unusual degree of congestion was observed in a clothing factory in which uniforms for the army were being made. This condition arose from the fact that the employer, in the absence of any properly adapted space for expansion, had to make use of rooms formerly designed for habitation, which were obviously unsuitable for the accommodation of the 145 persons of the working staff." X. 11.

Over and again we find that the deterioration in working conditions arises through the growth of industries connected with war. In these cases, we note that it occurs through the sudden advent of large contracts which can only be filled by employing far more workers than there is room for.

But such conditions are often expressly condoned by the governmental authorities, not only in the case of war industries:

"In many cigar factories in the Erfurt district, exceptions have again been granted for a larger number of persons to occupy the available space than is permitted by the federal regulations." I. 323.

However, it is not only a question of overcrowding.

"In the cigar factories of the Erfurt district, where stove heating is still customary, the heat in proximity to the stoves was absolutely unbearable during transition periods. . . . Complaints had to be made against inadequate or unsuitable heating in workrooms and rest-rooms. Even large machine buildings were insufficiently heated during the cold periods, and improvements could only be secured after the overcoming of considerable opposition, in many cases." I. 331.

"In the textile dye-works, the visibility in the workrooms in winter time left much to be desired, owing to the steam; for the required heating apparatus at the air-inlets was either not installed, because of lack of funds, or could not be kept functioning." VI. 41.

When the heating does happen to be satisfactory, the heating arrangements are often such that they constitute a real danger to the personnel.

"Steps often had to be taken against the use of unsuitable heating apparatus in factories specially liable to the danger of fire, such as varnish factories or works where clothing is cleaned by benzine. For instance, in two Berlin cleaning works iron stoves were used to heat the workrooms. . . . In two establishments, orders had to be made to remove iron stoves from spray-varnishing works." I. 330.

"In one workroom in a shoe factory celluloid was being pasted onto rubber, in close proximity to an iron coal-stove. In the same room was an apparatus for spraying nitro-brine as well as leather sewing and stamping machines. The workroom had only one exit; the walls and ceilings were in very bad condition." I. 321.

Worse, if possible, than the heating are light and ventilation. Few things in a factory can be more injurious to the health of the workers than too little light and air, particularly when too many are crowded together into one narrow space.

"In a button factory, hot dry air surrounded the steam-heated press . . . because the steam pipes had not been insulated. In a celluloid plant, the air was abnormally hot in the neighbourhood of the boiler because of lack of pipe-insulation." I. 454.

Nor was it claimed that the worst ventilation conditions were chiefly to be found in old buildings.

"Even in new buildings, the proper arrangements for ventilation are not included in the builders' plans." I. 450.

Nor that "special circumstances" are always the cause of these evil conditions.

"The grievous fact cannot be concealed that, in these questions (ventilation, etc.—J.K.), on the part of the factory managements . . . there still exists, unfortunately, a great deal of ignorance and indifference, so that the simplest considerations of the effect of air conditions upon the well-being, working capacity, and danger of fatigue or illness of many fellow-countrymen, have never been thoroughly thought out, nor the necessary consequences of such considerations drawn. With relation to the technical preparatory work, this accusation can also not be spared many architects, draughts-men and builders." IV. 68–69.

Frequently, also, lighting conditions are extremely bad.

"In old factory buildings . . . the supply of natural light is often quite inadequate." I. 456.

"In the boiler-room of a small saw-mill, the entire lighting consisted of one small portable carbide lamp, which in addition, was leaky." XI. 24.

As for rest rooms, etc., in factories we have the following evidence:

"In many factories, there are not yet any rest-rooms." XIV. 13.

"In a large number of concerns, particularly old ones, such as foundries, doll, paper and cloth factories, there were no washing and changing rooms at all. . . . A number of large factories in the Osnabruck district are still unprovided with rest-rooms and wash-rooms." I. 338.

"In one cement concern, there was only one wash-basin for 15 people. No running water was available. . . . Little satisfactory are the conditions in most brickyards. Often washing arrangements were merely improvised, or did not exist at all." I. 335.

"In one case, the obviously necessary installation of a pure drinking water supply had to take place against the opposi-tion of the firm." V. 97.

"The lavatories of the municipal workshops consist mainly of dark sheds built of boards. . . . Only through a police order, the proprietor of a newly-erected factory was induced to connect the lavatory basins with the existing water supply. The manager had previously required the workers to flush the basins with water-cans. . . . In a knitted goods factory, where previously only one common and inadequate lavatory existed for both men and women workers, the provision was ordered of separate and satisfactory accommodation." I. 345.

The above examples suffice to give us an indication of the appearance of those workrooms where the workers spend by far the greater part of their waking life. The reports themselves confirm the fact that these are by no means isolated examples.

B. SPEED-UP

Ninety per cent of Personnel Overworked—A Twenty-Four Hour Week too Taxing

In the workrooms above described, where the temperature is either too high or too low, and the air almost always thick and stale, labour many workers in Germany. These conditions, in themselves, would be injurious enough; but their effect is drastically enhanced by the speeding-up to which the workers were being subjected, in the period covered by these reports, and, of course, still are. This is a speed-up which, on the one side, is enforced by the management in order to get as much production as possible from each worker, and, on the other hand, is also enforced upon the "free" worker by the fact that he is inexorably compelled to make the total of his miserable piece-work earnings as high as possible, so as to bring some sort of sum home with him on pay-day, with which to ward off starvation.

In this connection also, we have ample material in the factory inspection reports.

"While piece-work is a means to enable the more capable, skilled and industrious to better themselves, the greatest care must be taken that such piece-work, when taking place in establishments where danger to health exists, does not lead to non-observance of protective regulations and to make physique less resistant to illness through too severe strain. . . . In general, the working speed is high; workers frequently complained that they felt that, through the high expenditure of energy, they had become more nervous and more liable to sickness."

"In one engineering works, overtime work was sanctioned, and until August 1936, they had been working 10-hour shifts, day and night. The medical officer of a sick benefit fund reported, in the middle of this year, that he had received from no other works as many cases of exhaustion as from this one. Dr. Betke, government and industrial medical councillor, followed up this complaint and ascertained that out of about 100 workers engaged on precision work at piece rates about 90 per cent complained of nervous irritability, fatigue and exhaustion, and that, in spite of their good muscular development and well-nourished condition, they showed extreme pallor and haggardness. Many of them complained of sleeplessness, in spite of great physical weariness, of headaches and attacks of giddiness; others complained of hysterical sobbing, lack of interest and lack of mental control; furthermore, there were many complaints of stomach trouble. An examination of their blood revealed, in several cases, light traces of lead poisoning, and in the course of the year, as a matter of fact, 13 cases of lead poisoning had been reported and confirmed. Statistics showed that from 1934 to 1935 the number of cases reported sick had increased by 45 per cent, and then from 1935 to 1936 by 90·7 per cent." I. 456–457.

That is one aspect of industry. Here we have a German armaments firm where the rate of work is frenziedly speeded-up, and where overtime has been worked daily for two years. By German standards, the wages are not very low, and the workers appear to be well nourished—yet they break down through general exhaustion. They have fallen victims to the mad tempo of armaments manufacture.

And now another case which reveals quite a different aspect but an equally horrifying one:

"In a textile mill complaint was made that the simultaneous tending of six looms per person led to over-exertion. Enquiries, however, elicited that it was not the actual tending of six looms which caused the trouble but the fact that, as some of the weavers were employed only 24 hours per week, they over-exerted themselves during this period in order to earn at least the minimum necessities." I. 457.

Here we have one of the miracles which Fascism has produced. A 24-hour week which is too much of a strain on the worker! The reason why is glaringly apparent in the above report.

C. FREQUENCY OF ACCIDENTS

Record Rise in Incidence of Accidents in Arms Industries—Speed-up and Rush Orders increase Accidents

It is obvious that, when work is performed at a highly speeded-up rate and in over-crowded and unhealthy factories or shops, the frequency of accidents must necessarily rise. Thus, in the factory inspectors' reports for the various inspection districts we find that the accident rate has increased in a higher proportion than that of employment. For instance, the Prussian inspectors report as follows:

"The number of accidents has increased in the period (that is from 1934 to 1936—J.K.) by 134,475 or 45·9 per cent, and that of fatal accidents, by 343 or 30·4 per cent, while the number of those employed increased by only 19·2 per cent." I. 175.

Among reasons given for the increase in accidents are the following:

"The packing of large numbers of workers into small spaces, which cannot always be avoided in these days of rapidly increasing production, higher rate of working speed, excess of zeal in working—particularly in the case of newly employed persons—night work in the building trade . . . have all contributed substantially towards the increase in accidents." I. 177.

Accidents, we note, have particularly increased in the arms industries.

"In the metal-working industry (of the Cologne district), in 1936 as compared with 1934, the number of accidents increased by 128 per cent, while the increase in those employed was only 36 per cent." I. 176.

"In a number of our industries in Saxony—and particularly in our metal industry—the increased speed of working and the lengthened working periods may have often contributed (to the increase in accidents—J.K.). Fatigue, owing to long hours, night work or Sunday work, in busily employed concerns, distracted the attention of employers and workers from the dangers of accidents. . . . While, for example, from 1934 to 1936, the sum total of accidents in all industry increased by 36 per cent, those in industrial groups V to VII— which embrace our Saxon metal industry—increased by 52·5 during the same period, a far sharper increase than all groups taken together." III. 66 and 69.

The Wurtemberg reports yield excellent statistics of accidents per working hour. According to these figures, the incidence of accidents for 100,000 working hours per year was as follows (IV. 51):

Year	Accidents per 100,000 hours
1932	121
1933	124
1934	143
1935	158
1936	160

"The still growing number of accidents is to be referred to the fact that more and more unemployed are returning to work, some of them quite new to the type of work, that working hours have increased, and thereby the number of accidents, and that the speed of work is a very rapid one." VII. 30.

"But even more contributory to the upward movement of accident figures has been the greater speed at work, which results from urgent orders, and the consequent greater susceptibility of the worker to fatigue." XI. 13.

The above quotations should suffice to show plainly that the accident rate in Fascist Germany rose generally, and on a considerable scale. They also show, as is frankly admitted in the reports, that one of the chief causes of increased accidents is augmented working speed, as well as fatigue, following on long hours of overtime. The reason for both these factors is given: orders—usually government orders for war materials—which have to be fulfilled at top speed. Being forced by Fascism to pile up war materials for a murderous attack upon the civilized nations, the German workers' health and safety deteriorated rapidly several years before the actual outbreak of the war!

D. Sickness

"Injurious Work Preferred"—Arms and Substitutes' Industries bring New Diseases
•

Closely related to the subject of accidents is that of sickness. The following lines, quoted from a Prussian report, treat the subject with remarkable, although, of course, one-sided, candour:

"The severe after-effects of protracted unemployment are being gradually overcome; the newly employed men and women are now able to pay their debts and make new purchases. These tasks are often very difficult, and the fear of losing employment leads to suppression of feelings of illness or exhaustion and also causes considerable reserve to questions by the industrial medical officer regarding occupational injuries. The long period of under-nourishment is now seldom regarded as the sole cause of weakened resistance; strain, caused by over-time and piece-work, can now to a certain extent also occasionally be reckoned with as an accompanying cause of occupational illness. Women tenaciously hold on to positions with the opportunity of earning good money, and physical troubles are denied by them, even when no doubts exist, that the work in question is unsuitable for women.

"The skilled workers usually earn better money and even during sickness, if the period be not too long, they do not suffer great needs. On the other hand, the unskilled workers' wage often just touches the existence minimum; when he is sick the current expenses of rent, heating and food cannot always be met from the scanty sickness benefit money. In factories where the work is dangerous to health, the temporary transfer of workers from injurious to non-injurious work is rendered difficult by the fact that the non-injurious work is not so well paid, and if the worker becomes sick after he has been transferred, his sick pay is very poor. . ." I. 448–449.

A rather long quotation, the above; but how much does it hold of suffering and exploitation, and the implacable struggle to obtain just a little bit more in wages!

Reports on the various separate types of industrial maladies do not generally differ particularly from those of earlier years. Frequently we find the figure of industrial sickness has risen; and, also, frequently that it has apparently diminished, for reasons given in the above quotation. But it is not sufficient to make the general statement that Fascism in Germany brought about an increase in the incidence of industrial disease. It also introduced completely new occupational diseases into the existence of the German workers, as we may see from the following:

"The construction of the national automobile roads through Baden brought in its train an increase in the appearance of 'shovel sickness,' which, however, was not at first always correctly diagnosed. It consists of the snapping (cracking) of the spine, usually the seventh cervical or first dorsal vertebra, to which are connected the back muscles. In the Mannheim and Heidelberg district, about 300 cases of this appeared. . . . The snapping can always be very clearly felt, and necessitates immediate cessation of work. It becomes quite impossible to raise the shovel. The worker comes to the doctor in a rigid attitude, the head held forward, and avoids all movement. . . . After five to six weeks work can be resumed." V. 86

Other occupational diseases are closely connected with the Fascist armaments plans and the policy of self-sufficiency—the production of "German raw materials":

"Carbon disulphide poisoning, which becomes apparent in stomach and digestive complaints, appeared originally in connection with workers engaged on the Xanthat-machines in the staple fibre factories." VI. 38.

"In the rubber industry, work on artificial rubber introduced new methods of using benzol (which is particularly dangerous because of the great risk of benzol poisoning— J.K.) and its homologues; it was, however, found possible, in a considerable number of processes, to use benzine." I. 452.

"In the pasting department of a gas-mask factory, the preparation of the paste required the use of benzol, as other substitute materials proved a failure. Two women working in this department were attacked by benzol poisoning." I. 295.

"The large scale use of German flax has been said to be responsible for the skin complaints which were apparent in a linen-mill." I. 478

"The number of cases of ophthalmic disease in the rayon, staple fibre and artificial sausage-skin factories has risen considerably in various districts. . . . The basis for this increase lies in the fact that, on the occasion of the great increase in production, starting in 1935, not enough attention could be paid to the demands of health protection." I. 272.

Once again, as in the case of other causes for deterioration in the workers' conditions, we see that the specifically Fascist causes—preparation for Fascist war and the effort after autarchy which involves the large-scale manufacturing of substitutes—play the chief part in this frightful process.

E. Working Hours

Twenty-Four Hour Week and Twenty-Four Hour Day—Sixteen-Hour Day is Legal—One Hundred Hours a Week—Exemption Measures for Army Contracts

We now add to the previous sorry list—over-crowded work-rooms, feverish speed-up, increased accidents, more sickness—an ever-increasing work day, which, in turn is one of the contributory factors to the foregoing evils.

In considering working hours, we must distinguish between the legal and illegal extension of working time. The first is perhaps more distinctive than the other, more characteristic of the spirit of Fascism. For a century past, the working class in all capitalist countries has fought for a shortening of the legal workday, and with a certain success. From the official 12-hour day, we progressed to the 11- and 10-hour day. At the beginning of the century, a large part of the working class of the world gained the nine-hour day, and, after the first world war, the general eight-hour day.

During the period under review, in Germany, the nine-hour day had already been re-introduced to a large extent, and, in some cases, the working day was extended legally much beyond that. Generally speaking, we may say that, by 1936, the German working class found itself back in the position, as regards working hours, which it had occupied some 30 years earlier. In reading the quotations below from the factory inspectors' reports it is obvious that a most important factor in the lengthening of working hours is the pressure of armaments orders, and government contracts and constructions in general.

"The more the object was accomplished of the first four-year plan—to give work to all fellow-countrymen capable of working—and the fewer were left to return to the factories, the more was the work-day lengthened." I. 55.

"Particularly in public building works, the skilled workers and supervisory personnel were often engaged in two 12-hour shifts, while the rest of the workers worked in three shifts. In some cases, one even encountered working hours of 15 to 16 hours per day, which were broken only by short intervals. Such long work periods were unavoidable if hold-ups in other departments or establishments were to be avoided. In one case, a turner was employed in a refitting shop for 24 hours consecutively." I. 64.

The Fascists can work "miracles," but even they have their limits. The 24-hour day is the maximum, in one day, to be found in Germany.

"In the metal industry also, overtime on the basis of hours regulations was frequently necessary, For this industry, the new hours regulations provided for a work-day of up to 10 hours daily (Berlin, Potsdam, Erfurt, Hildesheim). As the new regulations for the metal industry to a great extent met with the wishes of the employers for a lengthening of the working day, the realization that this was 'overtime' often disappeared; the 10-hour working day, with the shortened Saturday shift, was regarded as regular working hours and applications were made for working overtime beyond this." I. 65–66.

So now overtime began only when the 10-hour day was done.

"In many cases official consent, in accordance with Paragraph 9 of the A.Z.O. is not sufficient. So that, in a considerable number of instances, permission for additional overtime work, above 10 hours per day was granted on the basis of Paragraph 13 of the A.Z.O. . . . The duration of permitted overtime attained considerable proportions. For instance, a mosaic workshop, in order to execute an unusually big order of public importance, was permitted to employ 150 male workers over 20 years of age up to 13 hours per day for a period of two weeks; and another time, for the prompt execution of a public contract, 80 male workers over 18 years of age for 12 hours per day."

"Specialized workers, like engravers, specialized fraisers and turners had to work in some concerns from 12 to 16 hours per day. . . . In many machine-tool making establishments in the inspectorate district of Munich-Gladbach, which have orders till 1938, working hours are permitted from 60 to 72 hours weekly." I. 68–69.

"The thrashing works in the Wiesbaden district have been permitted to extend the regular working time up to 13 hours per day and even beyond this so long as it does not go above 156 hours in the working fortnight. I. 71.

"Through the labour trustees, a basic regulation was arrived at (for attendance in electrical switch and power stations—J.K.) to the effect that the daily working period, inclusive of rest intervals and stand-by periods, shall not exceed 16 hours, and must be followed by an uninterrupted rest period of eight hours. Every two weeks, a full free day must be granted." V. 15.

Let us note all the above cases are of hours worked with official approval and consent—in other words, legal overtime. Often, however, the working day is lengthened unofficially, "illegally," not in accordance with the official regulations regarding working hours. It is interesting in this connection to note the penalties which are inflicted for violations of the regulations.

"In the Osnabrück and Aurich district, on the other hand, a number of prosecutions of building employers, who had kept their men working as long as 18 hours daily on public building works, ended in the lower court where the proceedings were brought with an acquittal. The appeals were not considered on the grounds that they were disposed of by the amnesty law of April 25, 1936 (RGBl. p. 378)." I. 74.

"One lorry-driver was engaged until midnight, and then had to start again next morning at five, and from then work on until the following morning. As a result of over-fatigue he drove into a tree. He was fined 100 marks for careless driving and causing bodily injury and infraction of the traffic regulations. The employer, however, was fined only 70 marks for working the man over-long hours." I. 76.

"The owner of a machine-building concern—who had been ruthlessly working his turners, planers and horizontal borers in shifts of 17, 19, 20 and 24 hours for two weeks running, managed to escape any penalty because of the amnesty law. The proprietor of a sawmill and a metal goods manufacturer in the Cassel district worked their employees 80 hours per week for weeks on end, and sometimes even 100 hours in a week." I. 77.

"These workers worked from 8 to 10 hours in the workshop, and then, under another one of the company's foremen, for 9 to 11 hours on the building site" (that is up to 19 hours per day and more.—J.K.)." VIII. 6.

The above examples already show quite clearly the use of amnesty laws on the one hand, and the close connection between over-long hours of work and armaments production on the other hand. However, a few more examples will serve to underline the second point.

"The working of extra shifts was increasing even in concerns whose technical character did not demand several shifts and which normally would work with only one shift daily. However, occasion was now supplied chiefly by the Reich government's building programme, the great and urgent tasks of armaments, and the securing of economic independence from foreign countries." I. 59.

"Numerous construction undertakings in connection with the Reich automobile roads worked up to 60 hours per week, which is permissible in accordance with the regulations concerning the working conditions in unfavourable weather on the construction jobs of the Autobahn Company and the Army." II. 22.

"A master baker requested that he be permitted to begin work at 3 a.m. on the grounds that he had been entrusted with supplying a unit of the Air Force with morning bread and that the bread had to be delivered by 5.30 a.m." X. 8.

The Fascist régime in Germany removed in part the prohibition of night baking; and then, amazingly enough, it appears that infractions of the night baking regulations became fewer!

"The law of June 29, 1936 (RGBl. I. p. 521) on working hours in bakeries and pastry-cooks' establishments at last definitely settled the long disputed question of working hours in these trades. The advancing of the time for beginning work to four a.m. expresses the desire of the trade, and also the extension of the time between the beginning of baking and beginning of delivery to two-and-a-half hours. The factory inspectors have noted, as a happy result of this law, a considerable reduction in infractions already during the second half of the year." II. 21.

And, while from year to year in thousands of concerns the working hours became longer, in certain other establishments the number of hours worked was decreasing rapidly. These were the concerns which lacked raw material; particularly in the consumption goods industries, but by no means solely in them. For example, in the Aix-la-Chapelle cloth industry, 43 per cent of all the workers worked less than 30 hours per week. (I. 56).

"While one big shoe factory of the Sigmaringen district, with some 800 employed, has, since November, 1934, worked almost continually for only two or three days per week, in the Erfurt district the weekly working time was reduced to 32 hours for most shoe-factories, only at the end of the period reported." I. 57.

"The situation is similar in the Leipzig tobacco industry and in the printing trade, where the very occasional and short-termed orders compel the occasional reduction of even the 24-hour week." III. 32.

Incidentally, the wages are often so miserably low that the workers resist any suggestion that hours be reduced.

"Frequently the workers looked unfavourably upon the introduction of a third shift as this would mean that the extended week of 54 to 60 hours would now be shortened to 48 hours, resulting in a decrease in earnings." I. 63.

On the one hand, we see people working 24 hours in a day; on the other, 24 hours in a week. There were workers who demanded the preservation of two shifts per day, for fear that the three-shift system would not enable them to earn enough. There were army orders which called for work to start at 3 p.m. Public works contracts which compelled men to labour 16 hours per day for weeks on end. There were special laws regulating—or, rather, not regulating—working hours on the Reich's automobile highways and army orders. There were workers who were more severely punished than employers, but whose errors were due to the employer's compulsion. There were employers who were freed of all penalties by Hitler's amnesties, even freed of ridiculously small fines. Such is the verdict, distilled from these German factory inspectors' reports, on the situation in Fascist Germany as regards working hours.

3. The Working Woman

In general, the girl worker, as she grows older, shares the lot of the male worker. Her work is drastically speeded-up, her working days are spent in similar over-crowded and unhealthy premises where the air is similarly stuffy and stale, and where the same or similar employers drive her with equal ruthlessness.

However, for a great number of years in Germany the female worker, to some extent at least, was specially protected. This was manifested chiefly in two respects. Firstly, there existed a series of rules and regulations to prevent women from being given some forms of heavy work; and, secondly, women's working hours were less.

A. Protection of Women from Injuriously Heavy Work

Women's Work which is Too Heavy for Men—Driven to Over-Exertion by Low Pay

The inspectors' reports show with almost brutal clarity the type of work to which women are set under the Fascist régime.

"It has been reported from the Wiesbaden district that, in a felt shoe factory, young girls from the country were put to work on the turning machines. These were girls, many of whom had to come into town a long way from the country and who gave the impression, because of the long journey back and forth and the very exhausting nature of their work, of being in a highly nervous and fatigued condition. Later, when women were prohibited from working on turning machines, the men working on them complained after a few weeks because the work was too heavy. On investigation, it was discovered that it was not the expenditure of energy demanded by the particular operations that was too heavy but the heavy task set each operative: in each shift 8,400 shoes had to be turned, if the worker wanted to earn an hourly wage of one mark. (1 shilling—J.K.). I. 458.

' Not infrequently, it was established that women were

employed in brickworks at the prohibited task of carrying raw materials, and particularly the shovelling of loam . . . or the taking away of the big stones on barrows, without secure supports." I. 96.

Women's work is paid considerably less than men's, even when women perform absolutely the same tasks. This is one reason why the employers frequently evade the laws for the protection of female labour. And this work, which women are compelled to perform, leads often to illness or physical breakdown.

B. WORKING HOURS

A Thirty-Six-Hour Working Day

Nearly as injurious as work which is too heavy is work which goes on too long. It is characteristic of Fascism that, under its rule, reports of over-long working hours relate less to men than to women, who, in general, are less likely to offer resistance. Here, as previously, in the case of male workers, we can note that, not only are long hours worked illegally, but that Fascist law permits excessive overtime to be worked legally.

"In the Saar Palatinate, where the legal working hours (for women in the hotel trade—J.K.) can be extended to 14 hours per day, inclusive of meal hours, infractions of the regulations governing working hours have now practically ceased." II. 36.

Once again the Fascists discover the startling fact that, if you extend legally the working-hour limits, fewer employers break the regulations!

But quite often the legalization of ever longer working periods and the numerous exemptions granted to firms, do not suffice, and violations occur even of the regulations so broadened by the Fascists.

"In spite of the fact that in most districts, through orders of the Reich labour trustees, the permitted maximum working period has been extended to 10 hours per day (with shifts of

12 to 14 hours), the hours regulations were often ignored. For instance, cases of women workers in the catering trade working 16 hours, and hotel chambermaids working occasionally even 20 hours, have been established. During New Year celebrations and carnival periods, the women would actually work 24 or 30 hours on end." I. 96.

"In spite of the exertions, over a period of years, of the factory inspectorate, there have been numerous violations of the regulations regarding working hours in the pen, fountain-pen and propelling pencil trade in the Odenwald where examples were found of personnel, including female and juvenile workers, working as long as 14 hours." VII. 15.

"The owners of three tinware factories have been proceeded against because they employed female workers as long as 15¾ hours in one day, starting work before 6 o'clock, and, working double shifts, they also employed women after 10 p.m." XI. 8.

"Violations of the regulations for the protection of female and juvenile labour were comparatively numerous and related chiefly to length of working time and non-observance of the prescribed intervals and rest-pauses. How grave some of these violations are may be illustrated by the case of a large printing works in the inspection district of Nuremberg-Fuerth in which female workers were several times kept at work on urgent orders for 36 hours at a stretch, with only a few short rest intervals. . . . It was also found that women workers were given work to take home with them after work, contrary to the regulations." II. 39.

Women kept at work several times for 36 hours on end—truly this is the epitome of the insane greed and exploitation which Fascism permits to run wild under its protection! In no country but a country of Fascism could such cases be found.

4. THE WORKER IN OLD AGE

We have arrived at the conclusion of our description of the life of the German worker, male and female. Our entire description is based upon quotations from official reports of German factory inspectors. Our commentary has been sparse, for but little commentary was needed to point the picture.

In the entire world, there is no writing, German or otherwise, National-Socialist or Anti-Fascist, which contains such a remorseless indictment of "peace-time" labour conditions for Germans under Fascism, as the above reports. From them we perceive that the life of the German worker is a path of suffering and sorrow from cradle to grave. All that lacks is some description of the position of the worker who has become too old to work. To obtain some conception of how old age is placed under Fascism, we must depart, in this one instance only, from our rule of quoting from factory inspectors' reports, as, obviously, this does not come within their province. Instead, we will quote mercilessly revealing figures from another Fascist government publication: *The Statistical Yearbook of the German Reich.*

SPECIAL OLD AGE PENSION
(In Millions of Marks)

1932	13·4
1933	10·5
1934	9·1
1935	7·8
1936	6·7
1937	5·5

The above table is a fitting inscription upon the gravestone of the German worker under Fascism. Such is youth, life and old age under the rule of Fascism.

We have now come to the end of our review of the first five years of labour under Fascist rule. It has been a terrible tale indeed that we have had to tell. But the tragic content of this tale is dwarfed by the stark horror revealed by our survey of labour's history in the next five years of Fascist rule.

IN 1938 there were a number [of important changes in the] general economic and labour situation. For the first t[i]me Germany had conquered foreign territory and German indu[stry] was accumulating with unheard-of rapidity. At the same ti[me] armament production had increased to such a degree that t[here] were serious repercussions. German industry and econom[y in] general are now not only directed so as to give greatest sup[port] to the armament industry; but the armament industry is [so] absorbing so much capital and labour power, that a ser[ious] general labour shortage is developing, with its evil conseque[nces] under Fascism, that the squeezing of the small and med[ium] employers results in more and more bankruptcies, that fo[od] clothing and housing conditions are deteriorating more rapidly. Briefly, one is justified in likening this to a war economy. The phase of war preparation has passed, the war period has arrived. If we remember that 1938 was not only the first year of territorial conquest, in Austria and Czechoslovakia (Sudeten territory), but also the year of decision in Spain where German tanks and aeroplanes were used not only to frighten and terrorize peaceful citizens (as in the case of Austria and Czechoslovakia) but to shoot them, it will easily be understood why it is correct to call this year a decisive one in the history of German Fascism and its economy.

But that does not mean that it is possible to deal with the second five-year period as a whole, as we did in the previous chapter with the first. While we were right to study the five years, 1933 to 1937 as one single period in which Fascism laid its foundations and spread to embrace all fields of national economy, it is more correct to subdivide the period beginning 1938 into three phases. The first comprises the year 1938 and the first eight months of 1939, that is, from the period immediately preceding the rape of Austria up till the outbreak of war between

Germany and Poland, Great Britain and France. The second
phase comprises the years from September, 1939, to June, 1941;
that is the period when war was "easy-going" for the German
Fascist armies. The third phase begins in June, 1941, probably
as early as April or May, when the gigantic preparations for and
exertions of the campaign against the Soviet Union began to tax
German economy seriously

Each phase introduces new developments of Fascist economy.
Each phase shows a further development of the barbaric traits of
Fascism. Each phase spreads Fascism over new areas, subjecting
yet more tens of millions of people to the oppressive and cruel
regime of German Fascism. Each phase also brings increased
misery to millions of people both in Germany and degrades
labour and the workers generally.

1. FROM 1938 TO AUGUST, 1939—FROM WAR PREPARING
TO WAR ECONOMY

One of the most striking developments which distinguish
the period we are discussing from the first five years of labour
conditions under German Fascism, is the qualitative change in
the labour market and the measures which Fascism took to
combat it. A labour shortage is nothing new in the history of
capitalism. It has often existed in some specific section of the
labour market; in fact a labour shortage as regards skilled
workers is a fairly common phenomenon in the last phase of the
upward movement during the trade cycle in the nineteenth
century. Occasionally we find an absolute labour shortage; one
of the most marked instances of this is the one which developed
in the course of the first big gold rush in Australia, when Mel-
bourne was described as a city of women and children,* and
wages increased by 50 per cent and more within a single year.
But a prolonged labour shortage, affecting almost the whole of
labour, is rare in the history of capitalism, and the measures
taken by Fascism to combat it are unique. Let us briefly re-
capitulate the chief measures taken against specific shortages of
labour during the preceding years:

* Cf. vol. I, p. 181, of this *Short History of Labour Conditions*.

May, 1934: tying the agricultural workers down to agricultural employment;

December, 1934: keeping the skilled metal workers in the metal industry within the district in which they work;

November, 1936: extending the decree of December, 1934, to unskilled metal workers;

October, 1937: putting carpenters and masons under the same restrictions as metal workers;

November, 1937: women who had received marriage loans permitted to take employment;

December, 1937: raising of the tax upon itinerant trades in order to force as many traders as possible into industry.

By December, 1937, the number of unemployed had reached less than one million, that is less than half the amount on the December, 1928, level, the last December before the economic crisis. In the following months unemployment continued to decline so rapidly that long before the outbreak of the war it had reached an all time low for the last quarter of a century:*

UNEMPLOYMENT, DECEMBER, 1937, TO JULY, 1939

	Date	Number
December	1937	994,784
	1937	912,312
	1938	429,461
December	1938	455,656
First half year	1939	140,835
July	1939	38,379

The figure for 1938 already is abnormally low. And the figure for 1939 is so low that it shows quite clearly that the ordinary laws of capitalism are no longer affecting the labour market.

If we examine the measures taken by German Fascism we shall understand what has happened. The year 1938 began with another decree affecting the itinerant trades; but while this category may be considered a minor one, the inherent importance of the decree of January 29, 1938, is very great; it forbade the issuing of permits for these trades and even provided for the withdrawal of permits already issued if the person engaged in

* *Statistisches Jahrbuch für das Deutsche Reich, 1938*, and International Labour Office, *Year Book of Labour Statistics, 1941.*

this trade or asking permission to engage in it could be more usefully employed elsewhere. Here we have the first instance not of binding the worker to his trade or occupation but of compelling him to abandon his trade and transferring him to other work. The second measure of importance introduced another new development. A decree of February, 1938, forbade unmarried women under the age of twenty-five to enter "their chief industries," the clothing, textile or tobacco industries, or to become commercial or office workers before they had served at least one year in agriculture or in domestic service, or had been engaged for two years in nursing, welfare service or kindergarten work. At the same time a year of compulsory labour service for young women was introduced. In March, 1938, the Fascist régime began the compulsory direction of young workers to industries important in war preparations. A decree was issued to the effect that those desiring to enter an occupation as apprentices must obtain permission from the Employment Office, which in turn was advised to recruit as many young workers as possible for the armament industries. At the same time an order was made providing for the compulsory registration with the employment exchanges of children leaving school.

By the middle of the year the situation had become such that the Government decided upon a general labour conscription law. Issued in June, 1938, it gave power to the president of the National Employment Office to conscript all Germans of every age and occupation, whether man or woman, schoolboy or aged, employer or worker, civil servant or business man. The decree empowered him to draft anybody to any kind of work for a limited period of time, and also to compel anybody to undergo special training. This is the most sweeping conscription law introduced in any of the old capitalist countries (as distinct, for instance, from "native" legislation in some colonies) and gives almost unlimited power to the president of the National Employment Office who becomes the general recruiting officer of the Fascist war machine.

Two more measures of special significance for the labour market were introduced in 1938. The first is more significant of the thoroughness with which Fascism began to shackle almost everybody to the war machine. It antedates the general law just described by a month and refers to convicts. It provides for compulsory labour for all prisoners regardless of the crime they have committed and the length of their prison term. Convicts are to be employed in industries of importance to the war effort, and, in order to avoid "contamination" of free workers by prisoners, the prisoners are to work on special gangs. The prisoner is paid next to nothing, while the employer has to pay to the government 60 per cent of the normal wage. In this way, the employer gets cheap labour, the government makes money out of its prisoners, and war production is increased.—The last measure introduced in 1938 applied to women. It was issued in December, 1938, and enlarged the scope of the decree of February, 1938, by providing for a compulsory year of labour service for young women and forbidding them to enter any trade before having done so. This measure was issued chiefly because of the increasing labour shortage in agriculture.

Looking back upon the 1938 decrees we note that, after the preliminary steps taken during the first five year period of Fascism, within less than half a year a number of measures was taken, which with the June decree gave almost unlimited power to the State to order the labour of the citizens of the country as it desired. Every German had become liable to forced labour and the kind of work determined by the State. The State being an instrument in the hands of heavy industry and the party bosses this simply meant that every German had become potentially or in fact a compulsory worker for the heavy or armament industry. *Many of the special decrees actually transformed many Germans into workers in forced labour. More than a year before the outbreak of the war, all preparations had been made to make of Germany a forced labour camp in which the worker had not only lost his political liberties but also his character as a "free" wage earner, a wage earner who can sell his labour according to his choice (if he can find somebody to buy it) and who has freedom of movement.*

This employment policy is one of the various aspects of Fascist procedure, which shows us that the second phase of the process of war preparations, and war and oppression, did not begin with the actual outbreak of the war but some time before it. *The development of Fascism towards its fateful fruition is even quicker than the pace of general history. It leads in many fields to a state of war before war has actually broken out.* The actual outbreak of war, as we shall see, is not the decisive, all-changing factor, but almost an external incident. Once embarked on its way, Fascism developed with increasing rapidity into a society at war with the world, and took all measures the ruling dictatorship regarded as necessary—whether war had actually broken out or not.

The last eight months before the outbreak of the war were used to tighten up and supplement the measures taken in the preceding period. The new year was only a few hours old when another decree appeared, this time affecting the aged. If, according to the Fascist physicians, workers were in sufficiently good health when reaching the retirement age under the old age pension scheme, they were not allowed to retire but were forced to continue working; and if they had already retired they were forced to go back to work; otherwise their pension would be withdrawn.

In March, a circular was issued making it no longer a "crime against the German race" to employ Jews; on the contrary, it urged the employment of Jews—of course, in separate gangs, so that there was no danger of contamination for the "Aryan workers." In February an order had been issued designed to comb out the handicraft trades, which, it was estimated, drove 60,000 to 70,000 persons out of their occupations into the factories. The decree of February 13th and the order of March 2nd, enlarged the general conscription law to include aliens residing in Germany, and extended the time of service from a limited to an unlimited period. A decree of March 10th brought all members of a family who may be helping in the enterprise of one of them under the forced labour scheme by decreeing that from May 1st onward, each must have a work book like any regular worker; all members of a family, the grandmother who helps in the shop, the wife who helps on the farm were now drawn into the system of forced labour. This made it impossible, for instance, for the sister, who helped her brother on the farm, to leave her work and to obtain work in a factory, or even to marry and leave the farm without special permission by the authorities.

From April to August no new measures of special importance were taken. The net had closed over the German people. Men and women, old and young, convicts and handicraftsmen, "even" the Jews had been drawn in by it. The worker was bound to his job in many respects like a serf. Those who were small independent craftsmen or shopkeepers not only were without economic security, an evil from which they suffered long before Fascism came to power, but they had lost the right to carry on their business even when solvent; they were being forced into the factories.

Fascism was not merely ready for war. Fascism was virtually in a state of war. Its machinery was working in part as if war had already broken out. From the point of view of the worker the difference between peace and war under Fascism is small as compared with what this difference means to the workers in other countries. For the German worker, the difference between, let us say, the first quarter of 1941 and the last quarter of the same year was to be very much greater than between the first quarter of 1939 and the last quarter of 1939 or the first quarter of 1941.

*   *   *

How did wages, how did the purchasing power of the workers develop during his period? As we have seen, the first five years of Fascism meant almost no change in the standard of wages; it remained, on the whole, on the lowest level reached during the economic crisis preceding Fascism.

The wage stop policy of the Fascists remained in force on the whole. Wage rates remained stable; actual hourly earnings increased slightly because of the further shifting of workers into the slightly better paying armament industries and because of more overtime; and actual weekly gross earnings rose somewhat because of the lengthening of the working day and also because of the increasing proportion of armament workers. In a few cases only did the workers succeed in obtaining wage increases because of organized resistance—the two outstanding cases are the shipyard workers in the spring of 1939 and the fortification workers in the west in the summer of the same year.

The following table gives the main wage data : *

* *Wirtschaft und Statistik*, 2. Januar Heft, 1938 and 1939; International Labour Office, *Year Book of Labour Statistics, 1941*; and *International Labour Review*, May, 1940.

AVERAGE WAGE RATES, 1937, TO JUNE 1939

(Pfenning per Hour)

Year	Skilled	Men Unskilled	Women Unskilled	All Combined
1937	78·5	62·3	43·4	67·6
1938	78·8	62·5	43·7	67·9
1939, June	79·1	62·9	44·0	68·1
1939	79·1	62·8	44·0	68·2

The increase in wage rates was roughly 1 per cent during these two years—a negligible figure easily explained by the reasons given above; it definitely does not mean even so slight an increase for the workers in the individual occupation:—but does not exclude an occasional small rise in some branches of industry.

Weekly gross earnings which in 1937 amounted to 26·52 marks continued to increase slightly and amounted in 1938 to 27·84 marks.* No further statistics have been published. But other figures, showing the development of gross weekly earnings for industry only in index form, give more information:†

GROSS WEEKLY EARNINGS IN INDUSTRY, 1932 TO 1939

(1936 = 100)

Year	Index
1932	85·8
1933	87·7
1934	94·1
1935	96·4
1936	100
1937	103·5
1937, December	104·7
1938	108·5
1939, June	114·5
1939	112·6

Gross weekly earnings continued to rise after 1937, partly because of the increase in the number of hours worked, partly because of the shifting of workers from very low to less low paying industries.

During the same period the cost of living index, as computed officially, increased only slightly. Taking 1932 as 100 we know from former tables that it had risen by 1937 roughly to 104; during the following two years it rose by 0·4 per cent annually—

* International Labour Office, *Year Book of Labour Statistics, 1941.*
† *Wirtschaft und Statistik,* 1. Mai Heft, 1938 and April Heft, 1942.

an insignificant amount. From this one can conclude that, according to the official statistics, real weekly gross earnings rose from 1937 to 1939 by roughly 8 per cent; seemingly a not inconsiderable amount. But we have seen before that gross earnings give only a very inadequate picture of the movement of net earnings. During 1937, 1938 and 1939, deductions from wages for party organizations and similar purposes continued to rise, not only absolutely but relatively. For instance, during the period under review, contributions from wages and salaries to the so-called "Winter-Help" rose as follows: 1936–37, 69 million marks; 1937–38, 81 million marks; and 1938–39, 105 million marks. * This represents an increase of over 50 per cent while the total of wages and salaries increased considerably less. If we take all these deductions into account we shall arrive at an increase of wages considerably less than the official data indicate. But even taking this into account, we seem to come to a conclusion somewhat different from our survey of the change of conditions on the labour market; it seems that as regards wages and purchasing power, the years 1938 and the first eight months of 1939 have not brought any decisive change. Again, like for the years 1933 to 1937, it would seem that the purchasing power of the workers, on the whole probably stable, remained at the low level of 1932. As far as the history of wages and purchasing power under Fascism is concerned, the break which we made in 1937 would apparently not seem justified. But this is really not the case, for we have neglected one important factor, which began to play a slight rôle in 1935 and 1936, but whose gravity increased noticeably in 1937, and which attained full weight in 1938: the growing shortage of a number of foodstuffs and the deterioration in quality and the adulteration of food.

In 1938, we find, for the first time, frequent and long queues in Germany. In 1938, for the first time, the housewives all over Germany are complaining about the quality of the food, the scarcity of certain foodstuffs, the time it takes to obtain food, and so on. We also find, for the first time, an extensive black market for a number of foodstuffs. In 1938, according to the official statistics, the consumption of vegetables declined from 52 kilo-

* *Wirtschaft und Statistik*, 2. Februar Heft, 1941.

grammes per head of the population in 1936 and 50·3 in 1937, to 47 kilogrammes, while at the same time the consumption of fruits declined from 37·7 kilogrammes in 1936, and 42·5 in 1937, to a low of 27·3 kilogrammes in 1938. The first effects of vitamin deficiency, above that noticeable in pre-Fascist years, made themselves felt.

The effects of war preparations now began markedly to be felt on the food market. The stringent regulations reserving foreign exchange as far as possible for armament raw materials, the harsh treatment of the peasants inducing them to keep as much as possible of the food they grew and raised out of the hands of the collectors were also factors. To this must be added the fact that the quality of clothing had declined so much that even, had prices remained relatively stable (which they did not, clothing being the chief item to show a constant rise in prices), the worker would have had to spend more for this purpose, as he had to buy new clothing more frequently.

In fact, one may say, that with the beginning of 1938, we have to consider wages quite differently from formerly. The importance of wages has often been over-estimated in considering the standard of living of the workers. True, they are the most important single factor, but they are not an all decisive factor. If real wages increase, for instance, we cannot draw from this the conclusion that the standard of living has necessarily improved. Since 1938, however, one cannot even maintain that wages in Germany are the most important single factor in determining the standard of living of the workers. Just as Fascism has changed the status of the worker by depriving him of rights and liberties which he had enjoyed under capitalism—either as a formerly necessary characteristic of capitalism, like freedom of movement, or as the cherished result of a long struggle, such as the elementary political liberties—so has Fascism transformed the function of wages in determining the workers' standard of living. *With rapid and decisive changes in the quality of the goods supplied, with a shortage on the food market, with a black market for foodstuffs as well as for decent clothing, and also for flats or even small single rooms, as consequence of the growing housing shortage, money wages, even if measured against a so-called cost of living index, have lost their significance. They are interesting as one of many factors determining the standard* of living; their movement indicates aspects of the financial policy of Fascism; but they have definitely lost their importance as the most influential single factor determining the standard of living. Just as money wages in a period of rapidly changing prices must lose much of their significance, so *real wages, in a period of shortage and rapidly deteriorating quality of the goods, and also black market prices, have lost much of their significance.*

This does not mean that before Fascism came to power there had been no change in the quality of goods, nor that occasionally other factors have not temporarily reduced wages to a minor factor in determining the standard of living. But the changes in the quality of goods which previously took place, occurred gradually, and the periods when other factors singly over-shadowed the importance of wages have been rare and short. Fascism, therefore, has brought in something new in this respect. The elements of dissolution, decay or barbarism, which we have already noted as affecting the general status of labour have also undermined the wage structure and altered the character and rôle of wages. The worker is still paid wages, but the value of his wages—in peace time as a permanent policy!—is becoming the object of chance and can no longer be accurately measured. The fact that a worker may have relatives in the country, or that his wife is a friend of the butcher's wife, or that he lives in a town with many armament factories may considerably change the value of his wages. The fact that the government makes frequent changes in the quality of a number of goods, affects the value of a worker's wages much more than a rise or fall in their nominal amount or the development of market prices does.

Now, all these factors cannot be measured. Consequently our study of labour conditions is considerably handicapped and it is necessary to devote all the more care to the study of other than wage factors determining the standard of working and living under German Fascism.

*   *   *

We have seen some examples of very long and very short hours of work under German Fascism when we studied conditions during the period from 1933 to 1937. The average hours of work cannot give us a clear picture of conditions, for they include the extremes of working weeks amounting to a hundred hours and more and working weeks amounting to twenty-four hours or less. But, if average figures can give us no adequate impression of the variety of conditions and of the suffering this means for the workers, we can, once we realize their short-comings, obtain from them some impression of the general trend towards the longer working week. Once we realize that an increasing number of average hours worked per week, especially in 1938 and 1939, does not mean merely a lengthening of the working day in industries with short time, the following table, giving the average number of hours worked per week in industry, cannot be misinterpreted : *

AVERAGE WEEKLY WORKING HOURS IN INDUSTRY

Year	All Workers	Year	Men	Women	All Workers	All Workers Old Series
1932	41·46	1936	47·2	44·6	46·7	45·54
1933	42·96	1937	48·0	45·5	47·6	46·08
1934	44·58	1938	49·2	46·2	48·5	46·50
1935	44·46	1939	49·6	45·2	48·7	46·79†
1936	45·54					

Strictly speaking, these two sets of figures are not comparable, but both show the same tendency: a constant increase in the average number of hours worked per worker. If we compare data for 1937 in the first set of figures, for which we have data going further back, with those for pre-Fascist times, we find that by 1937 the number of hours worked in 1929 has been reached again : 46·02 in 1929 and 46·08 in 1937. Again we note that the year 1937 in certain respects concludes a phase in the history of Fascism. Up to 1937, the average number of hours worked—though including much longer and much shorter working weeks than in 1929—was approximately the same as that of relatively good trade periods in pre-Fascist times. In the phase which begins with 1938, the number of hours increases constantly, reaching new post-1914–18 heights. Before the outbreak of war, Germany had returned to the nine-hour day in the armament industries ! Again we see how the workers lost one after the other of their gains of the past. *The eight-hour day, achieved in 1919, and*

* International Labour Office, *Year Book of Labour Statistics, 1941*, and *Wirtschaft und Statistik*, April Heft, 1942.   † June, 1939.

gained also by the workers of other countries after the last war, was lost in Germany. In this respect too, Fascism was turning back the wheel of history.
But it was doing much more. While retrogressive in respect of the number of hours worked per day and per week, it was continuing the process ` begun by capitalism many decades ago, of constantly increasing the intensity of work. The chief difference which Fascism made in this respect was that, while the increased intensity of work in other capitalist countries was usually combined with a shortening of the working week, under German Fascism it is combined with a lengthening of the working day. Again we see Fascism combining the methods of former times with those of the present—if such combination means more oppression and bigger profits! The hardship caused by increased intensity of work without a corresponding increase in the standard of living of the workers, which we can find in many capitalist countries, has been augmented, by the additional factor of a constantly increasing working day. The methods of intensive and extensive exploitation are combined in a way we have never experienced before. For from 1750 to 1850 extensive exploitation (longer working days, employment of women and children, etc.) rapidly increased while intensive exploitation was neglected (this applies to all old capitalist countries); from 1850 to the present, the method of extensive exploitation gave way to that of intensive exploitation.* Only since 1919 do we find in some countries a very slight trend towards increases in extensive exploitation (e.g. lengthening of the working day in coal mining in Britain, as well as in pre-Fascist Germany) combined with continuously increasing intensity of exploitation. But it remained for Fascism to develop fully the system of exploitation in which both, intensive and extensive methods, play almost an equal part.

*   *   *

In addition to lengthening the working day Fascism has exerted every effort to enlarge the number of objects of exploitation, that is the number of workers. When we studied the forced labour measures of Fascism we saw how it combed out the whole community to find additional workers. Let us now consider the

* In Germany, the period of extensive exploitation lasted until about 1860.

results of this policy in terms of employment figures—figures which, for the years immediately following 1932 are, of course, chiefly influenced by the growing absorption of the unemployed.*

NUMBER OF EMPLOYED (WAGE AND SALARY EARNERS)

Year	Thousand
1932	12,580
1933	13,080
1934	15,090
1935	16,000
1936	17,140
1937	18,370
1938	19,520
1939 (First half)	20,340
1939 (June)	21,270

By 1937 the 1928 level of about 18 million employed had been reached while the crisis level of 1932 had been passed by roughly 50 per cent. In the period now under review, 1938 and the first eight months of 1939, two important movements took place. On the one hand, the number of employed continued to increase, for the first few months, perhaps, still partly by absorbing the remnants of the unemployed but then chiefly by recruiting those who either had worked independently or by forcing into employment people who normally would not have been working (young girls helping at home, housewives, etc.). On the other hand, Fascism began to expand outside Germany, occupying first Austria, then the Sudeten territory, and finally the whole of Czechoslovakia and the Memel territory. Through these conquests, the number of people employed under Fascist rule increased rapidly. Austria brought over two million workers; the Sudeten territory added over a million, and, if we count Czechoslovakia as a whole, Munich and its consequences implied a gain of over four million workers. However, in this volume we are dealing only with Germany proper. But while the lot of the Austrian and Czechoslovak workers under Fascism belongs to another volume of the history of labour conditions, we must also remember that numbers of them were deported from their own countries to Germany.

The number of foreign workers in Germany was already con-

* *Schriften des Instituts für Konjunkturforschung*, Wochenbericht, January 25, 1939, and August 10, 1939.

siderable before the war of 1914–18. Many of them were Polish agricultural workers who had come over from Czarist Russia. After the war, the number of foreign workers declined rapidly and never reached a figure approaching that of the first fourteen years of this century. During the crisis of 1929–32 the number of foreign workers showed a further decline. In the beginning of 1934, after one year of Fascism, it was still less than 200,000; in 1935 and 1936 it rose slowly, and during 1937 it rose to over 350,000. These foreign workers were usually engaged in unskilled labour; one-third were employed in agriculture, and slightly less than 10 per cent were in domestic service. All these had not been imported by force from their home countries into Germany.

The first forced importation of workers, though on a relatively small scale, took place some time after the conquest of Austria. The scale of deportations rose rapidly with the conquest of Czechoslovakia. By 1939 the number of foreign workers had risen to roughly three-quarters of a million and their composition had changed considerably: first, there were the Polish, Italian and other low-paid and unskilled workers who had come voluntarily; their number was probably slightly above 400,000. Then there were 250,000 workers deported from Czechoslovakia and about 100,000 workers deported from Austria. The Austrian workers formed a special group, similar in position to the workers who had come voluntarily* from other countries, in so far as there was not the slightest economic discrimination against them, on the contrary, having a higher percentage of skilled workers they were paid on the average, much better than the other foreign workers. On the other hand, their position resembled that of the workers from Czechoslovakia inasmuch as they did not come voluntarily and were robbed of the political liberties they had enjoyed before Fascism conquered their country. The workers from Czechoslovakia were deported largely by force (economic compulsion by withholding unemployment insurance benefits from them, etc., or by pure and simple terrorism!) Here

---

* By "voluntarily" I mean that they were not deported by German Fascist force. The Italians, for instance, while not being forced by German Fascism to come, while not being treated as slaves from a conquered country, were forced by Italian Fascism to go to Germany.

the *element of slavery* begins to enter openly the status of the workers working in Germany.

What was the effect upon production of all these measures: the increase of employment by the driving of people out of independent livelihoods, the compulsory recruitment of women, by importing workers from conquered countries into Germany and the lengthening of the working day? Production continued to increase, the armed strength of Fascist Germany rose rapidly, and production in the consumption goods industries, which also furnished more and more goods for the army, rose too. *

INDUSTRIAL PRODUCTION, 1937 TO 1939†

(1932 = 100)

Year		Total Production	Production Goods	Consumption Goods
	1937	199	276	132
	1938	212	297	138
First half	1939	224	313	146
June	1939	227	322	142

The increase in production is impressive. But the increase in employment was impressive too, and the rise in the number of hours worked was also very considerable. How has production per worker changed during the period under review?

PRODUCTION PER WORKER, 1937 TO 1939‡

(1932 = 100)

Year		Total Production	Production Goods	Consumption Goods
	1937	111	124	97
	1938	112	124	99
First half	1939	113	125	100
June	1939	112	125	97

Productivity per worker and per day, then increased very little during 1938 if it increased at all; and during 1939 it developed a tendency to decline. Also in the production goods industry, which comprises almost the whole of the armament

* Part of the rise is due to the need to produce more consumption goods because of the wear and tear of the low quality goods produced.
† Based on figures given in *Schriften des Instituts für Konjunkturforschung, Statistik des In- und Auslandes*, 14. Jahrgang, 1939–40, Heft 2, August, 1939, and *Statistical Year Book of the League of Nations*, 1939–40.   ‡ Ibid.

industry, production per worker showed no further increase. The situation had changed fundamentally as compared with the preceding period. True, during the years from 1932 to 1937, productivity per worker and day in the consumption goods industries had a tendency to decline slightly and slowly. On the other hand, productivity in the armament industries, in fact, in the whole of the production goods industry rose rapidly and was in 1937 higher by about one quarter than in 1932. The rapid and constant rise of productivity per worker in this section of industry forced up the average for all industry by more than 10 per cent, in spite of the poor showing of the consumption goods industry. This changed in 1938 and 1939. *Productivity per worker did not continue to increase. The limit of exhaustion had been reached: in spite of slave-driving and terror, and the lengthening of the working day production per worker did not rise further.*

This does not mean that, in the subsequent years, Fascism did not make every effort further to increase production per worker. Nor does it mean that, although this tendency had become obvious by the end of 1937, Fascism did not continue to lengthen the working day, and to intensify production by speed-up methods. It does, however, mean that, if Fascism wanted further to increase production, it had to rely more and more on extensive exploitation, on increasing the number of workers. This explains in part the drive for more workers in 1938 and 1939, and also the large-scale importation of foreign workers, begun in 1938 and intensified in 1939.

The picture of the exhaustion of the working power of the worker under Fascism is thrown into even sharper relief when we study production per worker, per hour.*

PRODUCTIVITY PER WORKER PER HOUR, 1937 TO 1939

(1932 = 100)

	Year	Total Production	Production Goods	Consumption Goods
	1937	100	108	91
	1938	98	104	91
First half	1939	98	105	90
June	1939	98	105	88

* Based on figures given in *Schriften des Instituts für Konjunkturforschung, Statistik des In- und Auslandes*, 14, Jahrgang, 1939–40, Heft 2, August, 1939, and *Statistical Year Book of the League of Nations*, 1939–40.

In spite of technical and organizational progress in the heavy industries (the armament industries) since 1932, in spite of terror and slave-driving, productivity per worker and hour is on the way back to the 1932 level. The consumption goods industries showed in 1937 productivity by almost 10 per cent below the 1932 level, and since then it has further declined. In industry as a whole productivity per worker and hour worked is definitely below the 1932 level.

The German worker, under Fascism, has become an industrial wreck. With the finest industrial production apparatus in the heavy industrial sector, especially in the armament industries, driven to ever increased haste by the most cruel and refined system of supervision, under constant pressure of political and physical terror, and at the same time played upon by clever propaganda which has not remained without effect—he is still less able to stand the pace, and his productivity now begins to drop generally. A decline in productivity is nothing unusual under capitalism. In the nineteenth century it usually declined during a crisis, and in the twentieth century it sometimes declined during an unusual rise in production. But under Fascism all the causes making for declining productivity on these other occasions are absent. There is really only one main cause for it: the worker has reached the limits of physical endurance. *Under Fascism for the first time the entire working class of a country reached in peace time the limit of physical endurance* and slightly increased production is possible only by rapid technical progress, organizational progress or by increasing the number of workers.

*   *   *

Very little information, unfortunately, has been published with regard to other aspects of working class conditions. The rate of accidents, the sickness rate and similar figures are either not available, or the figures are incomplete, or they are not comparable with those for former years. One of the most interesting sets of figures, illustrative of an important aspect of the standard of living is the development of housing construction. Fascism was in a difficult position in this regard. Housing construction had declined rapidly during the 1929–1932 crisis while the population continued to increase. When Fascism came to power, it inherited a housing shortage. Housing conditions are an important factor not only affecting the worker's general standard of living but also his productivity—not as important a factor as his food standard, but probably more so than his clothing standard. If the worker's rest is affected by congested housing conditions, if he has to travel far from home to the factory and back, his working capacity is lessened. For this reason, Fascism took some interest in better housing conditions. But even more important than the productivity of the worker were the raw materials, which Fascism needed for the armament industries. Munitions, therefore, had a definite priority over housing. In the course of time, however, not only such, somewhat remote, industries as gun and tank and grenade production diverted steel and similar materials from housing construction, but, much closer industries, as fortification works absorbed much building material, such as concrete and bricks, and encroached upon house-building. No wonder that under Fascism housing construction took the following course:

NET ADDITION* OF DWELLINGS, 1932 TO 1938†

Year	Number
1929	317,682
1932	141,265
1933	178,038
1934	283,995
1935	241,032
1936	310,490
1937	320,057
1937‡	340,392
1938‡	305,526

In 1939 the net addition of dwellings was less than 200,000. After a considerable rise from 1932 to 1934, construction declined in 1935 (chiefly because of a decline in the reconstruction of existing buildings), increased again in 1936 and 1937, and then declined rapidly in the following two years.

As in so many other respects, the year 1938 is a turning point in the history of workers' housing conditions under Fascism. They were worse than in pre-Fascist days during the first five

---

* Construction, after deduction of demolished and dilapidated and uninhabitable flats.
† *Statistisches Jahrbuch für das Deutsche Reich, 1938*, and *Wirtschaft und Statistik*, 1. Juni Heft, 1939.   ‡ Without deducting demolished, etc., flats.

years, but they were incomparably worse in the following five years. Just as in the case of food, 1938 brought for the first time a very real and general shortage, so for housing; 1938 brought about a change inasmuch as the growing congestion became an absolute shortage. This means that people with small incomes were unable to get even the most congested accommodation. Newly-married couples had to wait for months until they could set up house, or couples had to postpone marriage because they could not find accommodation. Sub-letting increased rapidly and rents rose—of course, this was not shown in the official cost of living index. A black market for rooms began to develop. The strain under which the workers lived was increased by the rapid deterioration of housing conditions. The journey between home and place of work became more lengthy, means of transport grew more congested, the number of persons per cubic room increased, and the physcial effects of all this became more marked.

*   *   *

In concluding this survey of labour conditions we can do no better than study the few figures we have on the development of the social insurance system in Germany:*

THE PENSION SYSTEM IN 1937 TO 1939

Pensions	1937	1938	1939	1932
For the sick—				
Number, 1,000 ..	12·9	12·2	11·7	18·4
Benefits, million marks	2·9	3·0	—	4·2
For the aged—				
Number, 1,000 ..	18·0	14·7	12·2	40·2
Benefits, million marks	5·5	4·6	—	13·4
For the widows—				
Number, 1,000,000	0·63	0·65	0·72	0·65
Benefits, million marks	151·3	164·1	—	141·4
For the sick widows—				
Number, 1,000 ..	1·5	1·4	1·3	2·1
Benefits, million marks	0·3	0·3	—	0·5
For the orphans—				
Number, 1,000,000	0·29	0·28	0·33	0·55
Benefits, million marks	38·3	44·5	—	58·6
For all—				
Number, 1,000,000	0·96	0·96	1·08	1·26
Benefits, million marks	198·3	216·6	—	218·0

* *Reichsarbeitsblatt, 1939*, Heft Nr. 20.

On the whole, these figures show the same tendency indicated by a similar table covering the years 1932 to 1937. A ruthless cutting down of the number of pensioners and severe restrictions in the amounts of pensions paid. But 1938 brings one decisive difference, which we can already observe in 1937 and which becomes even clearer in 1939: with all the cutting down in the number of pensioners, with all the callousness developed by the Fascist officials, they do no longer succeed in reducing the number of pensioners. The rapid increase in accidents, the growth of permanent disability because of industrial and other diseases have created so many victims of industry that even if the proportion of refusals of pensions grows, it is nevertheless impossible to check an absolute increase in the number of pensions. The Fascist officials were beaten by the magnitude of the misery they had created.

Similarly, the number of recipients of invalidity pensions increased from 2·46 millions in 1937 to 2·48 in 1938 and to 2·57 in 1939 while the benefits paid rose from 925·9 in 1937 to 965·0 in 1938.

The financial development of the social insurance system as a whole followed the lines observed in the previous years: expenditure rose slightly, from 3,816 million marks to 4,181, while the income rose much more sharply, from 4,709 million marks to 5,480, and the funds reached an all time record of 8,746 million marks in 1938 as compared with 7,439 in 1937.*

* * *

When we survey the twenty months of the Fascist régime preceding the outbreak of the present war we find that quantity has turned into quality, that many features which were only in their beginnings—though already quite discernable—during the first five years of Fascism are now fully developing in 1938 and the first eight months of 1939. The worker has been wholly caught in the network of employment regulations; he has completely lost his freedom of movement; the wage system has been definitely undermined; food, clothing and housing have become scarce and of poor quality; the productivity of the worker in spite of increased driving is beginning to decline; workers are

* *Wirtschaft und Statistik*, 2. Juli Heft, 1939.

brought compulsorily, like slaves, from foreign countries into Germany; the social insurance system is accumulating vast sums and the "beneficiaries" of this system are treated worse than ever. Fascism has definitely entered a new stage, more brutal and barbarous even than the preceding one.

2. FROM SEPTEMBER 1939 TO JUNE 1941

The outbreak of a war always means a rapid deterioration of working and living conditions for the workers. If the workers realize that it is a war in their own interests, they accept this deterioration as necessary and justified in order to achieve an object, the defence of their country against an aggressor, their liberation from a foreign oppressor who occupies their country, and so on. If, or rather when, the workers realize that a war is being fought against their interests, they resent this deterioration of working and living conditions—but deterioration there will always be.

When the war broke out in September, 1939, the German workers had already lived for about two years under what can be termed war-time conditions. Much of the hardships which war must inevitably bring about had been anticipated under German Fascism, had, in fact, deliberately been introduced before war broke out. Many of the conditions war always brings for civilians, such as a housing shortage, a food shortage, clothing shortage, and so on, existed in Germany since 1938. It is no wonder, therefore, that the actual outbreak of war meant less change in Germany than for the workers in other countries. In fact, it is one of the characteristics of life under Fascism that the outbreak of a large scale war does not imply a radical change in the conditions of the workers.

*　　　　*　　　　*

As a first object lesson in this respect, let us study the development of conditions on the labour market. By the summer of 1938 it was obvious that there was a serious and widespread labour shortage in Germany, and that in order to counter this shortage Fascism had introduced a variety of measures which made of the German worker in many respects a serf, restricted in movement, bound to his occupation and region. Furthermore, workers in "peacefully conquered" countries had been deported to Germany like slaves. When war came regulations in Germany were tightened up, a further step in the oppression of the German worker was made, but no fundamental change took place. On September 1, 1939, drastic control over changes of employment was introduced, affecting not only movement from one district to another and from one occupation to another, but from one factory or working place to another. The worker was no longer permitted to leave his place of employment in any branch of activity, except mining, agriculture and domestic service, without the permission of the local employment office. At the same time the restrictions still in force limiting the employment of women in night work, and of juveniles and children were abolished. The order relating to women and juveniles and children was partially revoked in December, 1939, since accidents had increased to a degree which alarmed even the Fascists, while productivity had declined rapidly.

The order of September 1, 1939, relating to the mobility of labour only completed the transition to "industrial feudalism." All other measures in the field of employment introduced up to June 1941 are of little importance; some illustrate the callousness of Fascism, such as the orders of March and April, 1941, which drove women into the mines; but as far as the German workers are concerned, none brought any major changes. The German worker is now bound to his factory just as the serf was bound to the land of the lord of the manor. Two factories, possessing the same machinery and not differing in other respects, will still be valued differently, according to the percentage of skilled workers "belonging to the factory"—just as, in the Middle Ages, apart from fertility and other considerations, the number of serfs on a piece of land was an important factor in determining its value. In fact, in some cases, the number of workers attached to an establishment constitutes almost its sole value. For in a number of cases, especially in the building industry, the industrial serfs are all that is left to the employer, since he cannot carry on production either because of shortage of raw materials, because machinery has broken down and cannot be replaced, or for some other reason. In such a case, as the employer can get no profit from his workers in his own establishment, and since other establishments are short of labour, he hires them out. For the first time in the history of capitalism, workers are being "farmed out." The borrower pays the wages and a charge, based on a percentage of the total wage bill, to the "owner" of the working power, that is to the original employer. Not a few articles have appeared in the National Socialist Press, some written by officials of the Labour Ministry, dealing with the ethical and financial problems involved; whether it is ethical to lend workers at all, how much the price per head should be, where usury begins, and when the relations between employer and worker begin to be affected by such procedure, and so on. *

While the position of the German workers during these years resembles in many respects that of serfs, we have another category of workers in Germany whose position is more like to that of slaves: the workers imported into Germany from foreign countries.

We have noted that the conquest of Austria and Czechoslovakia was accompanied by the large scale recruitment of labour power—hundreds of thousands of workers were deported from these countries, with more or less compulsion, to help to overcome the labour shortage in Germany. When war began the total number of foreign workers in Germany was probably little less than three-quarters of a million. No accurate figures are available since the Fascist statistics do not treat Austrians and Sudeten Germans, sent to Germany, as foreign workers; they are counted as German workers. I am, therefore, forced to leave them out of account when discussing the number of foreign workers, and also am unable to exclude them from the total of the German (proper) working population. Since the number of foreign workers has risen rapidly, and since the number of Austrians and Sudeten Germans working in Germany is small as compared with the total of German or foreign workers, this defect is not of great importance statistically.

* Cf., for instance, *Berliner Boersenzeitung*, February 21, 1942. Such practices have not been confined to Germany; they are also reported from other countries under German domination. See, for instance, a report from Denmark in *Jydske Tydende*, Koelding, September 1, 1942.

The rapid conquest of Poland was followed by a wholesale deportation of Polish workers into Germany. Here again, the full extent of this deportation cannot statistically be assessed, since part of Poland was converted into a German district, and Polish workers in this district are not regarded as foreign workers, though an increasing number of them have been deported into the non-incorporated part of Poland in order to free the acquired district from these "sub-humans." The attitude of the Fascist régime to the workers in the occupied countries was defined quite early in the war. In its issue of October 15, 1939, the official Journal of the Ministry of Labour (the *Reichsarbeitsblatt*) stated: "*The working class of the entire occupied territories must serve not only to maintain the economic life of the occupied areas, but also to strengthen German economy. This aim necessitates the most effective exploitation possible.*"

According to this policy within a short time hundreds of thousands of Polish people, workers and intellectuals, men, women and juveniles, were deported to Germany where the labour shortage had grown more serious. In some cases a quarter or more of the adult population of a town would be arrested and sent to Germany, where they usually live in barracks and are fed either by the employer or by an official authority—the cost being deducted from their wages. The foreign workers who followed the Poles, the French, Norwegians, Belgians, Dutch and Luxemburgians, later the Yugoslavs, Greeks and others, were treated similarly in these respects. It is rare for foreign workers to live in rooms like other people (except when employed as domestics) and to work individually rather than in gangs. The exceptions are workers from satellite countries, such as Spain, Bulgaria, etc.

The first official statistics of foreign workers after the out-break of the war refer to the turn of the year 1940–41;* they do not give the number of foreign workers employed at that time in Germany, but the number of workers imported up to that time (including those who may have returned in the mean-time because their period of service was terminated or because

---

* *Wirtschaft und Statistik*, 1. Maerz Heft, 1941. A global statement by Dr. Syrup (*Frankfurter Zeitung*, October 25, 1940) gives a total figure, excluding prisoners of war, of 1.1 million.

they had fallen sick). The workers are subdivided into those employed in agriculture and otherwise.

FOREIGN WORKERS IN AGRICULTURE AT TURN OF 1940–1941

Poles	..	..	..	..	469,000
Italians	..	..	..	..	47,000
Slovaks	..	..	..	..	32,000
Dutch	..	..	..	..	4,650
Jugoslavs	..	..	..	..	4,400
Hungarians	..	..	..	..	2,500
Others	..	..	..	..	2,000
Czechoslovakians*		..	..	..	150,000
					711,550

To these must be added:

FOREIGN WORKERS IN NON-AGRICULTURAL OCCUPATIONS
AT THE TURN OF 1940–41

Building and Construction	..	..	380,000
Iron, Steel and other Metal	..	..	90,000
Mining	..	..	65,000
Stone Quarrying, Clay, Sand, etc.	..		29,000
Others, Men	..	..	81,000
Women ..	..	..	25,000
Total	..	..	670,000

To these official statistics add 180,000 freed Polish prisoners of war who are alleged to work voluntarily in agriculture, and finally (this figure refers to the end of September, 1940) 650,000 prisoners of war. The majority of the prisoners of war worked in agriculture, although, in the course of time, more and more of them were put to work in industry.[†]

PERCENTAGE DISTRIBUTION OF PRISONERS OF WAR

Occupation	Beginning of 1940	Middle of 1940	Beginning of 1941
Agriculture ..	95	65	52
Industry.. ..	5	35	48

The total number of imported workers amounts after somewhat more than one year of war to over one and a quarter million. A few months later, on April 1, 1941,[‡] the number of

* Workers from Bohemia and Moravia only; imported since Spring of 1939.
† *Reichsarbeitsblatt*, May 25, 1941.
‡ *Reichsarbeitsblatt*, July 15, 1941. This figure refers to those imported **and actually working in Germany, that is excluding those who have died or returned in the preceding months.**

civilian forced workers imported from other countries had risen to one and a half million, one and a quarter million men and a quarter of a million women; while the number of prisoners of war had risen to almost one and a half million. Five countries provided more than 50,000 workers each:

Poland	873,000
Bohemia and Moravia	150,000
Italy	132,000
Holland	90,000
Belgium	87,000
Slovakia	69,000

But these figures do not show the full number of deportations because workers were deported to other countries besides Germany. Belgium, Poland and Holland had to send workers to France who, with 25,000 workers in Germany* at that time, thus received more civilian workers than she had to send away—not counting, of course, the terrific loss in man power represented by the prisoners of war in Germany. One can estimate that, at the end of the period under review—that is before the outbreak of the war against the Soviet Union—Germany had within her

NUMBER OF PEOPLE EMPLOYED IN GERMANY†

Period	Civilians	Prisoners of War	Total
1938	20,543,349‡	—	20,543,349
June, 1939 ..	21,874,593§	—	21,874,593
August, 1939	22,000,000‖	—	22,000,000
December, 1940	21,550,000¶	1,000,000**	22,550,000
May, 1941 ..	22,050,000††	1,400,000‡‡	23,450,000

* Excluding workers from Alsace-Lorraine.

† The figures refer to Germany proper, excluding all conquests since 1938; they include temporarily sick workers.

‡ *Reichsarbeitsblatt*, March 5, 1939.

§ *Reichsarbeitsblatt*, August 25, 1939.

‖ Estimate of *Wirtschaft und Statistik*, Februar Heft, 1942.

¶ The official figure of 22,670,000 (*Wirtschaft und Statistik*, 1. Maerz Heft, 1941) refers to a larger area than Germany proper.

** *Wirtschaft und Statistik*, 1. Maerz Heft, 1941, gives an estimate of 650,000 for the end of September, 1940; Reichsminister Seldte gives an estimate of 1,100,000 for an area larger than Germany proper, for the end of 1940 (*Reichsarbeitsblatt*, January 5, 1941).

†† The official figure of 23,083,000 (*Reichsarbeitsblatt*, May 25, 1942) refers to an area, larger than Germany proper.

‡‡ Based on material collected in E. M. Kulischer, *The Displacement of Population in Europe*, International Labour Office, Montreal, 1943.

frontiers probably one and a half million workers working under actual slave conditions, and about one and a half million prisoners of war, of whom a large part had to work under conditions worse than those usually imposed on prisoners of war.

Because of the ruthless employment of all potential labour forces in Germany, of retired old age pensioners, of the very young, of the injured and disabled who are of no use at the front, of prisoners of war, and through the importation of labour, the labour forces in Germany continued to grow considerably in the course of the war—a unique phenomenon.

According to the above figures the total number of employed workers (including salary earners) has increased from year to year* in spite of the mobilization of an army which can be estimated at roughly five million men during the Polish campaign, at roughly four million when the campaign was ended at the turn of the year 1939–40, at over six million men at the height of the 1940 campaign against the West, and over five million at the turn of 1940–41; the campaign against the Soviet Union was preceded by a mobilization of a total of probably seven million men.

Apart from imported workers and employed prisoners of war,

EMPLOYED WOMEN†

Year	Number	Percentage
1929	6,721,296	33.1
1933	5,691,371	31.2
1934	5,547,351	30.5
1935	5,590,433	30.1
1936	5,775,324	30.1
1937	6,055,528	30.6
1938	6,401,752	31.2
1939 June	7,075,439	32.3
1939 August	7,300,000‡	33.2
1940 December	7,600,000§	35.3
1941 May	8,000,000‡	36.3

* Most studies of the development of employment in Germany (e.g. the oft-quoted article by Balogh and Mandelbaum in Bulletin Vol. 3, No. 12 of the Oxford Institute of Statistics) give much too high figures for pre-war years, mixing up Germany proper and a constantly changing area of "Greater Germany."

† The figures refer to Germany proper.   ‡ My estimate.

§ Estimate based on information given in *Wirtschaft und Statistik*, 1. Maerz Heft, 1941.

women were the chief source of additional labour. The total number of employed women and the percentage of employed women of all employed workers, during the years from 1933 to 1941 were as shown in table at foot of page 193. *

In industry proper the employment of women developed as follows :†

WOMEN EMPLOYED IN INDUSTRY AS PERCENTAGE OF ALL WORKERS, 1933 TO 1938

Year	Percentage	Year	Percentage
1933	29·3	1936	24·7
1934	27·0	1937	25·3
1935	25·5	1938	25·2

From the outbreak of the war to the beginning of the campaign against the Soviet Union the employment of women has increased by roughly one-tenth, or about 700,000. That is, *the number of women pressed into employment was lower than that of foreign workers*. All in all the number of additional workers gained during the period from the beginning of the war to the beginning of the Soviet campaign was roughly as follows :

> 1,000,000 imported workers
> 700,000 women
> 1,400,000 prisoners of war

The additional labour force, thus, amounted to over three million workers. To this must be added a considerable number of young workers who were pressed into employment earlier, at a younger age, and more completely than was the case before the war—while those who were conscripted for military service have to be deducted.

All in all employment during the war had developed as shown in table on page 195.

In spite of the fact that the number of serving soldiers has doubled between August, 1939 and May/June, 1941, the number of employed workers in Germany has increased by almost one and a half million. But this increase in employment is due exclusively to increased importation of forced labour and to the

---

* *Reichsarbeitsblatt*, Heft Nr. 7 and Nr. 24, 1939.
† *Statistisches Jahrbuch für das Deutsche Reich*, 1938. and *Wirtschaft und Statistik*, 2. Mai Heft, 1939.

ESTIMATE OF EMPLOYMENT AND ARMED FORCES (Millions)*

Category	August 1939	End of 1939	End of 1940	Before War against S.U.
Armed Forces	3.5	4.0	5.50	7.00
Civilian Employment ..	22.0	21.8	21.55	22.05
German Workers ..	21.3	20.9	20.15	20.35
Men ..	14.0	14.0	12.60	12.35
Women	7.3	6.9	7.55	8.00
Foreign Workers ..	0.7	0.9	1.40	1.70
Men	0.7	0.9	1.35	1.40
Women	†	†	0.05	0.30
Employed Prisoners of War	—	0.2	1.00	1.40
Total Employment ..	22.0	22.0	22.55	23.45

fact that a rising number of prisoners of war is employed in industry and agriculture. In spite of the fact that the number of German women put to work has been raised to eight million, the total number of German workers employed is in May/June, 1941 by one million lower than in August, 1939.

Moreover, these figures would be even less impressive if one could put beside them others, indicating the productivity per worker. Though we have no such figures, we can, even in their absence, assert that productivity per worker has declined. The composite physical standard of the workers deteriorated through the conscription for military service of many of those who were in their best working age. The repeal, as early as the end of 1939, of a considerable number of provisions in the first war decrees regarding the lengthening of the working day, reductions in wages, etc., proves a serious decline in productivity, at least for the first four months of the war. The untoward length of the working day, in spite of the repeal of the early war measures, combined with a deterioration in nutrition, are further factors contributing to a decline in productivity. Finally, we must remember that the imported workers are working, of course, at a lower rate of productivity than German workers; partly because slave labour always is less productive; partly because of the poor physical condition of these workers, which became even

* For sources see the above tables.   † Number of women very small.

worse under the poor working and living conditions imposed upon them in Germany; and partly because of the passive resistance inspired by political motives, which these workers endeavour to practice. As the proportion of these workers increases in Germany these factors increase in importance.

Let us first study the general development of the working day during the war:*

AVERAGE NUMBER OF HOURS WORKED PER WEEK

Year	Men	Women	Average
1938	49·2	46·2	48·5
1939	49·6	45·2	48·7
1940	50·4	44·5	49·2
March 1941	51·4	44·8	49·9

From previous acquaintance with such statistics, we know the pitfalls we have to avoid when examining them. We know, they embrace both very long and very short working weeks; we know that, with the growing raw material difficulties in the consumption goods industries, the working week declines while continuing to increase in the armament industries. But we also know that, if the average number of hours worked by men (who to a very large proportion are employed in the armament industries) and by all workers combined increases, this is indicative of a lengthening of the working day for the mass of the workers.

When the decrees issued at the beginning of the war, permitting an unlimited working day, were repealed in December, 1939, the 10-hour day became the normal working day. Only after the tenth hour was overtime paid. Thus, after having, in the years preceding the present war, gone back to the conditions prevailing before the 1914–1918 war, *Fascism, in its legislation affecting working hours, has now reverted, for industrial workers, to the latter half of the previous century, and has re-introduced the 10-hour day as the normal working day.*

But for millions of workers the "normal 10-hour day" was a minimum, and this became more and more the case. In the armament factories, the 11 and 12-hour day became normal. For transport workers, for instance, after the repeal of the

* *Wirtschaft und Statistik*, April Heft, 1942.

September orders, the working day up to 14 hours was not unusual, and the employers were expressly allowed, without application to any authority, to introduce the 98-hour week. * In some branches of transport even the regulation that a transport worker should not customarily be employed for longer than 14 hours per day, 7 days per week, was repealed. Workers employed in shipping on the Danube, for instance, can be employed for any length of time, up to 24 hours per day.† While we have seen a case, even before the war, when a working week of 104 hours was officially introduced,‡ this, apart from the panic legislation at the beginning of the war which was so quickly repealed, is the first order making an unlimited working day and working week legal, and leaving it exclusively to the employer to determine the length of the working day.

Conditions in this respect were at their worst for the workers imported from other countries. For them, the 12-hour day was normal. Often they had to work longer; and when they had become physical wrecks, they were sent back again to their homeland to die. There were plenty of others to take their place. And when it becomes difficult to obtain sufficient adult workers, they impress the children. As early as in February, 1940, the official German slave-herders in Poland were advised that, if they had difficulty in rounding up a sufficient number of adults, they would have to take juveniles. Polish boys and girls, aged 14 and 15, could be used in German agriculture.§

*   *   *

While the number of hours worked was increased, wage rates remained on the pre-war level, which was the level of the deepest point of the crisis 1929–1932. Wage rates by categories of workers developed as shown in the table on page 198.‖

Since the beginning of the war, wage rates have practically remained stable, rising by only 1 per cent. But the increase in

---

* *Deutscher Reichsanzeiger*, January 20, 1940.
† *Reichsarbeitsblatt*, Heft No. 5, February 15, 1940.
‡ See p. 159 of this book.
§ Cf. *Reichsarbeitsblatt*, Heft Nr. 6, February 25, 1940.
‖ International Labour Office, *Year Book of Labour Statistics*, 1941; and *International Labour Review*, February, 1941, and August, 1942.

the number of hours worked per week has led to an increase of actual weekly gross earnings. The following table gives the

AVERAGE HOURLY WAGE RATES, 1939 TO 1941

(*Pfennig*)

Year	Skilled Men	Unskilled Men	Unskilled Women	Average All
1939	79·1	62·8	44·0	68·2
1939 September	79·1	62·9	44·0	68·2
1940	79·2	63·0	44·1	68·2
1941 June	79·9	63·7	44·4	68·9

development of these earnings, and, in addition, that of hourly gross earnings which have risen too, chiefly because of the shifting from low to less low-paying industries.*

INDEX OF GROSS WAGES, 1939 TO 1941

(*1936 = 100*)

Year	Hourly Gross Earnings	Weekly Gross Earnings	Cost of Living
1938	105·6	108·5	100·9
1939	108·6	112·6	101·3
1939 September	107·3	110·6	101·0
1940	111·2	116·0	104·5
1941 March	115·5	122·2	106·1

According to these statistics, hourly earnings rose during the first eighteen months of the war by roughly 8 per cent, while weekly gross earnings rose by about 11 per cent. If we compare these wage figures with the official cost of living index we find that the latter has risen less than wages. But it is not worth attempting, on this basis, to compute something like a gross real wage index since these figures are useless for such a purpose. Firstly, we have already seen that the index of the cost of living does not take into account the deterioration in the quality of the goods included in the index, a deterioration which has been intensified in the course of the war; secondly, the rapid growth of the black market is not taken into account.

But even if the cost of living index were reliable, we could not compute a real wage index since the gross wages are not indicative of what the worker actually finds in his pay envelope. There are considerable deductions from his wages, and these have tended

* *Wirtschaft und Statistik*, April Heft, 1942.

to increase during the war. The decree of September 4, 1939*—
which provided for wage stability during the war, encouraged
the lowering of piece rates when they seemed too high to the
labour trustees, abolished overtime rates and higher rates for
night work, Sunday work and holiday work—had also increased
'the tax on wages, for incomes of 2,800 marks and over, by 50
per cent. While an order† of November 16th, little more than
two months later, reintroduced payment of higher rates for
night, Sunday, and holiday work, and another,‡ dated December 12, 1939, reintroduced overtime rates above 10 hours of
work, the tax increase remained in force. Furthermore, the
pressure upon the workers to contribute to the various Fascist
organizations and to the frequent national collections was substantially enhanced. Contributions from the workers (both, wage
and salary earners) to the "Winter-Help," for instance, rose
from 105 million marks in 1938–1939 to 131 million in 1939–
1940 and to 179 million in 1940–1941.§

For all these reasons it is impossible to compute real wages
which would indicate even approximately the development of
the purchasing power of the worker. How fruitless such an
attempt would be is obvious from the fact that the official
statistics show a slight increase in real wages, while even Fascist
officials were, at the same time, conceding that the purchasing
power of the workers had declined.||

But this does not mean that it is impossible to get some kind
of a picture of the development of the standard of living in
Germany. Before we attempt this, however, with the help of

---

* *Reichsarbeitsblatt*, 1939, Heft No. 26.   † Ibid., Heft No. 33.
‡ *Reichsgesetzblatt*, December 12. 1939.
§ *Wirtschaft und Statistik*, 2. Februar Heft and 1. Oktober Heft, 1941.
|| In the Report of the Bank for International Settlements for 1941 we
read (p. 13): "How much has consumption fallen since the war began? An
official of the German Institute for Economic Research arrives at the conclusion that the actual amount of money spent in Germany on consumption
was about the same in 1941 as in 1938 (Dr. W. Bauer in *Europa-Kabel*, May 22,
1942). But in the latter year the population in the 'Altreich' was 75·4 million,
while in the present 'Reich' area it amounts to 92·7 million; moreover, the
cost-of-living index rose from 1938 to 1941 by 6·7 per cent, and account has
also to be taken of the fact that, during a war, some deterioration in the
quality of the goods sold is unavoidable. The author points out that the
reduction in consumption implied by these facts has been most uneven . . ."

other means, it is necessary, first, to investigate the development of the wages of certain specific groups of workers in Germany.

The largest group whose wages we shall examine are the women. If we were to base our findings on the official statistics of wage rates, it would appear that the relation between the wages of men and women has remained the same during the war. There are, however, two factors which have tended to raise wages for women more than these figures indicate. Firstly, the tendency among German employers to evade the wage regulations by paying (against the law) wages above the rates fixed in order to obtain labour, is most pronounced in the case of women. Women are not so much affected as men by the regulations tying them down to a particular place of work, as they are often just entering industry. Another reason why there is a tendency for women's wages to increase nominally more than men's is that many women entering industry accepted jobs which were chiefly occupied by men before the war and for which, consequently, no special rate for women's labour existed. In such occupations women's wage rates were usually fixed at 80 per cent of the men's—in case of time rates—and in cases of piece rates the wages of women occasionally touched the men's rates.

The second special category are the foreign workers. In the period now under review, their importance has increased considerably. These foreign workers fall into three groups: foreign workers in general, Polish workers, and Jewish workers (foreign as well as German).

In general foreign workers receive the wages of German unskilled workers in the particular industry in which they are forced to work. Deductions from wages, except for Fascist party organizations, are the same for them as for the German workers. But they do not receive the same social insurance benefits. Moreover, they are usually not free to feed themselves at their own choice. In the factories they usually eat at special tables or in special rooms, and their food is worse than that for the German workers. At home, that is in their barracks, they are fed by either the employers, the municipality or the State, again without the freedom to choose their food, even within the limits of the rationing system. The cost of their feeding and housing is deducted from their wages. Furthermore, considerable pressure is brought to bear upon them to send money back home; this is done for two reasons: first, the money sent home cannot be used to buy commodities on the German market, and this leaves them for Germans to buy; and second, it is hoped that the sending of savings home will favourably impress the people in the occupied countries and thus soften the resistance of foreign workers to the recruitment for Germany.

Conditions among the Polish workers are worse. They have to pay a special tax, a "social equalization levy," corresponding to the amount by which Fascists assume the alleged lower Polish racial level can be expressed in terms of wage percentages. Furthermore, since it is in the interest of mankind, according to Fascist theory, that the Poles shall die out in the course of time, nothing in the general regulations affecting foreign workers which might help to keep the family alive or to increase it, applies to the Polish worker. Polish juveniles are excepted from the protection applicable to other young workers.

Legislation regarding the status of Jews consists chiefly of orders and decrees indicating the "privileges" which Jewish workers are not allowed to share with other workers. The special racial tax, levied upon the Poles, is imposed also upon the Jews. The family benefits, of which the Poles are deprived in the interest of their more rapid extermination, are also withheld from the Jews, who must be eliminated even more quickly. In some cases the Jewish workers are in an even worse position than the Poles, though usually their conditions are about the same. While Poles, for instance, receive compensation for wage losses incurred during air raid alarms, or because of a stoppage of production caused by damage to the factory through air attack, Jews do not receive such compensation.

While it is not possible to make a detailed study of the living conditions of these foreign workers, it is evident that they live under conditions markedly worse than those of the German workers, and that *for the majority of the foreign workers during this period—namely the Polish and Jewish workers—the standard of living is deliberately fixed at so low a level as to cause them to die out in the not very distant future.*

In conclusion, it is perhaps of some interest to compare some wage data for German and Polish workers in Poland itself although, as I have indicated before, figures cannot show the whole difference even in the purchasing power, to say nothing of the status : *

HOURLY WAGE RATES IN THE GOUVERNEMENT POLAND

Workers and Region	German Workers	Polish Workers
Unskilled Workers—		(Zlotys)
Warsaw and Cracow	1·16	0·58
Elsewhere	1 to 1·08	0·50
Semi-skilled Workers—		
Warsaw and Cracow	1·22	0·72
Elsewhere	1·05 to 1·13	0·62
Skilled Workers—		
Warsaw and Cracow	1·30	1·02
Elsewhere	1·20 to 1·30	0·88

The table shows two things of importance. The first we have noted in the foregoing pages : the wages of the Polish workers are considerably lower than those of the German workers. But the second point is equally significant : in the lowest wage category, that for unskilled workers who have to live at the lowest standard, the Polish workers' wages are exactly half those of the German workers. Unskilled Polish workers are cheap and relatively plentiful—what matter if many starve to death. If a Polish worker is semi-skilled he gets a wage which is some 20 per cent higher than that of the unskilled worker and "only" about 40 per cent lower than that of the German worker. When we come to the skilled workers we find that the Polish workers are paid wages which are "only" about 25 per cent less than those of the German worker, and roughly 80 per cent higher than those of the un-skilled workers, while the German skilled workers' wages are only about 20 to 25 per cent higher than those of the German unskilled workers.

Here we find the application of a principle which we shall study in more detail when investigating the German rationing system : the more useful a worker to the armament industry, the higher his wages, the fuller his rations, the better his standard of living. This applies even to Polish workers where the unskilled are condemned to death, the semi-skilled have a chance of clinging to life if their constitution is strong, and the relatively

* Cf. Verordnungsblatt des Generalgouverneurs fuer die besetzten polnischen Gebiete, February 1, 1940.

small number of skilled may enjoy permanent slavery under conditions which just enable them to produce for the German war machine.

*   *   *

On the whole, the study of wages here is not very fruitful. It gives us no real insight into the living conditions of the workers, although it gives us some into the barbaric character of Fascism, its campaign of extermination against a whole people and its carefully calculated system of hellishness by which it spares at least temporarily those workers who are producing weapons of destruction and are thus engaged in strengthening the chains which hold them, while preparing new chains for their comrades in other countries.

A considerably better insight into the life of the workers can be gained by a study of the rationing system in Germany.

Many foodstuffs in Germany were rationed directly or indirectly before war broke out; many foodstuffs were already scarce in 1938 and during the first eight months of 1939; some commodities, which were part of the normal diet of the people before Fascism came to power, had completely disappeared from the market by 1939 in favour of armament raw materials. When war came, an extensive rationing system was introduced, covering not only food but many other commodities. Rationing of soap and shoes, for instance, began in Germany on August 27, 1939, before the outbreak of war. Rationing of clothing began in November, 1939, and within a short time almost all commodities appertaining to the standard of living were rationed, either directly, by coupons, or indirectly through the "wise and just distribution among his customers" by the retailer.

Let us first study the ration of the normal consumer in Germany, of the worker, male or female, who does normal work, neither specially heavy nor requiring night work or extensive overtime. The following table compares his rations during the period under review (there were no important changes in the quantities allotted under the rationing system before the war against the Soviet Union) with the average consumption of a German male person above the age of 15 in 1937:*

* *Statistisches Jahrbuch für das Deutsche Reich*, 1938, and League of Nations, *World Economic Survey*, 1939–1941.

WEEKLY CONSUMPTION OF SOME IMPORTANT FOODSTUFFS
(Grammes per Week)

Commodity				1937	1939–1941
Bread and Flour*	..			1,200	2,400
Meat†	..	..	..	1,060	500
Milk‡	..	..	..	2·1	none
Cheese	..	..	..	120	50
Eggs§	..	..	..	2¾	1½
Fats	..	..	..	585	270

Except for bread for which the ration is double as high, the normal consumer during this period of the war got only about half as much as he did before. If we add to this the fact that during the war vegetables and fruits became even scarcer than they were before, it would appear that the standard of feeding in Germany declined rapidly, the war making a sharp turning point in the nutrition of the German worker.

But this conclusion would be incorrect. To imagine the German worker living chiefly upon bread and potatoes during those years would be a mistake, and the gigantic exertions of the Fascist war machine, especially in the field of armaments production, would be inexplicable. First, the rations for 1937 exaggerate the consumption, since this is an average for the whole population and not for the workers only; second, the pre-war consumption is computed for the male worker, while war rations apply to every adult, including female workers. Furthermore, the above war-time figures apply only to a limited number of workers. The Fascist rationing system is graduated for various age groups of children and juveniles, giving to the older boys and girls higher rations of some foodstuffs than to the normal consumer. It also provides varying rations for the following groups of workers:

> Normal workers.
> Workers doing much overtime, or night work.
> Workers doing heavy work.
> Workers doing very heavy work.

* From July, 1940 on, the bread ration was shortened by 150 grammes per week for all adults, and increased by 200 grammes for all between the ages of 10 and 20.

† Three weeks before the outbreak of war against the Soviet Union the meat ration was reduced by 20 per cent, doubtless to provide for the troops on the Eastern front.   ‡ Litre.   § Pieces.

These last three categories of workers receive higher rations than the normal consumer or ordinary worker.

Rations of some important foods for the four categories of workers during the period under review were as follows:*

RATIONS FOR VARIOUS CATEGORIES OF WORKERS
(Grammes per Week)

Worker	Bread	Meat	Fats
Normal Worker	2,400	500	270
Worker doing overtime and night work ..	3,000	750	290
Heavy worker	3,800	1,000	395
Very heavy worker	4,800	1,200	740
Adult Male, 1937	1,200	1,060	585
Ruhr Miner†	3,250	1,440	814

Now the picture looks quite different. For those doing heavy and very heavy work the war has brought probably only a slight deterioration, as far as meat and fats are concerned. For the worker doing overtime and night work, the standard of living has definitely deteriorated.

But even the above qualifications of our first findings with regard to food standards are insufficient. They do not take into account two other important factors. One tends towards a worsening of the standard of feeding; it is the progressive deterioration in the quality of foodstuffs. The other makes for an improvement in nutrition standards. It became operative only in the summer of 1940, but definitely affected living standards up to the spring of 1941. The conquests in the West and the ruthless looting of stocks combined with a rapid depression of the standard of living of the people in the conquered territories, definitely improved food conditions in Germany. Vegetables and fruits came in larger quantities on the market, and some commodities which had for long been absent now reappeared in noticeable quantities. To this must be added the considerable individual loot sent to their families by German soldiers from the occupied territories. *A German soldier between June, 1940, and May, 1941, rather than being a source of anxiety to his relatives—the*

---

* League of Nations, *World Economic Survey*, 1939–41, and current German press.

† According to a study by Ziegelmayer "Die Kost der Schwerarbeiter" in *Zeitschrift für Volksernaehrung*, July, 1937.

losses during the campaigns were very small* indeed—was a source of largesse, bringing chiefly gifts of food and clothing.

One can perhaps conclude as follows this survey of food standards in Germany from the beginning of the war until just before the campaign against the Soviet Union:

From September, 1939, to May, 1940, a further deterioration but no rapid decline.

From June, 1940, to May, 1941, a slight improvement especially for non-rationed goods through state pillage of the occupied countries, and through private looting by German soldiers. It is doubtful whether, during this period, food conditions were much worse than before the outbreak of the war.

May and June, 1941, a new deterioration of conditions, partly because of exhaustion of stocks in occupied countries, but chiefly because of preparations for the attack on the Soviet Union.

*   *   *

The development of the clothing situation was not fundamentally different from that of food; quality deteriorated and quantity became smaller. Probably the introduction of the clothing card meant a somewhat sharper reduction in consumption of clothing than it did for food. During the year from June, 1940, to May, 1941, the situation improved for the reasons mentioned in connection with the food situation. There was probably not so noticeable a deterioration during the months preceding the campaign against the Soviet Union as was the case with foodstuffs.

As to housing, the situation deteriorated from year to year without relief. The construction of new houses continued to decline. The number of dwellings newly built or reconditioned, which had declined from about 300,000 in 1938 to little more than 220,000 in 1939, dropped to only about 100,000 in 1940.†
During the first half of 1941, building activity declined further.

This development in the standard of living must be considered side by side with the development in working conditions. With

---

* Being about equal to traffic casualties!

† *Wochenbericht of the Institut für Konjunkturforschung,* December 28, 1940, quoted in Sweezy, l.c., p. 223.

increasing hours of work, much night work, and increasing pressure to speed up, even a slight deterioration in the standard of living means much; it means all the more if in peace-time the standard was already a very low one.

There was only one group of workers at this time who were well fed. *The German soldier, during the period under review, was excellently fed, and many workers who served temporarily in the army—when a new campaign was undertaken—were able to build up considerable physical resistance during this period and returned to work during the winter (1939–1940 and 1940–1941) with renewed vigour.* The importance of this fact must not be under-estimated since these workers represented a force of at least a million in the first winter, and probably more than that in the second, and numbered among themselves a high percentage of skilled workers, especially armament workers.

*   *   *

Perhaps we can best conclude this account of labour conditions during the first twenty months of the war with mention of a report by the *Angriff* of May 1, 1940, which stated that of 45,000 workers who were assembled from Berlin factories for fortification work in the West, 21,000 had to be sent back, because even the official Fascist doctors found them physically unfit. They were, of course, unskilled workers, not employed in the armament industry—and, therefore, physically unfit. Only the workers directly concerned with armament production remained fit.

3. FROM JUNE, 1941, TO THE PRESENT DAY

The campaign against the Soviet Union brought about a radical change in the conditions of the German worker. As far as his working and living conditions are concerned (apart from political conditions and terrorism), the campaign meant a rapid deterioration, much more rapid than that occurring on the outbreak of the war in September, 1939. The change is more comparable to that which occurred in 1938. *While in 1938 many turns from quantity into quality occurred, the campaign against the Soviet Union changed conditions from the serious to the desperate.*

*   *   *

In investigating the conditions of the workers we have usually begun with a study of employment. Partly because the question of man-power is one of the most important and partly because the study of this problem has served as a useful introduction into the study of what one understands by the infiltration of the elements of barbarity, of slavery and serfdom, into the status of labour.

The campaign against the Soviet Union was preceded by military preparations surpassing anything hitherto accomplished. During the winter of 1940–1941, and during the spring of 1941, more workers were employed in Germany than ever before. While the productivity per worker, and especially per worker and hour, declined, the growth in the number of workers employed—probably 10 per cent as compared with the previous spring—the "acquisition" of foreign patents and especially the increasing use made of the factories in Western Europe, contributed to a rapid rise of armament production. There is no doubt that, during the months preceding the war against the Soviet Union, armament production reached new records, both in the rapidly enlarged area dominated by German Fascism as well as in Germany proper.

During the last few weeks before the attack upon the Soviet frontiers, the number of employed actually declined, because of heavier conscription for the army, and production followed suit. The Fascists expected to finish the campaign rapidly and victoriously, and thought they had a sufficient superiority in weapons to be able to risk such a diminution in industrial man-power. During the second half of 1941, the number of employed continued to decline as more and more men were needed at the front.

When, in the beginning of December, 1941, the Soviet troops had not only not been decisively defeated but had begun a winter offensive, the Fascists were forced completely to revise their man-power policy. On the one hand, it was impossible to bring a million or more skilled workers temporarily back from the front, as had been done in the previous two winters. And, on the other hand, it became difficult rapidly to augment the influx of foreign workers from the occupied countries: the political resistance in these countries grew with the failure of the campaign against the Soviet Union; those skilled workers, who could be taken away without diminishing armament production in the occupied territories, had already been deported during the preceding year; unskilled workers were needed for agricultural work. Thus, German Fascism would have had at its disposal fewer workers in Germany proper in the winter of 1941–1942 than in the preceding years, had it not concentrated on a large scale recruitment in Germany itself. Armament production probably continued to increase, though not so much because of an increase in Germany proper but because of the progressive use being made of the armament factories in the occupied countries of the West, where many initial difficulties were now being overcome.

It was only in the course of 1942 that the man-power shortage was slightly relieved by the import of great numbers of civilians from the Soviet Union. Men, women and children were arrested, thrown into concentration camps, and there sorted out according to their state of health and skill to be sent to Germany. While in its annual survey of economic conditions in Germany, the *Frankfurter Zeitung*, December 25, 1941, contrasts man-power conditions with the situation in raw materials, armament production and nutrition, in favour of the latter three factors, during the last months of 1942 German papers published unofficial estimates of the number of foreign workers employed in Germany which, even if untrustworthy because of their exaggeration,* do indicate a large influx of workers from the Soviet Union. During the winter campaign and especially after the loss of the battle of Stalingrad German man-power losses at the front were so big that factories and fields, mines and offices were combed out for men who could be sent to the front. But if this vast conscription for military service was not to reduce man-power in production, new millions of people had to be sent into industry and agriculture. This was the basis of the so-called total mobilisation orders. On January 28, 1943, Sauckel, the director-general of labour, issued a decree requiring all men down to the age of 16 and up to the age of 65, and all women between 17 and 45

---

* *Frankfurter Zeitung*, September 15, 1942, gives an estimate of 5½ to 6 million foreign workers and prisoners of war which may be correct for the beginning of 1943, but not as early as the autumn of 1942.

to do national defence work. Even convicts, serving up to twelve years penal servitude, were granted immediate release if they were ready to serve at the Eastern front. This total mobilization did not have inconsiderable success as far as the number of men and women mobilized is concerned. Over a million additional people were driven out of small shops, schools (juveniles), small establishments, retirement (invalids, the aged), and so on into production. It was a failure as measured by the simultaneous loss of man-power at the front up to November, 1943.

The number of people employed as workers can be estimated as follows: *

ESTIMATE OF EMPLOYMENT
(Millions)

Category			May/June 1941	End of 1941	End of 1942	October 1943
Civilians	..	..	22.05	22.80	24.30	24.30
Germans	..	..	20.35	20.70	19.80	18.80
Foreigners	..	..	1.70	2.10	4.50	5.50
Prisoners of War		..	1.40	1.50	1.70	1.70
Total Employment		..	23.45	24.30	26.00	26.00

The figures show that the total number of employed increased during 1941 and 1942—but that during 1943 there was no further rise from the beginning to the end of the year. Employment could be maintained only by increasing the number of foreign workers imported into Germany. The number of German workers employed, after a small increase from May to December, 1941, declined in 1942 and 1943. The average total employment for the year 1943, however, is higher than for any preceding year.

The herding of the German people into the factories can best be illustrated by three examples. On March 17, 1942, the Munich press published a short obituary concerning a 72-year-old woman who was killed by a tram; the press said that she had come to Munich "to start work, as ordered, in a large

---

* Same sources for material, as for estimates for previous years, and in addition *Frankfurter Zeitung*, December 25, 1941, *Reichsarbeitsblatt*, December 5, 1941, and June 25, 1942, *Die Zeitung*, March 13, 1942 (quoting an estimate given over the German wireless) and the data given by Wagemann (German statistician) over the German wireless at the end of October, 1943.

establishment."* On January 4, 1942, the *Muenchener Neueste Nachrichten* published a report† that girls, aged 16 and 17, are being forcibly sent from home into the country to agricultural work. One year later, in 1943, boys of 14 and 15 were employed in manning the A.A. batteries. On May 13, 1942, the *Frankfurter Zeitung* describes how disabled soldiers are being trained for war work at home: "One has on his left hand only one thumb and the little finger, but he also tried to do his work."

The ways and means chosen by the Fascists to force foreign workers into slavery and serfdom in Germany are varied. In some occupied countries unemployment is deliberately created, partly by the closing down of consumption goods industries; then unemployment insurance benefits are denied—and so the workers are forced to accept employment in Germany. Or, an order is issued that no ration cards are to be given to workers not doing war work, if they do not come "voluntarily" to the labour-recruiting centres for Germany (Poland, Norway). Or, more officially and covering the whole country, the number of war prisoners to be released (France) and the tonnage of food-stuffs imported into a hungry country (Norway) are related to the number of workers prepared to go to Germany. In some countries, as in Poland, workers are simply ordered to appear at a certain place at a certain time, and are then packed into railway carriages and sent to Germany, without an opportunity even of notifying their relatives. The worst treatment is meted out to the Soviet citizens. Hundreds of thousands of Soviet people are driven into huge concentration camps; the best are chosen for work in Germany, and many others are simply left to die of hunger and cold. The Second Molotov Note on the barbarous acts of the German armies in the Soviet Union‡ describes how the Soviet workers are first assembled in prison camps in the Soviet Union:

> "In the camp for 'war prisoners' near Kiev, where 7,000 men are kept, the number of Red Army men constitutes

* *Fascism*, May 18, 1942 (published by the International Transport Workers' Federation), quotes from a letter: "Father had already for four years his old age pension. In spite of his 70 years, they forced him to go back to work. This he could not stand and had a breakdown. Now he can stay at home. But he is very weak."   † Quoted in *Fascism*, January 26, 1942.
‡ *Soviet War News Weekly*, May 7, 1942.

only 15 per cent; all the others are peaceful Ukrainian civilians doomed to slave labour and extinction."

The process of assembling these workers and transporting them to industrial work in the rear, including in Germany, is "necessarily a cruel one." An order of the day of December 2, 1941, of the 37th Infantry Regiment of the 6th Division, entitled "On the transfer of the civilian population," says:

"A certain amount of cruelty in carrying this order into effect is unavoidable."

After the workers from the Soviet Union have been transferred to Germany they are either sent in gangs to the factories or they are used for agricultural work. How they are chosen for agricultural work is graphically described in a report in the *Muenchener Neueste Nachrichten*, August 5, 1942:

"The local peasant leader comes to the barrier behind which a recently arrived shipment of Eastern workers stand . . . to the right by the wall, in two rows the girls and women; to the left, already divided, the boys and men. An experienced official makes the choice, accompanied by the critical gaze and occasional comment of the peasant leader. When a small Polish boy is handed to him, the peasant leader is obviously very little pleased. But he is satisfied when, with the help of an interpreter, a hefty, strong Ukrainian girl is selected from among the women."

The description is similar to others we have from the slave market in ancient times. Like cattle, the Soviet people are checked upon and distributed among the German employers.

The means used by the Fascists to drive foreign workers into Germany, as well as to comb out the German population for more workers, have, since the campaign against the Soviet Union, become much more drastic than ever before. The desperate need to increase production, to maintain the offensive, and later the defensive, against the Red Army, drove the Fascists to ever more frantic efforts. Within one year the official responsible for the recruitment of labour was changed twice; three men tried in vain to solve the labour shortage problem.

This is a problem which cannot be solved only by increasing the number of people working. It is mainly a problem of efficiency. In this connection it is of interest to study a table circularized by the present man-power dictator in Germany Sauckel (June 3, 1942):*

EFFICIENCY OF PRISONERS OF WAR
(Normal German Worker = 100)

French	..	.. 80 to 90	Serb	..	.. 60 to 70
Belgian	..	.. 75 to 85	British	..	.. 45 to 55
Polish	..	.. 65 to 75	Russian	..	.. 40 to 50

In order to replace one million German workers about two to two and a half million prisoners of war from the Soviet Union are needed!

Part of this "inefficiency" of the prisoners of war is due to political sabotage. Part of it is due to their terrible living and working conditions. It is the latter factor which we must now study in some detail for the German as well as for the foreign workers.

*   *   *

Food conditions in Germany began to deteriorate slightly even before the war against the Soviet Union was begun. The meat ration was cut by 20 per cent in the beginning of June. Fruits and vegetables which had arrived in surprising, though not over-large, quantities during the preceding year from the occupied countries had grown scarcer and continued to do so all through 1941 and 1942. The winter of 1941–1942 was worse than any other since the appalling years of war and inflation, 1917 to 1923. When the spring came, rations were cut, the first all around cut since the beginning of the war. The table on page 214 indicates the extent of this cut for the three most important rationed commodities, bread, meat and fats:†

The cuts, especially as far as meat and fats are concerned were very severe, indeed. While the very heavy workers probably still had enough to work fairly efficiently, it is doubtful whether the heavy workers did. Those working much overtime, and

---

* Quoted in *Fascism*, November 18, 1942.
† Cf. German Press, March 20, 1942.

night workers, could not maintain their working power, and a
rapid decline in their productivity must have resulted. While

RATIONS BEFORE APRIL 6, 1942 (A), AND AFTER (B)
(Grammes per Week)

Category	Bread		Meat		Fats	
	A	B	A	B	A	B
Normal consumer	2,250	2,000	400	300	269	206
Worker doing overtime and night work..	2,850	2,600	600	450	289	226
Worker doing heavy work ..	3,650	3,400	800	600	394	306
Worker doing very heavy work	4,650	4,400	1,000	850	738	575

the German soldiers at the front continued to be well fed, the
vast mass of the German workers lived during the summer of
1942 under conditions which seriously incapacitated them, and
led to a considerable decline of their working power. Since the
free market, providing vegetables and fruits, was also very small,
since potatoes were so scarce that, in June, 1942, they had to be
rationed, the prospects for war production during the autumn,
and winter were bleak indeed. Under these circumstances the
Fascist régime decided to change its policy. As the speech by
Goering* indicated, the government resolved to bleed the
occupied countries even further in order to be able to increase
rations in Germany. In this way it was hoped to secure at least
for Germany, a relatively decent standard of production. As
the German press of September 16, 1942, announced, rations
were to be restored to the level prevailing before April 6th,
except for meat, where they were as follows:

MEAT RATIONS IN GERMANY IN 1942 AND 1943
(Grammes per Week)

Category	Before April 6th	April to October	October, 1942 to May, 1943	May, 1943 to 1944
Normal consumer	400	300	350	250
Worker doing overtime and night work	600	450	550	450
Worker doing heavy work	800	600	700	600
Worker doing very heavy work ..	1,000	850	950	850

* The Harvest Thanksgiving speech of October 4, 1942, in which Goering
expounded the German policy: "I have firmly resolved and have since
adhered to the principle that, while I do not want to see the populations of
the occupied territories suffer hunger and privation, if through enemy measures
privation is unavoidable, it will in no circumstances affect Germany."

The meat shortage is such that even at the expense of the peoples of the occupied territories, the Fascist régime did not want to risk a full restitution of the meat cuts in October, 1942, and had to order a new cut in May, 1943.

The partial restitution of the cuts of April, 1942, probably brought about sufficient improvement to enable heavy workers to stand the same working pace as during the previous winter. On the other hand, while there are no indications that the supply on the free market has been improved, there are evident signs that the quality of goods has further deteriorated. Bread, in fact, has in the summer of 1942 already become of such poor quality that the sale of fresh bread had to be forbidden. The Reich, June 28, 1942, admits that "bread has lost in quality and wholesomeness" and that the water content of flour has increased by as much as 40 per cent. Perhaps the best proof for the general deterioration in food is the fact that a new special category of workers was to be set up: namely, the miners. Even the rations for very heavy workers were insufficient to maintain production levels in the coal mines, so Goering announced in his above-mentioned speech of October, 1942, that the miners would receive special rations. In 1943, the very good harvest somewhat improved conditions. The bread ration was increased in June and September, 1943, by 75 and 100 grammes per week for the normal consumer, raising the ration above the 1939/40 level, and the general quality of the bread became better. One can say, perhaps, that to-day, at the end of 1943, the food standard in Germany is sufficient for armament workers to maintain output on the present level of efficiency, while the increasing strain and the poorer nourishment must have a cumulative effect upon the output per person in non-armament industries and occupations.

During all this time the quality and quantity of rationed clothing continued to decline. Even if a new ration card contained the same number of points, and the number of points for individual articles of clothing was not increased, the period covered by the clothing card was increased. Housing conditions deteriorated further, in part owing to the attacks of the R.A.F. and the difficulties of reconstruction and repair.

*   *   *

In spite of these factors contributing to a further weakening of the physical resistance of the German workers, working hours were in 1941 still further increased and the drive in the factories to accelerate labour processes was intensified. According to the official statistics the number of hours worked developed as follows : *

AVERAGE NUMBER OF HOURS WORKED PER WEEK

Period			Men	Women	All
March, 1941 ..	..	..	51·4	44·8	49·9
September, 1941	..	..	52·2	44·6	50·4
March, 1942 ..	..	..	51·1	43·6	49·2
September, 1942	..	..	51.2	42.8	49·2
December, 1942	..	..	51·5	42.8	49·5

But, as the table shows, in 1942 it began to become impossible to lengthen the working day further. Exhaustion and passive resistance began to set a limit to the extension of the working day.

More impressive than these average figures is the speech of one of Germany's worst slave drivers, Gau-leader Buerkel (responsible for the "Westmark"—Lorraine, Saar, Palatinate), in which he said that it was extremely doubtful whether it was possible further to lengthen the working day in Germany; he also mentioned that *miners and railway workers sometimes work without interruption for 30 to 40 hours.*†

But when it becomes impossible further to lengthen the working day production must be intensified. The year 1942 is characterized by a general drive for further rationalization. Only one day after the *Frankfurter Zeitung* wrote‡ that "many employers and workers have for years been working to the utmost of their capacity," the man-power dictator of that time, Dr. Mansfeld, introduced the two-for-three plan§, that is to have two people do the work of three. 1943 brought a new acceleration of the rationalization process—partly under cover of the total mobilization campaign and the consequent closing down of ten thousands of small firms.

In order to drive the workers harder considerable changes

---

* *Wirtschaft und Statistik*, April Heft, 1942, and Maerz and Juli Heft, 1943.
† Speech at the middle of May, 1942, quoted in *Fascism*, June 15, 1942.
‡ February 4, 1942.   § *Reichsarbeitsblatt*, February 5, 1942.

were introduced into the method of wage payments in Germany. True, wage rates remained roughly stable:*

AVERAGE HOURLY WAGE RATES, 1940 TO 1942
(Pfennig)

Period	Skilled Men	Unskilled Men	Unskilled Women	Average Wage Rates
1940	79·2	63·0	44·1	68·2
1941	79·9	63·8	44·4	69·0
June, 1941	79·9	63·7	44·4	68·9
December, 1941 ..	80·0	63·9	44·5	69·1
December, 1942 ..	80.8	64.1	44.6	69.5

While wage rates remained the same, hourly and weekly gross earnings continued their slow upward trend, due chiefly to increasing overtime† and the shifting of workers from consumption to armament industries.‡

GROSS EARNINGS, 1941 AND 1942
(1936 = 100)

Period	Hourly Earnings	Weekly Earnings	Cost of Living
1940	111·2	116·0	104·5
1941	116·4	123·6	106·6
1942	118.2	124.3	108.9
March, 1941	115·5	122·2	106·1
September, 1941 ..	117·3	125·0	107·1
March, 1942	117.5	123.6	109.2
September, 1942 ..	118.9	125.0	108.6
December, 1942 ..	119.5	126.4	109.1

But these figures also do not show what is really happening to the German wage system. What actually is happening is that, firstly, in numerous industries (building trades, for instance) and occupations, piece instead of time rates are being introduced; secondly, the classification into skilled, semi-skilled and unskilled workers is being replaced by the introduction of more categories (dilution); and thirdly, while the total wage sum is remaining the same, the minimum is being lowered in order to pay higher

---

* *Wirtschaft und Statistik*, 1. Februar Heft. 1941, Februar Heft, 1942, and Maerz Heft, 1943.

† When the increase in the number of hours of work was halted in 1942, earnings began to remain practically stable.

‡ *Wirtschaft und Statistik*, April Heft, 1942, and Juli Heft. 1943.

wages to those workers who work more efficiently. In this way the employer has greater freedom to play the workers off, one against the other, or as the *Frankfurter Zeitung* expresses it:* "The two motives behind the revision of the wage structure which is now taking place are the creation of a really just wage and piece-rate system, and the mobilization of hidden output reserves." The *Voelkische Beobachter*† is franker: "The factory leader will be able to pay particularly efficient workers on time rates a correspondingly higher wage than the less efficient in the future." While pitting one worker against the other, this new wage system at the same time gives much more power to the individual employer. The employer is also better enabled to foster a labour aristocracy of lackeys and spies irrespective of the skill of the worker. *The whole system of collective wages (after the abolition of collective bargaining) has been undermined for the sake of intensifying the working process, and of creating a labour aristocracy of boss-lovers.* The same principle is applied by whole industries: the miners receive, on the whole, a wage increase, beginning with December, 1942, while the new wage regulations for the metal industry (October, 1942) provide for a relatively smaller wage sum in that industry.

*   *   *

It is not surprising that under these conditions the health of the workers deteriorated rapidly. This was due partly to overstrain and exhaustion, and partly to the actual drugging of the workers in order temporarily to increase their working capacity. It is by no means unusual for workers in Germany to find in their pay envelopes, in addition to their meagre pay, tablets containing Pervitin, Benzedrin, or similar stimulants.

According to the *Reichsgesundheits-Blatt*‡ the tuberculosis rate increased from 1940 to 1941 by almost one quarter. Meanwhile the rate of employment of those suffering from tuberculosis also increased. According to the *Deutsche Tuberkulose-Blatt*§ about 60 per cent of Germans with open tuberculosis (about a quarter of a million people) are in employment, often working overtime

* November 17, 1942; cf. also I.N.G. Publications, December 17, 1942.
† November 11, 1942.
‡ *Reichsgesundheits-Blatt.* January 28, 1942.   § April Heft, 1942.

or on night work. Of the possibly (fakultativ) open tuberculosis cases 80 to 90 per cent are employed.

During 1942 and 1943 the deterioration in health conditions continued. In 1941 about 200,000 cases of diptheria were notified; in 1942 the number of cases increased by one-third above the 1941 level; the number of cases of scarlet fever increased from 160,000 in 1940 to 275,000 in 1941, and to 400,000 in 1942; the number of cases of typhoid more than doubled between 1941 and 1942.*

*   *   *

The description of working and living conditions in the preceding pages refers only to German workers. Workers deported to Germany from occupied countries are living considerably worse, and their working conditions are much more cruel.

To begin with, foreign workers receive lower wages and less rations. Just as German workers employed in the occupied territories receive higher rations than the "native workers," so are the foreign workers deported to Germany fed worse than the "native Germans." A reporter of a Swiss paper,† commenting on the living and working conditions of foreign workers in a factory which he had visited under official guidance, revealed that, in this establishment at least, the rations for foreign workers were 11 per cent less for bread and 7 per cent less for fats than those for German workers. As to wages, there are numerous official documents available to show the large difference in the wages of German and foreign workers during the period under review. In a previous section of this chapter we have shown how inhumanely Polish and Jewish workers are treated in this respect as in so many others. Since July, 1941, there is yet another category of foreign workers treated with extreme cruelty, those from the occupied territories of the Soviet Union.

Like all other foreign workers deported to Germany, the Soviet workers usually receive the same wages as German unskilled workers. Like the Polish workers, they must pay a special

* *Reichsgesundheitsblatt*, January 20, and April 7, 1943.
† *Neue Zuercher Zeitung*, December 8, 1941.

tax which is designed to reduce their wages by the amount which the Fascists consider the normal Soviet standard of living is below the German standard. It is not surprising that the Fascists assume that the Soviet standard is, not only considerably lower than the German, but even lower than the Polish standard. The Poles, like the Jews, have to pay a special tax of 15 per cent, the Russian workers have to pay taxes which in certain circumstances are as high as 75 per cent. A considerable proportion of the Soviet workers were at first employed in construction work. Both the Soviet and the German unskilled worker in this occupation earned about 35 marks gross per week. But, while the German worker receives roughly 25 marks net, after all deductions, the Russian worker has to pay about 25 marks in taxes and other deductions, so that only about 10 marks are left to him. He has to hand over these 10 marks to pay for his palliasse in his barrack and for the food which is given to him. Not a penny is left to him—if he is lucky enough to work the seventy hours necessary to earn 35 marks. If, because of illness or, more often, bad weather, he is not able to work his seventy hours, the Russian worker accumulates debts. Since a considerable number of the Russians are skilled workers, the Fascists, in the course of time, transfer them to more important work than construction. But, in order to avoid paying the Soviet workers higher wages in such cases, a rule was introduced that, if the nominal gross wage of the Soviet workers amounts to more than 70 marks, deductions are so heavy that under no circumstances are more than 17 marks left to him per week. If a French prisoner of war, for instance, does skilled work for 60 hours per week, he may earn a gross amount of 78 marks, from which is deducted something over 40 per cent; thus, he usually receives about 46 marks. A Russian civilian worker for the same work receives 17 marks net; but from these 17 marks further deductions are made for "social insurance," and for his palliasse and food.*

* See *Reichsgesetzblatt*, January 27, 1942, *Deutsche Allgemeine Zeitung*, March 4, 1942, and *Fascism*, March 23, 1942. A new regulation, dated June 30, 1942 leaves in some cases a higher minimum wage for the Russian worker from which, however, "savings" are now deducted in order to provide "for his future."

Under such conditions the Russian workers began increasingly to fall into debt. They worked 10, 11 and more hours per day, and yet often finished the week owing more than before. All this required a good deal of book-keeping, which absorbed more clerical work than the Fascists wanted. A special decree was, therefore, published on February 9, 1942, which provided that deductions for bed and food should not be so big as to leave the Soviet worker in debt. If possible (!), the worker should be left with pocket money (!) amounting to 20 pfennig (2¼d.) per day (except Sunday, for which pocket money was evidently regarded as undesirable).* More recently (May, 1943) a new "concession" was made to the Russian workers. The lowest wage is increased from 12·00 marks in January, 1942, and 12·04 marks in June, 1942 to 12·25 per week from May 1943, and the money these workers receive in cash is now 1·75 marks per week.

Just as the food and wages of the foreign workers are worse than those of the German workers, so are their clothing and housing. Their clothing cards (if they get them) have fewer points, and, as to their housing, a most interesting order and circular were published in October, 1941. They expressly prescribe worse conditions for the foreign workers than for the Germans and state that what are to be regarded as the minimum sanitary conditions for German workers are by no means identical with those for the foreign workers. The same circular points to the advisability of avoiding "contamination" of the German people by associating with foreign workers.†

Health conditions among the foreign workers have rapidly deteriorated. If a foreign worker falls ill, he very rarely receives medical attention. In order to reduce medical attention for those workers who are not housed in barracks (the barracks' officials can usually be relied upon to keep the doctor away), that is chiefly agricultural workers, the Gau-leader of the Stettin district in December, 1941, notified the Pomeranian employers that, if a Polish worker fell ill, the doctor should be called only in cases of extreme need, and even then only if no German patient needed his attention at the time. As all German doctors

* Unless the Soviet worker worked on Sunday.
† Quoted in *Fascism*, January 26, 1942.

are over-worked, this means virtually that Polish workers are to receive no medical attention.

If a foreign worker is ill for more than three weeks, he is sent back to his home country as quickly as possible (order of October 8, 1941 *). He has become useless to the German war machine and may die at home if he does not succumb on the way.

*   *   *

This short description of some aspects of the living and working conditions of the foreign workers in Germany is sufficient to show the appalling state in which they are living. True, there is a labour shortage in Germany. But, on the other hand, as far as unskilled labour is concerned, there are roughly three hundred million people on the Continent, aged 15 years and more, the vast majority of whom can do unskilled work. That is, there is an enormous reservoir of labour power. *The Fascists, therefore, not only treat the foreign workers as slaves, but treat them without any regard to losses through sickness and death. They treat them as the Romans treated their slaves during a period when slaves were still available in large quantities and when a rich Roman did not mind occasionally cutting up a slave in order to feed his gold-fish.* The skilled slaves, on the other hand, are treated somewhat better. They are fed and clothed sufficiently just to keep them alive and able to work with a certain degree of efficiency in the armament industry. "Even" Jews and Soviet workers, if they are highly skilled, are fed sufficiently to enable them to continue working.

There are to-day about seven million foreign workers and prisoners of war in Germany. *More than every fourth worker in Germany to-day is working under slave conditions, just kept alive if he is a skilled worker, doomed to death if he is an unskilled worker.*

*   *   *

And the German workers? We have seen above how their conditions have deteriorated, especially during the last 2½ years. We have seen, how the elements of slavery and serfdom have penetrated their lives. We have seen, how Fascism has

---

* Quoted in *Fascism*, March 9, 1942.

chained them to the war machine which must inevitably lead them to death and destruction—if they do not break the chain. There is one new measure which the Fascists recently introduced, of which little is known outside Germany, but which is perhaps more indicative of the position of the German worker than any other. On April 14, 1942, the supreme German Labour Court, the Reichsarbeitsgericht, decided that *the German employer has the right to levy money fines upon his employees, thereby assuming police powers, and that no German labour court is justified in interfering. The German employer has thus become like the feudal lord or the slave holder, to a certain extent the judicial master of the German worker.* The German worker is not free to change his employer but the employer is free to inflict fines upon the worker without that worker having any judicial recourse. *Such is the German workers' position under German Fascism. A slave and a serf in many respects, an oppressed and degraded human being in every respect.*

INDEX

I.—INDEX OF TABLES

II.—INDEX OF NAMES
(INSTITUTIONS, PERSONS, PLACES, PEOPLES)

III.—GENERAL INDEX